LIKE
WHAT
WE
IMAGINE

PITTSBURGH SERIES IN COMPOSITION, LITERACY, AND CULTURE

DAVID BARTHOLOMAE AND JEAN FERGUSON CARR, EDITORS

LIKE
WHAT
WE
IMAGINE

WRITING *and the* UNIVERSITY

DAVID BARTHOLOMAE

UNIVERSITY *of* PITTSBURGH PRESS

Published by the University of Pittsburgh Press, Pittsburgh, Pa., 15260
Copyright © 2021, University of Pittsburgh Press
All rights reserved
Manufactured in the United States of America
Printed on acid-free paper
10 9 8 7 6 5 4 3 2 1

Cataloging-in-Publication data is available from the Library of Congress

ISBN 13: 978-0-8229-4672-4
ISBN 10: 0-8229-4672-6

COVER ART: Modified photo by Jaredd Craig on Unsplash

COVER DESIGN: Alex Wolfe

For Joyce: *La ruta nos aportó otro paso natural*

CONTENTS

PREFACE

This book is made up of ten essays drawn from writing I did over the last decade of my career. Some of these chapters were previously published, some began as the texts of talks or lectures, and some were written specifically to complete this volume.

This is an end-of-career book—a looking back, a taking stock, a series of reflections on writing and the teaching of writing. It is not meant as a final statement; for me, it was a way of thinking things through one last time, seeing where I had been, reflecting on where I find myself now, saying thank you, and paying respects. These essays, then, are not driven by argument or thesis. They are, rather, intent on remembering, on gathering and sorting. This is, perhaps, a "late style." One of the early readers of the manuscript said that the prose "lets readers in on [my] ways of thinking, reading, writing, engaging with students."

I very much liked this formulation, that the book's style is designed *to let readers in* on something. For me, the chapters were meant as an invitation rather than an intervention, an open door rather than a forced march. And, as part of this strategy, I wanted the collection to be unified by a thread of memoir—not an account of my personal or private life but a revisiting of some of the books and ideas, people and places, students and courses that have shaped and sustained my work as a teacher of writing over a long career. The writing led me to encounters (or reencounters) that I could not shake and dared not ignore. One thing would lead to another. That is a quick summary of the book's method and style: one thing leading to another.

And I wanted there to be a *documentary* quality to the chapters. I wanted student papers and classroom handouts to be at the center (rather than behind or below) any account of my work or my place in the field. I have often felt that much of the most important writing I do is published only by xerox; it has circulated primarily among my students and colleagues. (As a documentary history, *Like What We Imagine* is an homage to two books that I read and taught and loved early in my career: Bill Coles's *The Plural I* and Roger Sale's *On Writing*.)

You will find that I rely heavily on block quotations. This has been true of my writing and teaching throughout my career, although it is perhaps more pronounced at this late date. The block quotations are meant to be moments of pause and of close concentration. They are not offered simply as evidence. (You will find that I use set passages more than once. For me, the repetition is always bringing something new into focus.)

These long passages are part of the terrain through which I travel. I think about them and I think through them. And it is an oddly populated terrain, since the extended passages are drawn as much from students' writing as they are from the major figures of our profession. My writing and my teaching have always been shaped by extended passages that I hold dear and that I return to again and again. Lessons. I use them as headnotes, both in published essays and in daily assignments. I build classes around them.

They are drawn from writers (published and unpublished) who have spoken to what I see as the fundamental problems of writing, reading, and teaching. And while the ideas have been important to me, I go back to these passages for the sentences, for the sentences and what they do or don't do—for their articulation and for their possible use, extension, or translation. The writers and passages have changed over time, but I am always working with block quotations. One thing leading to another. That is the style and method of this book. It was my job to maintain a reasonable pace, essay by essay, to make the most of the connections, and to be sure that there was an end in sight. There may be some unexpected leaps or turns along the way, somewhat in the manner of John McPhee, whose sense of the essay has shaped my own, but I think these leaps and turns can be among the true pleasures of reading.

The essays were certainly a pleasure to write. I have never before written so much so quickly, nor have I had such a good time of it.

CHAPTER OVERVIEW

The Introduction moves between Pittsburgh and Bilbao, river towns that have marked the odd trajectory of my career. I also use this occasion to present a poem by Elizabeth Bishop, "At the Fishhouses." I have taught this poem often—and in both settings. I invite the line, "it is like what we imagine knowledge to be," to provide the terms for my account of my career—and the teaching of freshman composition. Semester after semester, and week by week, I have worked closely with first year students, reading their sentences, suggesting revisions both large and small, trying to find a way of saying: "Well, yes, interesting—I think this is close; this is like what we imagine knowledge to be."

Chapter one, "Everything Was Going Quite Smoothly until I Stumbled on a Footnote," opens with an invitation I received to give the inaugural David G. Osborne lecture at Ohio Wesleyan University, where I received my BA in English and where Professor Osborne was my teacher. He taught courses in the Romantics and the Victorians; he was known for his commitment to the lower division and to freshman composition; he was my favorite teacher, the one who made the major make sense for me. This essay was originally published in *Writing on the Edge* (Fall 2009). It was a finalist for the 2009 National Council of Teachers of English Donald Murray Prize, and it was selected for *The Best of the Independent Rhetoric and Composition Journals* (Parlor Press, 2011). I am grateful to my editor, John Boe, and to the journal for permission to republish.

Chapter two, "Teacher Teacher," considers the writing and the teaching careers of Richard Poirier and William E. Coles Jr. Both had taught with Theodore Baird and Reuben Brower at Amherst. Both were key figures in my formation as a teacher and a scholar, and both, I feel, represent commitments to the "work of knowing" that might continue to inform new generations of teachers and scholars. I am probably the only person in the world who would (or could) bring these two figures together. It was a delight to try to do so. This was first published in *Raritan* (Winter 2017). I am grateful to Jackson

Lears, who followed Richard Poirier as the editor of this journal, for his support and encouragement. In a letter to me, he said, "I don't think I've ever heard RP come so alive on the page."

Chapter three, "'Inventing the University' at 25: An Interview with John Schilb, Editor, *College English*," looks back at "Inventing the University" twenty-five years after publication. The piece had traveled widely and the *College English* editor, John Schilb, invited this interview for the journal as part of a series of "Reconsiderations," pieces that looked back on the profession. He asked great questions, and I was pleased to have the chance to think retrospectively. The interview transpired as an exchange of emails while I was on sabbatical leave and serving as a visiting professor at the University of Deusto, in Bilbao. This essay was originally published in *College English*, vol. 73, no. 3 (January 2011), pp. 260–82 (©2011 by the National Council of Teachers of English. Used with permission).

In the 2016–2017 academic year, I taught two courses that I had taught in 1975–1976, my first year at the University of Pittsburgh, and I taught them with the thought that I would write about them, using them as a way of thinking forward and back. Chapter four, "Contest of Words," is the first of those two essays; it is an account of my teaching in our required, first-year composition course, Seminar in Composition.

Chapter five, "Back to Basics," is the second of the two. In the spring term of 2017, I taught Workshop in Composition (once called Basic Writing). When I taught that course in 1975, my students were primarily African American, first generation, and/or working class. In 2017, they were all Chinese. Chapter five, "Back to Basics," is a reflection on that course, its past and present. The essay was first published in the *Journal of Basic Writing* (Spring 2020). I am grateful to my editors, Cheryl Smith and Hope Parisi, for their support and to the journal for permission to republish.

Chapter six, "The Historians of Cape Town: On Teaching Travel Writing (with Rene Lloyd)," opens with the text of a student essay. In fact, this chapter reverses my usual practice. In the early chapters, I embedded student writing in an essay of my own. Here, my comments are embedded in the full text of an essay by one of my undergraduate students.

For several semesters, I taught a travel writing course to students who were traveling in a special University of Pittsburgh study abroad program called PittMap. The semester-long course had a focused curriculum. The first year, with colleagues from Economics and the School of Medicine, our topic was public health, with a focus on HIV/AIDS. We spent five weeks each in Buenos Aires, Cape Town, and Beijing, meeting with doctors, patients, researchers, and public health officials, and visiting clinics, hospitals, research centers, and pharmaceutical companies.

The writing course, as I conceived of it, would serve two purposes. It would provide a motive to be out on the streets, paying close attention to people and places, and it would create a quiet, reflective space each week in the middle of a demanding and chaotic travel schedule.

Much contemporary travel writing, minus some of the very best, tends to be self-centered and dismissive of others. And so I found it difficult to follow my usual practice and to work from published, professional models. I wanted a genre that would honor detail over generalization and that would take students outside of themselves (and their preconceptions) and onto the streets and into the world. I quickly developed a library of exemplary student papers. This is one of them.

Chapter seven, "From Arrigunaga to Yoknapatawpha: Ramiro Pinilla and William Faulkner," thinks about writers and their sources, about literacy and learning. It takes as its subject Ramiro Pinilla's encounter with *As I Lay Dying* in the Casa Americana (a library run by the US State Department) in Bilbao in the early 1960s. Although Pinilla had been writing genre fiction, Faulkner (he said) opened up *un hueco*, a space that allowed him a new sense of the possibilities of narrative. Pinilla's next novel, *Las ciegas hormigas*, won a major national award and launched the career of one of Spain's most important twentieth-century writers. "From Arrigunaga to Yoknapatawpha" traces the routes and outcomes of this productive exchange. The essay was first published in *Critical Quarterly* (October 2016). I am grateful to my editor, Colin MacCabe, for his support and encouragement and to John Wiley and Sons for permission to republish.

Chapter eight, "In Search of Yasuní," opens in July, 2017, when I was teaching in the Amazon basin, in the rain forest along the Napo River in Ecuador. I spent the month of July 2017 teaching in the Amazon basin, in the rain forest along the Napo River in Ecuador. I had the opportunity to travel by motor canoe six hours downriver, deep into the Yasuní National Park. The Yasuní contains one of the richest and most diverse ecosystems on the planet. And it sits on the largest untapped oil field in Ecuador. Although mostly narrative, the essay also considers conservation as a writing problem (and a conceptual problem), as well as a problem of national and global politics. This essay was first published in *The Smart Set* (November 2017). I am grateful to my editor, Melinda Lewis, for her support and encouragement, and to the journal for permission to republish.

Chapter nine, "That Went for a Walk/On the Camino de Santiago," is a photo-essay and is the most memoir-like of the collection. On the pilgrimage route to Santiago, I was thinking about distance, age, and time—and my final year in the classroom. This essay, too, was first published in *The Smart Set* (May 2019).

REFERENCES

There are no footnotes or endnotes or in-text citations in these essays. In my experience, these conventions disturb the exchange between a reader and a writer. I was working toward something else.

It was also the case that in the past decade I had been happy to publish with a variety of journals and editors who did not insist upon MLA-style documentation. As a result, I had a mixed bag of essays, some with such apparatus but most without. I decided to cut the endnotes from everything and so I revised accordingly.

This was actually surprisingly easy, with the single exception of the essay on the Spanish novelist Ramiro Pinilla, first published in *Critical Quarterly*. There I had used endnotes to provide additional commentary, to establish an extended context for the contemporary reviews (in local magazines and newspapers), and to provide the original Spanish for the various translations of his work into English. If you are interested in a further search into these materials, you can find the original essay in the Wiley Online Library at https://onlinelibrary .wiley.com/doi/pdf/10.1111/criq.12296.

ACKNOWLEDGMENTS

I am writing at the end of a long career. I can't begin to name all those who have been my teachers, students, colleagues, editors, readers, supporters, counselors, and friends. Please know that I am forever grateful for your good company and for all that you did on my behalf.

I spent ten years as a Writing Program Administrator and fourteen as a department chair, and all at a time when the University of Pittsburgh was a site of remarkable energy, experimentation, and growth. I couldn't have asked for a better place to begin (and end) a career. I had the privilege and good fortune of riding the crest of a wave created by the brilliant leadership of Chancellor Mark Nordenberg, with the support of senior administrators: Provosts James Maher and Patricia Beeson; Deans Peter Koehler, John Cooper, and Robert Marshall; Department Chairs Robert Hinman, Mary Briscoe, and Philip Smith; Robert Glaser, founding director of the Learning, Research and Development Center; and the senior administrative staff of the English department—Annette Galluze, Sandy Russo, and Gerri England.

I joined Pitt's English department in 1975. It was a rare department in that it was (and remained) a department deeply committed to reading and writing in general education, where composition was understood to be one of the essential areas of research and teaching. In my day, we had a wonderfully open and collegial mix of colleagues across ranks and programs, including graduate students. We swapped courses and ideas, students and their papers. We hung out together. We made sure to have a good time of it. The essence of this spirit was provided and maintained by many, but especially by Jean Ferguson Carr, Steve Carr, Phil Smith, Susan Harris Smith, Paul Kameen, Mariolina Salvatori, Nick Coles, Jim Seitz, Joe Harris, Tony Petrosky, Bill

Smith, Richard Tobias, Jim Knapp, Chris Rawson, Colin MacCabe, Jonathan Arac, Lucy Fischer, Lynn Emanuel, Jen Waldron, Marah Gubar, Jean Grace, Beth Matway, Lois Williams, Geeta Kothari, Cindy Skrzycki, Jennifer Lee, Marylou Gramm, Bruce Horner, Richard Miller, Min-Zhan Lu, Donna Dunbar-Odom, Steve Parks, Stacey Waite, and Peter Moe.

I served in leadership positions for the National Council of Teachers of English, the Conference on College Composition and Communication, and the Modern Language Association and its Association of Departments of English. These professional organizations were crucially important to me as part of my continuing education. They provided a home and broadened my horizons. David Laurence (of MLA and ADE) became a good friend as well as a trusted mentor. There were also colleagues from across the profession who became good friends and coconspirators: Jim Slevin, Susan Miller, Jacqueline Jones Royster, Nancy Sommers, Don McQuade, Mike Rose, Andrea Lunsford, Erika Lindemann, John Gage, and John Boe.

With my old pal, Tony Petrosky, I was the author of a textbook, *Ways of Reading*, now in its twelfth edition. We had the great good fortune to have Stacey Waite join the team with the tenth edition. Chuck Christensen, Joan Feinberg, and John Sullivan (originally with Bedford Books, later with St. Martin's Press and Macmillan) taught us how to write in this genre and for this large and impossible audience. They were and remain the best in the business.

After I stepped down as department chair, I became deeply involved in Pitt's Study Abroad Program. This provided some of the most important, difficult, and exhilarating teaching of my career. I am grateful to the program director, Jeff Whitehead, and to the brilliant work of my colleague Nancy Condee, a professor of Slavic languages and literatures and a former director of our programs in both cultural studies and global studies. Nancy created the PittMap course that I describe in the pages that follow. I want to also name my colleagues on those trips, wonderful teachers and brave companions: Peter Veldcamp (from the School of Medicine), Svitlana Maksymenko (from Economics), and Michael Goodhart (from Political Science).

This book includes two travel essays. As I was working on these (and writing in this genre) and thinking about finding a place to publish, I turned to old friends from our Creative Writing program and beyond: Jeanne Marie Laskas, Michael Meyer, Geeta Kothari, Bill Lychack, Michael Steinberg, and Ben Lerner. They were generous in their support and encouragement.

I am very grateful to my editors, Josh Shanholtzer and Jean Ferguson Carr, for their help and encouragement. Alex Wolfe was the editorial and production director. I am grateful to him for all his care and attention, but particularly for the very striking page design. Paul Kameen and Peter Moe were my first readers from beginning to end. The manuscript was reviewed for the press by Pat Bizzell and Jackie Royster, a dream team. Their encouragement made the book possible and their comments provided the terms for the final revision. In addition, Jean Carr, Josh Shanholtzer, and Richard Miller read all of this manuscript as it was in process. Barry Qualls, Jonathan Arac, and Richard Miller read early versions of "Teacher Teacher." Mike Rose, Suresh Canagarajah, Bruce Horner, and Min-Zhan Lu read "Back to Basics." Aitor Ibarrola, Joyce Bartholomae, Gayle Rogers, Colin MacCabe, and Keith McDuffie read versions of the essay on Ramiro Pinilla. I wish all writers the blessing of such generous, attentive, and honest readers.

I want to thank our friends in Algorta for inviting us into the community and into their lives: Aitor, Isabel, Anton, Maite, Maite, Juanma, Amaia, Angel, Maria Asun, Manola, Luis, Tonio, Maribel, Carlos, y Loles.

This book is dedicated to Joyce Dunlop Bartholomae, who makes an appearance of her own in the final pages. She stands alongside everything I have ever done that mattered—and has for more than fifty-five years.

And I am offering this book to my children, and to their children and spouses. I would love to think that they will all read it, someday:

Jesse (and Mireia Brancos), Daniel (and Lauren Elson), Katie (and Bjorn Liese), and Jack, Keira, Dylan, Lily, Jordan, and Torin. The book represents a part of my life that they have seen mostly from the outside and largely in passing. My career was never as important to me as my life was with them, but my career was important to me, and I would love them to know both how and why.

I have permission from all of the students whose work I include in this volume. I gratefully acknowledge permission to reprint the full text or an excerpt from the following poems. "At the Fishhouses" from *POEMS* by Elizabeth Bishop. Copyright © 2011 by The Alice H. Methfessel Trust. Publisher's Note and compilation copyright © 2011 by Farrar, Straus and Giroux. Reprinted by permission of Farrar, Straus and Giroux. All Rights Reserved. Excerpts from "In English in a Poem" from *Then, Suddenly—* by Lynn Emanuel ©1999. Reprinted by permission of the University of Pittsburgh Press. Excerpts from Tony Hoagland, "Commercial for a Summer Night" from *What Narcissism Means to Me* ©2003 by Tony Hoagland. Reprinted with the permission of The Permissions Company, LLC, on behalf of Graywolf Press, Minneapolis, Minnesota, graywolfpress.org. Excerpts from "In Sofia" from *Crazy Love* ©2003 by Anthony Petrosky. Reprinted by permission of the Louisiana State University Press. Joyce Bartholomae provided all the translations from Spanish.

LIKE
WHAT
WE
IMAGINE

Introduction

Like What We Imagine Knowledge to Be

In the spring of 1982, I was promoted to associate professor with tenure in Pitt's English department. That fall, I began a year as a Fulbright lecturer in American literature at the University of Deusto, in Bilbao, Spain. I had trained as a Victorianist, and I had just spent six years at Pitt teaching freshman composition. I didn't hide any of this when I wrote the application for a position in American Literature.

In the application, I said that I had been teaching contemporary American literature for the past six years, which I had, teaching it both as literature and as writing. (I took time to explain what that distinction meant to me.)

And I said that I had been working on the front lines of American literacy, preparing courses for thousands of students, eighteen, nineteen, twenty years old, semester after semester, including a substantial number of first-generation college students, mostly working class, some African American, but all of them learning to be writers in America in the mid-1970s, early 1980s, even though these were writers for whom the label *writer* had a difficult or tenuous hold. I knew it was a stretch, but this was an argument I believed in, and so it was easy to write.

I may have used a line from Raymond Williams' essay "Culture is Ordinary." It was hard for me then, as it is hard for me now, to write anything without quoting or channeling Williams. Here is the section of that essay that has had abiding importance for me: "Culture is ordinary: that is the first fact. Every human society has its own shape, its own purposes, its own meanings. Every human society expresses these, in institutions, and in arts and learning. The making of a society is the finding of common meanings and directions, and its growth is an active debate and amendment under the pressures of experience, contact, and discovery, writing themselves into the land."

He goes on: "A culture has two aspects: the known meanings and directions, which its members are trained to; the new observations and meanings, which are offered and tested. These are the ordinary processes of human societies and human minds, and we see through them the nature of a culture: that it is always both traditional and creative; that it is both the most ordinary common meanings and the finest individual meanings." The common, the known, the ordinary—these labels came easily. It is harder for Williams to name what is poised outside: the "creative," the "new," the "the finest individual meanings," the institutions of the arts and learning.

I had been taking the first-year writing course as a primary site of contact and debate and would sometimes label this other arena of knowledge as "academic," a decision I often regret. Williams's point was, however, that "what we imagine knowledge to be" is a product of the meeting of diverse practices and expectations and not the erasure of one by the other. No one of them was, he said, sufficiently articulate.

My dissertation was shaped by his account of Thomas Hardy. In "Notes on English Prose: 1780–1950," Williams locates the debate between ordinary common meanings and "the finest individual meanings" in the differences between narrative language and reported speech, the diverse voices in, say, the novels of Charles Dickens, Elizabeth Gaskell, and George Eliot. Hardy, however, served (as my students have served me) to embody these moments of contact, these active and fundamental debates, within the work of a single writer:

> But Hardy as writer was mainly concerned with the interaction between . . . the educated and the customary: not just as the characteristics of social groups, but as ways of seeing and feeling, within a single mind. And then neither established language would serve to express this tension and disturbance. Neither, in fact, was sufficiently articulate. An educated style, as it had developed in a particular and exclusive group, could be dumb in intensity and limited in humanity. A customary style, while carrying the voice of feeling, could be still thwarted by ignorance and complacent in repetition and habit. Hardy veered between them.

I don't have a copy of my Fulbright application, but whatever it is I wrote, it worked.

Now, in applying for the Fulbright lectureship, I was fulfilling a promise Joyce and I had made to each other when we married, in 1969, a promise that we would use the opportunities of an academic career to live and teach abroad. We wanted our children to learn their Spanish on the streets and on the playgrounds, from the ground up. Joyce, a Spanish teacher, had spent a considerable amount of time studying outside the United States—a summer at the University of Guanajuato in Mexico and a junior year (1967–68) at Complutense, the University of Madrid. I knew if I wanted to keep this beautiful woman in my life, I'd better get with the program. And so I did.

In the fall of 1967, I was working as a waiter at Bunn's Restaurant in Delaware, Ohio, the home of Ohio Wesleyan University. I saved my money. At Thanksgiving I told my parents that I wouldn't be home for the three-week Christmas break, that I was going to Spain to visit Joyce. We had plans to travel south to Granada and Cordoba and then north to ski in Andorra. My father said, "You can't go to

Europe. I've never been to Europe." My mother cried and bought me a raincoat, a trench coat. I lived in Akron, Ohio. I had never been on an airplane, and I had never traveled farther than my parents' hometown, Winona, Minnesota. The trip to Spain changed my life. It's that simple.

In 1982, when I told my senior colleagues what I was doing, that I had been awarded a Fulbright to teach in Bilbao, there was some considerable skepticism. Why would I take a year in Spain? Spain, the Spanish language, Spanish literature, the Basque country—these weren't my "subjects." I wasn't working in that field.

Bob Whitman was the most senior of the seniors. He had a 1956 Harvard PhD. His wife, Marina von Neumann Whitman, was a well-known economist, later a member of Richard Nixon's Council of Economic Advisers. Bob joined Pitt's English department in 1960 as an assistant professor and was promoted to professor in 1967. And in 1967, he became department chair, a post he held until 1973, with a year or two off in Washington, DC. Whitman's subject was drama. He was concerned that I might lose my focus and lose my discipline, that I might fall out of sight.

And I thought, *Well, yeah, that sounds like a plan.* I was eager for breathing room and thinking room. I didn't want to keep doing the same thing over and over again. (At this point in my career, my "subject" was error analysis.)

On my sabbatical, I wrote "Inventing the University," a much-traveled essay that was initially unreadable to my editor (and good friend), Mike Rose, who couldn't figure out why I didn't write what I was supposed to write for a volume on cognitive approaches to writer's block. I started it on the third floor of an old stone house in the old port, the Puerto Viejo, in Algorta, a small town on the coast north of Bilbao. As the weather improved, I moved out onto a balcony cut into the red tile roof, where I could watch the fishing boats as they came in and out, following the rhythm of their workday.

Bilbao is an old industrial city on the north coast of the Iberian Peninsula, on the southern edge of the Bay of Biscay. It is, in fact, Pittsburgh's sister city. I taught American literature at the University of Deusto, a Jesuit school and one of the few private universities in Spain. In 1982, Deusto was across the river from an abandoned shipyard—rusted oil drums and cranes like giant praying mantises. If you stand at that spot now, you will see the iconic Richard Gehry Guggenheim Museum and, all around it, green parks, landmarks restored, and new skyscrapers.

In 1982, the river was filthy and stunk of sewage and dead fish. Now the river is clean, and you can see both small racing shells and the larger *traineras*, the oceangoing shells with a crew of thirteen that are raced in bays and harbors, or from island to island, in towns and villages along the coast.

The river is the Rio Nervión, which in English is pronounced *Monongahela*. It is the home of *Altos Hornos de Vizcaya*, the high ovens where steel was made for pre- and postwar Europe. In 1982,

Romano Salvatori, a Westinghouse engineer and the husband of my dear colleague Mariolina, hooked us up with Leroy Sauter, an engineer with US Steel, who was serving as a consultant to Altos Hornos as these mills, like the Pittsburgh mills, were shutting down. Leroy and his wife, Lillian, put us up while we looked for a place to live.

Joyce and I (and, for a while, our children) have returned to Bilbao and to Deusto every sabbatical year, for a year, from 1989 to 2018, eight years total, with many side trips in between and with time spent hosting Spanish kids studying abroad and Spanish scholars on sabbatical leave. In 2000, we bought a flat in the town of Algorta, once a fishing village to the north of Bilbao, now a bedroom community. We live in a 1960s-style building on a cliff above the rocky coast of the Bay of Biscay, which we see from our windows and balcony. I retired from teaching in August 2018, and we now do our best to split our year between there and here (or here and there).

I give this brief bit of biography to provide some context to the essays that follow. All are about reading and writing, literacy. Most take as their subject the teaching of writing in required composition courses. But there is also an essay on the Spanish author Ramiro Pinilla (whom I met and interviewed at his home in Algorta). And there are a series of essays on travel writing. I'll have more to say about travel and travel writing later. But, for now, let me give just a brief account of how I understand the lived connection between the genres.

I was formed as a teacher and a scholar within the traditions of Cambridge English, where the key question to ask—to ask as a reader, a writer, or a teacher—went something like this: Where, with this text, do you locate yourself? Or, Where, within this text, might you find yourself?

When you read, write, and teach, in other words, you locate yourself (or not) in relation to a discursive environment: ways of reading, structures of feeling, cultural contexts, local history, new languages, the work of knowing. The problems of finding one's way as a reader or writer come quickly to focus when you are also trying to find your way around a major city, like Beijing, in a language you don't understand, like Mandarin. For me, as a teacher (and writer), I was lost and found in Spain, Argentina, South Africa, Ecuador, Brazil, China, India, Cuba, and (not surprisingly) England.

The title of this book comes from a poem by Elizabeth Bishop, "At the Fishhouses." The poem is set in Nova Scotia, and not Algorta, but I find it easy to bridge the gap, since much of the writing here was done at a desk that looks across to Santurce, where the fishing boats tie up at the fishhouses, and where we go to eat fresh sardines cooked over a wood fire.

I often use this poem in my composition courses. It is, I say, an exercise in (and a defense of) attention to detail. And it has something important to say about the relationship between examples and conclusions.

At the Fishhouses

Although it is a cold evening,
down by one of the fishhouses
an old man sits netting,
his net, in the gloaming almost invisible
a dark purple-brown,
and his shuttle worn and polished.
The air smells so strong of codfish
it makes one's nose run and one's eyes water.
The five fishhouses have steeply peaked roofs
and narrow, cleated gangplanks slant up
to storerooms in the gables
for the wheelbarrows to be pushed up and down on.

All is silver: the heavy surface of the sea,
swelling slowly as if considering spilling over,
is opaque, but the silver of the benches,
the lobster pots, and masts, scattered
among the wild jagged rocks,
is of an apparent translucence
like the small old buildings with an emerald moss
growing on their shoreward walls.
The big fish tubs are completely lined
with layers of beautiful herring scales
and the wheelbarrows are similarly plastered
with creamy iridescent coats of mail,
with small iridescent flies crawling on them.
Up on the little slope behind the houses,
set in the sparse bright sprinkle of grass,
is an ancient wooden capstan,
cracked, with two long bleached handles
and some melancholy stains, like dried blood,
where the ironwork has rusted.
The old man accepts a Lucky Strike.
He was a friend of my grandfather.
We talk of the decline in the population
and of codfish and herring
while he waits for a herring boat to come in.
There are sequins on his vest and on his thumb.
He has scraped the scales, the principal beauty,
from unnumbered fish with that black old knife,
the blade of which is almost worn away.

Down at the water's edge, at the place
where they haul up the boats, up the long ramp
descending into the water, thin silver
tree trunks are laid horizontally
across the gray stones, down and down
at intervals of four or five feet.

And then, at this point in the poem, there are gestures toward the kinds of meanings poems are supposed to have, big statements, but these don't take. They are quickly dismissed, or the speaker is distracted, again, by detail:

Cold dark deep and absolutely clear,
element bearable to no mortal,
to fish and to seals . . . One seal particularly
I have seen here evening after evening.
He was curious about me. He was interested in music;
like me a believer in total immersion,
so I used to sing him Baptist hymns.
I also sang "A Mighty Fortress Is Our God."
He stood up in the water and regarded me
steadily, moving his head a little.
Then he would disappear, then suddenly emerge
almost in the same spot, with a sort of shrug
as if it were against his better judgment.
Cold dark deep and absolutely clear,
the clear gray icy water . . . Back, behind us,
the dignified tall firs begin.
Bluish, associating with their shadows,
a million Christmas trees stand
waiting for Christmas. The water seems suspended
above the rounded gray and blue-gray stones.

Colm Toíbín is one of the best readers I know of Elizabeth Bishop's poems. I learned much from his lovely, short book, *On Elizabeth Bishop*, part of the Princeton University Press series Writers on Writing. I read his book as I was revising this manuscript. Since I was using "At the Fishhouses" in my introduction (and for my title), and as I had written about Toíbín in my last chapter, I was curious to see what he had said about this poem.

Toíbín noticed what I think most readers would notice—that at about this point in the poem, the tone begins to change. From detail and everyday language, Bishop begins to use a tone, he says, "rich in cadence and lifted language."

"Lifted language." I find this phrase particularly useful for the ways it combines theft with transcendence. As a writer or speaker, you get out by breaking in. That is what I am thinking when I read this. And, tellingly, Toíbín then turns to Seamus Heaney (and Heaney's essay on Bishop in the collection *Finders Keepers*) to let Heaney say what he (Toíbín) is now prepared to say. That is, he uses Heaney's words in place of his own to describe this moment in the poem. (Why does he do this? I don't believe it is because he lacks, or worries he lacks, the authority to speak for himself. I think he values the company.) He says, "What we have been offered, among other things, is the slow-motion spectacle of a well-disciplined poetic imagination being tempted to dare a big leap, hesitating, and then with powerful sureness actually taking the leap."

Here are the concluding lines of the poem. This is where the leap is taken:

I have seen it over and over, the same sea, the same,
slightly, indifferently swinging above the stones,
icily free above the stones,
above the stones and then the world.
If you should dip your hand in,
your wrist would ache immediately,
your bones would begin to ache and your hand would burn
as if the water were a transmutation of fire
that feeds on stones and burns with a dark gray flame.
If you tasted it, it would first taste bitter,
then briny, then surely burn your tongue.
It is like what we imagine knowledge to be:
dark, salt, clear, moving, utterly free,

drawn from the cold hard mouth
of the world, derived from the rocky breasts
forever, flowing and drawn, and since
our knowledge is historical, flowing, and flown.

It is *like* what we imagine knowledge to be. Bishop leaves us two steps away from what knowledge *is*. The line says that the cold saltwater or taste of the water (or this, this precise act of description, becoming metaphor) is "like what we imagine knowledge to be."

That is how I would sum up my career. Semester after semester, and week by week, I have worked closely with first-year students, reading their sentences, suggesting revisions both large and small, trying to find a way of saying: *Well, yes, I think this is it—this is like what we imagine knowledge to be. Yes. Interesting.*

Most of the essays in this book were efforts to describe how I organize such a course and what, over time, I have learned to do as a teacher of writing. What is the point of the required first-year writing course? Where do you begin? Where do you end? What do you do along the way?

Here is a long passage from *On Elizabeth Bishop*, where Toíbín is providing a general description of Bishop's work as a writer. I find it to be a useful laying out of terms, perfect for this introduction. The key terms for me are *little* and *much*, *irony* and *futility*, *precise* and *exact*, *essence*, *stability*, and *resonance*, *limits* and *failures*, *odd delights*. Here is the pivot: *A word was a tentative form of control. Grammar was an enactment of how things stood.*

She began with the idea that little is known and that much is puzzling. The effort, then, to make a true statement in poetry

—to claim that something *is* something, or *does* something—required a hushed, solitary concentration. A true statement for her carried with it, buried in its rhythm, considerable degrees of irony because it was oddly futile; it was either too simple or too loaded to mean a great deal. It did not do anything much, other than distract or briefly please the reader. Nonetheless, it was essential for Elizabeth Bishop that words in a statement be precise and exact. "Since we do float on an unknown sea," she wrote to Robert Lowell, "I think we should examine the other floating things that come our way carefully; who knows what might depend on it." . . .

A word was a tentative form of control. Grammar was an enactment of how things stood. But nothing was stable, so words and their structures could lift and have resonance, could move out, take in essences as a sponge soaks in water. Thus language became gesture in spite of itself; it was rooted in simple description, and then it bloomed or withered; it was suggestive, had a funny shape, or some flourishes, or a tone and texture that had odd delights, but it had all sorts of limits and failures.

I think student writers take in essences as sponges soak up water. "Little is known and much is puzzling"—a student's command of that pairing falls quite short of ours and our expectations for serious work. Student writers want conclusions and they want to get to them as quickly (and easily) as possible. This is one of the ways the written language of these writers becomes gesture in spite of itself. I think student writers can learn to apply terms like these to all that is happening in their sentences. I believe that grammar matters and must be taught. I have learned that such invitations to revision or rewriting are necessary lessons; they can define the stages of a writer's education (and may define the structure of a syllabus). I know that student writing can produce odd (and significant) delights, even in the midst of its limits and failures. It has been my job to help my students to see this, and to insist that they act on the basis of such understanding.

On April 25, 1983, almost thirty-five years ago to the day before my retirement, Raymond Williams presented one of four lectures on the occasion of *his*. It was titled "Cambridge English, Past and Present" and published first in *The London Review of Books*, later collected in *Writing in Society*. The lecture is a tribute to the work of a Cambridge faculty committed to a redefinition of English as a school subject. It is also elegiac, lamenting the passing of Cambridge English and regretting its failures along the way, the most recent being the very public sacking of my good friend and colleague, Colin MacCabe.

For my conclusion, I want to read aloud (so to speak) a passage from this essay. It comes at an interesting moment toward the end, one where Williams struggles to find the words for what Cambridge English might have been—and for what we have lost in its undoing. You'll hear the language falter, collapse, and then draw itself back together. It is a telling moment—for me, unforgettable. And a bit scary. He has reached his limits as a writer and teacher. The grammar enacts how things stood.

What is English's proper subject, he asks?

Language in history: that full field. Even within a more specialized emphasis, language produced in works through conventions and institutions which, properly examined, are the really active society. Not a background to be produced for annotation where on a private reading—naked reader before naked text—it appears to be relevant and required. Instead, the kind of reading in which the conditions of production, in the fullest sense, can be understood in relation to both writer and reader, actual reading and actual writing. A newly active social sense of writing and reading, through the social and material historical realities of language, in a world in which it is closely and precisely known, in every act of writing and reading, that these practices connect with, are inseparable from, the whole set of social practices and relationships which define writers and readers as active human beings, as distinct from the idealized and projected "authors" and "trained readers" who are assumed to float, on a guarded privilege, above the rough, divisive and diverse world of which yet, by some alchemy, they possess the essential secret.

What is our subject? He asks such a seemingly easy question and then struggles to compose an answer that doesn't fall back on cliché, on standard terms. Still, around midparagraph, as he works toward a possible reformulation, he turns to such surprisingly common terms: "actual" and "active." Actual readers actively reading; actual writers actively writing. *That* is our subject, he says, as though perhaps he was closer now, here at the end of his career, to finding a way of saying what he wants to say. He is trying to make these ordinary words make uncommon sense. It is such an odd and dramatic moment.

And then at the end of the paragraph, he brings himself back to form as he characterizes those professionals who don't get it (some his colleagues), the trained readers who float on guarded privilege and who enforce the borders between literature and the rough, divisive, and diverse world where students are partners in the struggle to read and to write—here and now, week after week, moving toward the end of term.

As always, I choose to read this as though I had written it. It says, this is your job. Pay close attention to students' sentences as they are being written. This is what we do. And the "we" here means student and teacher. And it says: think of this writing as like what we imagine knowledge to be, what we might imagine knowledge to be right here and right now, in this place and at this moment, and for this actual, active writer and this actual, active reader. Do this for now. Next week we'll be somewhere else.

And then, because knowledge is not just repetition, and because revision is the only way to engage writers with their writing, as a teacher I think hard, I try again to imagine where we are and where we might go next, and I begin to write comments to direct revision, and I begin to write out the assignments that will shape the work of the following few weeks. That is the big leap.

This book collects a set of essays I wrote over the last decade of my career. I completed the manuscript and submitted it to the university press in mid-September 2019, when our Pittsburgh campus was truly an international meeting place, and when our study abroad program was booming, developing both new courses and new sites.

I could never have imagined the Pittsburgh campus now, under the shadow of the coronavirus pandemic. It is early summer 2020. I am at my desk preparing the manuscript for production, while my university struggles to make plans for the upcoming academic year. Although students will be coming to campus in August, it seems certain that there will be far, far fewer international students. It will be a different place. Our study abroad programs for the fall semester have been already canceled. Students will travel less and less widely.

With the 2016 general election, our national politics had already begun to isolate us from the rest of the world, despite the best efforts of those in opposition. Now, with the pandemic, it will be some time, I suspect, before we can again present convincing arguments to reengage. I believe that we must, and I hope that we can, and it is in that hope that I send this book out into the world.

CHAPTER ONE

Everything Was Going Quite Smoothly until I Stumbled on a Footnote

From a Lecture in Honor of David Osborne (1930–1996), Professor of English at Ohio Wesleyan University

The grand work of literary genius is a work of synthesis and exposition, not of analysis and discovery; its gift lies in the faculty of being happily inspired by a certain intellectual and spiritual atmosphere, by a certain order of ideas, when it finds itself in them; of dealing divinely with these ideas, presenting them in the most effective and attractive combinations,—making beautiful works with them, in short. But it must have the atmosphere, it must find itself amidst the order of ideas, in order to work freely; and these it is not so easy to command.

> — Matthew Arnold, "The Function of Criticism at the Present Time" (1865)

I was invited to give the inaugural David G. Osborne lecture at Ohio Wesleyan University, where I received my BA in English and where Professor Osborne was my teacher. He taught courses in the Romantics and the Victorians; he was known for his commitment to the lower division and to freshman composition; he was my favorite teacher, the one who made the major make sense for me. The Osborne Lecture series was established in 2003 through the generous gift of a former student, Julianna Ebert ('74). The audience was mostly faculty and undergraduates (many of them, I suspect, on assignment). This is what I said.

I came to Ohio Wesleyan as a freshman in 1965. To most of you this probably seems like a long time ago (to me, it seems a *very* long time ago), and I was prompted by the occasion of this lecture to think back to where I was—where I was in my life, where I was in history (in the period we call the 1960s), and to where I was, in Matthew Arnold's terms, within a certain order of ideas.

In 1965, we were the last freshman class to wear dinks, little multi-colored beanies you wore to remind you of what you already knew—that you were foolish and awkward and stuck out on campus like a sore thumb. Women had to be in the dorms by ten thirty on weeknights, one o'clock a.m. on the weekends, and they locked the doors if you were late. Women could not wear pants unless the temperature fell below freezing. We went off to "barn" parties, driving home at night with dozens packed into the back of rented trucks, everyone loaded to the gills with 3.2 beer, loaded to the gills or unloading—and this to save us from the dangers of drinking on campus.

We were either the last class or among the last classes to have compulsory chapel. Once a week, with a lecture or presentation, more Unitarian in spirit than Methodist, our attendance was recorded through the new technology of the IBM punch card. As a freshman, I would carry stacks of them hidden in my jacket to stuff into the box to record the presence of the absent upperclassmen in my fraternity house. At our first chapel meeting, we were greeted by the President (I think) who welcomed the class of '69. One young woman, Liz Dumbleton, shouted out from behind her program: "69 is not a class; it's a position." And I thought to myself: *Wow. Welcome to the big leagues.*

By the time we graduated, drugs had come to Delaware, Ohio; women had to be in by five o'clock a.m. (five *a.m.*, go figure); and the senior who recruited me during fraternity rush, Jack Dawson, was killed in action in Vietnam. We came clean for Gene McCarthy and took leaflets to unsuspecting Ohioans. I was working as a waiter at Bunn's restaurant when the news came through that Martin Luther King Jr. had been shot, and I was stunned by what I heard spoken over the breakfast tables.

I had some truly wonderful teachers. Anna Macias, who taught Latin American history and whom I got to know again years later, since she was a close friend of a colleague of mine at the University of Pittsburgh. Ben Spencer, who was the very image for us of the scholar: silent and kind, confident of what he knew, which seemed to be everything, and with the ability to read American literature out loud to us in a manner that was, itself, a form of criticism—the pace and inflection, the phrasing and emphasis, all did as much for us as the critical essays we read. Ron Rollins, who led us into a passion for Joyce and for Irish literature and who had the ability, which I cannot imitate, to speak for minutes at a time in alliterative phrases: Bloomsday, June 16, a dismal day in dear dirty Dublin.

And David Osborne, in whose name we are gathered today. The most vivid classroom memory I have of David are of those moments when he would suddenly sing in class, with a dear, true voice; he would do it without warning—a period song, a ballad, a song from the Victorian stage would interrupt a lecture or discussion to illustrate a point—or, perhaps just to remind us that there was more there than we knew. He was a surprising teacher; his classroom was a quiet place where we learned to listen carefully, where we were expected to remember names and dates and to read documents that were neither novels nor poems, and the reward was a surprising insight, a Victorian moment that suddenly made vivid sense of the present. I was inspired to memorize Arnold's "Dover Beach," thinking it would be a good way to impress my girlfriend, Joyce Dunlop, a Tri-Delt.

These teachers and their colleagues, this lovely and historic campus, these old buildings and the memories they contain, all provided a certain intellectual and spiritual atmosphere, a certain order of ideas—and it was here that I found myself in 1965. I first read Arnold as a student of David Osborne (my copy of *Essays in Criticism* is heavily marked and annotated); I can remember struggling to read these long, strange sentences. And the passage I used as my epigraph is one of the passages I had heavily marked on its first reading: The gift of literary genius "lies in the faculty of being happily inspired by a certain intellectual and spiritual atmosphere, by a certain order of ideas, when it finds itself in them."

Well—nostalgia is the blank check issued to a weak mind. I am waxing nostalgic and it is time to stop and to get this lecture moving.

I love that line: "Nostalgia is the blank check issued to a weak mind." It comes to me from a poem ("Commercial for a Summer Night") by a friend and former colleague, Tony Hoagland, in a book with a wonderful title, itself a small poem: *What Narcissism Means to Me.* This is the opening of the poem:

That one night in the middle of the summer
when people move their chairs outside
and put the TVs on the porch
so the dark is full of murmuring blue lights.

We were drinking beer with the sound off,
watching the figures on the screen—
the bony blondes, the lean-jawed guys
who decorate the perfume and the cars—

the pretty ones
the merchandise is wearing this year.

Alex said, *I wish they made a shooting gallery
using people like that.*

Greg said, *That woman has a Ph.D. in Face.*
Then we saw a preview for a movie

about a movie star who is
    having a movie made about her,
and Boz said, *This country is getting stupider every year.*

Then Greg said that things were better in the sixties
and Russ said that Harold Bloom said
that Nietzsche said Nostalgia
is the blank check issued to a weak mind,

and Greg said,
    They didn't have checks back then, stupid,
and Susan said It's too bad you guys can't get
Spellcheck for your brains.

Russ said Harold Bloom said Nietzsche said—this is my theme: transitions, legacy, the way things are handed down over time, how words and ideas are used and reused, and what schooling and teachers might have to do with that process.

Hoagland's poem draws its language and inspiration from the poet's lively, critical, mean-spirited engagement with both academic and popular culture. You hear the poem and you hear *Cheers* and *Friends* (and maybe Bordo and Baudrillard). You think of all those shows where people are prettier and wittier than we ever get to be in our everyday lives. Carl Dennis, in his book *Poetry as Persuasion*, categorizes Hoagland as a political poet; he says Hoagland's poems are all about America as she shapes and determines who we are, what can be said, thought, and done. And that's how this poem ends, with a reference out to America and to its people, and not only to the pretty ones the merchandise is wearing this year:

and we sat in quiet pleasure on the shore of the night,
as a tide came in and turned and carried us,
    folding chairs and all,

far out from the coastline of America

in a perfect commercial for our lives.

You hear *Cheers* and *Friends* and then *Real World* or MTV reality shows (where bored kids watch bored kids complain about being bored). Stepping back you can hear Frank O'Hara or even Robert Frost. I also hear two other friends and colleagues, two other Pittsburgh poets.

This is Tony Petrosky, from his last book, *Crazy Love.* The poem is titled "In Sophia," and it is set in a café in Bulgaria. It makes characters of Nietzsche and Proust and turns on slogans, setting them against a bleak Eastern European background. In a café in Sophia:

> Nietzsche loves to eat here with Proust on Tolbulchin
> in the nameless restaurant in the dimness and smoke,
> unnerved through the representations of time,
> contesting life right back to its lack of sense.
>
> . . . .
> Nietzsche nods
> and picks at the bread.
>
> Proust sighs.
>
> The trees grow distant shaking their arms.
> The birds disappear and all the creatures
> fold up into the magician's books.
>
> *And as for happiness*, Proust broke in,
> *it has almost a single usefulness*
> *to make unhappiness possible.*

Suffering almost all the more deeply hollows out the heart.

Almost.

The next is Lynn Emanuel from her book *Then, Suddenly*—. The poem is titled "In English in a Poem," and it, too, has sharp edges and the move to slogan and to dialogue and to theory; and it, too, has the one great line, the one you wish you had thought of:

> I am giving a lecture on poetry
> to the painters who creak like saddles
> in their black leather jackets; in the study,
> where a fire is burning like a painting of
> a fire, I am explaining my current work
> on the erotics of narrative. It is night.
> Overhead the moon's naked heel dents
> the sky, the crickets ignite themselves
> into a snore, and the painters yawn
> lavishly waiting for me to say Something
> About Painting, the way your dog, when
> you are talking, listens for the words Good Dog.
>
> "Your indifference draws me like horses draw flies,"
> I say while noticing in the window the peonies
> throbbing with pulses, the cindery crows seething
> over the lawn. "Nevertheless," I continue, "I call
> your attention to the fact that, in this poem, what was
> once just a pronoun is now a pronoun talking about
> a peony while you sit in a room somewhere unmoved
> by this."

I hear our theorists butting heads with the MFA students and being butted in return; I hear Frank O'Hara, again, and Tony Hoagland; in the capital letters, turning clichés into allegorical dragons, I see the work of Bill Coles, a former colleague of ours and a legendary teacher of composition, and through him the now legendary freshman course at Amherst College and then to Robert Frost, one of Amherst's presiding spirits. This is the order of ideas, the atmosphere I find myself in when I sit at my desk or enter a class in Pittsburgh. These poems, these lines, are in the atmosphere, as are others, and when we are attentive, when we are taken by them, when we find ourselves there, we make each other's work possible. This is one of the things I want to say. Even when the footnotes aren't there, there are footnotes.

All of these poems think about poetry's affection for the epigrammatic line, for the slogan, and they do so in a climate that is suspicious of sloganeering. (These poems have a certain resonance during the presidential primary campaigns.) And all of these poems think about the relationship of literary theory to everyday life and everyday language. I'm not saying that these poets agreed upon a common theme or set of concerns. Influence is much more subtle than that. And if asked about influence, my guess is that they all would be quick to deny making use of the others. And I am not talking about either theft or plagiarism but about paying attention, about how our work as writers and thinkers is always, even when we don't know it, even when we don't want it to be, informed by what has come before, by what sticks, by what shapes the ways we speak and think—and what sticks sticks because the words matter. The work enters our lives and we are shaped and, hopefully, shaped for the better.

This was one of the great hopes of David Osborne in his teaching, and it was articulated for him a century before by his great hero, Matthew Arnold, in the essay I spoke from earlier, "The Function of Criticism at the Present Time." Arnold said that the purpose of criticism (choosing what to read and preparing others to read it) was to "learn and propagate the best that is known and thought in the world." And later, "Simply to know the best that is known and thought in the world, and by in its turn making this known,—to create a current of true and fresh ideas."

Sentences that echo sentences. The presence of the past in the work of the present. A current of ideas. I love to see this in my students' work. Several years ago Richard Ford came to our campus to read from his new book, *Women with Men*. I was teaching a group of first-year students, and I assigned the book so that they could be prepared for the visit. And I assigned a recent *New York Times* review by Michael Gorra and asked my students to write a book review, one that spoke from the perspective of their generation, its reading and its values.

Here was the opening of the published review:

> Richard Ford is among the most traditional of contemporary American writers and also among the most original. Original because traditional: in the sense that T. S. Eliot meant when he wrote that "not only the best, but the most individual parts" of a writer's work "may be those in which the dead . . . his ancestors, assert their immortality most vigorously."
>
> Ford's sinewy and distinctively American voice contains the echoing tones of many ancestors. . . . And Ford's title does indeed signal an allegiance to the Hemingway legacy, or at least a part of it—his fascination with a world of male rituals that has, in the past, led him to write about duck hunting and car theft and fishing and football.

Here is the opening of the student essay I reproduced for class discussion—you will hear it rework not only the idea but the syntax of Gorra's review, and it keeps the performance moving along quite convincingly until, with the last sentence, it comes undone, and the student reminds us that he is a student:

> Richard Ford's *Women with Men* speaks in a strong, unrepen-
> tantly male voice enriched with a smoky sense of Americana
> and a slanted, self-deprecating wit. Ford's intelligent yet unas-
> suming prose wraps around his characters and places them in
> the timeless sensibility of classic American writers like J. D.
> Salinger or Ernest Hemingway. The short stories "Jealous" and
> "Occidentals" both focus on male protagonists and decidedly
> male issues. . . . Together, the two characters and stories serve
> up a diner-sized heap of commentary on knowledge, wisdom,
> experience and growing up.

The other students in my class were furious over this essay. It was
cheating; it was copying; the writer wasn't playing fair.

The writer, on the other hand, was completely floored by these
accusations. It had never occurred to him that there were parallels; he
thought of the opening as his, he thought the gesture toward literary
history (Salinger added to Hemingway) was an achievement, and he
thought of the review as one of his very best pieces of writing. He
was proud of it.

As he should have been—it was his, as much as any of us ever own
our writing, and it was smart (a gesture toward the kind of thinking we
think of as smart), it was stylish and voiced, and it was the best thing
he had done all term. And, I said to the class, it was the first paper
of theirs I had read that sounded like writing rather than the dreadful standard issue of the English class: "When one reads the short
stories of Richard Ford, one can be transported to other worlds. . . ."
That language, too, is prepared, learned, available; it is just that it is
not the language of adults speaking about things that matter, and so
it is not a language I want to encourage. And the reason the students
all felt so angry, so betrayed, although I didn't say this to the class,
was that one of their own had broken out and tried to do something
more interesting—not more original, that's not my claim for it, but
more interesting. The grand work of literary genius, says Arnold, is
synthesis and exposition, not analysis and discovery.

If there is a lesson here, and I believe there is, it is that you have to be ready to be taken by the words of others—learning, including learning to write, is not about invention, about being creative. It is not about having ideas on your own; it is about finding yourself in relation to the work of others, having a voice in intense conversation with other voices, learning to listen and to read in ways that allow the rhythms and cadences of other people's prose to dance at the ends of your fingers while you type away at the keyboard.

I came to Ohio Wesleyan the year after Alfred Ferguson left to teach at the University of Massachusetts, Boston. I was told that I missed out on a great teacher. He left, as I later came to learn, because this university, like most universities in the 1960s, had difficulty finding room in the faculty for women, especially wives with PhDs. His wife was Mary Anne Ferguson, and their daughter, Jean Ferguson Carr, is now my colleague and good friend.

It is a small world. Mary Anne Ferguson became the Chair of the English department at UMass Boston; she was also one of the first women in the country to bring women's studies into the curriculum, and because women's studies has always been concerned with who has access to knowledge and authority, that English department has always had a strong interest in composition. While he was teaching as an adjunct in an academic support program at UMass Boston, Richard Miller decided he wanted to work for a PhD with a focus on composition and pedagogy. Our faculty were well known to the faculty at UMB; one of our students, Judy Goleman, was teaching there, and Richard applied to Pittsburgh, where I became one of his teachers and the director of his dissertation. Richard went on to chair the English department at Rutgers, where, many years before, I had completed my PhD.

There is a circle here—OWU, Pitt, UMass, Rutgers—and I want the loop to return to David Osborne, who was hired by Alfred Ferguson, and this turns out to be surprisingly easy, although you will have to allow me a few minutes of what might seem like a digression.

Richard Miller's dissertation began as a study of the ways in which several educational initiatives, like the Great Books program in the United States or the Open University in Britain, imagined and represented the student—or the position that would be occupied by a young person who would then take on the role of the student. The dissertation became a book, published by Cornell University Press in 1998, and it is titled *As If Learning Mattered: Reforming Higher Education*.

In the opening chapter, Richard tells the story of the early stages of the research project, the dissertation, when he was thinking about Matthew Arnold, since Matthew Arnold had become the fall guy or the punching bag for those interested in radical educational reform, as Richard was. Arnold became the punching bag largely because of the broad circulation (and misreading) of his statement that the function of criticism and education should be to "learn and propagate the best that is known and thought in the world." This had come to stand as the representative slogan of elitism, and Arnold as spokesman for colonial power; his essays had come to stand as an argument for closing the canon to the work of emerging writers, or minority writers; for Edward Said, in *The World, the Text and the Critic*, it rationalized the hegemony of "an identifiable set of ideas, which Arnold honorifically calls culture, over all other ideas in society." And Matthew Arnold came to stand for the English (and Western) desire to colonize the world and to impart strict controls over thought, speech, and writing.

Here is Richard telling the story of his dissertation project. I am going to present a lengthy passage, since it tells a story of scholarship that I take to be representative:

> [W]hen this research began, I had meant for Matthew Arnold to figure, as he does throughout much of the academy,

as the whipping boy whose whipping would inaugurate my own "oppositional" project. I would identify him as a bookish elitist, out of touch with the world, blind to the needs of real students. All that remained for me to do was connect the dots and move on to the next exercise in critical historiography. And, as it happened, I discovered there was no shortage of evidence to support such a project: opening "Culture and Anarchy" to almost any page effortlessly provided me with all the damning quotes I would ever need; contemporary work that decried Arnold's influence, such as Chris Baldick's *The Social Mission of English Criticism* and Edward Said's *The World, the Text, and the Critic*, was everywhere ready to hand. Everything was going quite smoothly until I stumbled on a footnote that brought my developing argument crashing to the ground.

As it turns out, Arnold was not the wealthy aristocrat I assumed him to be. Rather, he spent his life as one of Her Majesty's inspectors of schools, traveling the country to visit the nation's poorest schools and to inspect the often gruesomely disappointing results. This unwanted discovery led me to read in parts of the Arnoldian corpus that originally had held no interest for me—Arnold's book-length reports on foreign education, his annual inspection reports on British schools, his anonymous tracts concerning the Revised Code. In order to understand these works, I had to move to other parts of the archive altogether: parliamentary papers, histories of popular modes of instruction, handbooks describing the duties of school inspectors. . . .

To be confronted with how little I knew about the history and the mechanisms for disseminating mass education was embarrassing, and my failure even to consider these matters important to my study was a further sign of the "conceptual crudity," as Silver would put it, of my original approach to these materials.

With this insight in mind, I realized that I could use my own ignorance and expectations as signs of a state I shared with many others. This, in turn, enabled me to historicize the connections between what I knew and didn't know and the areas of thought I had and hadn't been introduced to in school, as well as the teachers, writers, and ideas that I had and hadn't been given access to through the educational system; the autodidactic pursuits that that system had and hadn't given rise to; and, most important, the ways I had and hadn't been taught to define, think about, and respond to ignorance.

There is a way in which this is a conventional story. A scholar heads out with a fixed idea, a thesis, but stumbles on a footnote (or a document in the archive, or a line in a book), and, if this is a good scholar, a serious one, everything stops and the project reorganizes itself and the scholar realizes how unprepared she is for the work that must be done. She has to teach herself (to become an autodidact) to read things she is unprepared to read and to think things she has not yet thought. It is exciting; it is necessary; it is conventional and predictable; and it must be staged (and experienced) as a surprise. Richard found himself in a position to make the most of what he didn't know rather than to avoid the unknown or to skirt the unmanageable. As I often say to freshman—the problem with the thesis is that it often comes before you know what you are talking about. More than anything else, you need to learn to think of ideas as provisional and strategic; of the opening as a way of getting started with a topic; of the summary as a point to push off from. If you are lucky, you will find that the thesis doesn't hold, that you have come upon counterexamples or sidetracks too interesting and too compelling to ignore.

Richard says, "Everything was going quite smoothly until I stumbled on a footnote that brought my developing argument crashing to the ground." As I remember the progress of the dissertation, he didn't stumble on a footnote; I put something in his path—or, to be precise, I put a book in his hands. The book was Fred Walcott's *The Origins of Culture and Anarchy: Matthew Arnold and Popular Education in England.* This was a book that was given to me by David Osborne, who had worked for years with the letters Arnold wrote as a school inspector.

In the late 1970s, in fact, when I was a brand-new Assistant Professor at the University of Pittsburgh, David had written to see if I would be interested in editing these letters with him. He turned to me, I think, as a gesture toward a young person in his profession, a profession that requires research projects and publications, and he turned to me, I think, because I was at a large research university, with collegial and travel and library resources that are not available to scholars working at the smaller, liberal arts colleges. He was a brilliant teacher, but he was not a published (or publishing) scholar, and he felt this as burden. We never did collaborate on this project, but over the period of half a year we did share notes and books, and one of those books made its way into the path of Richard Miller, who stumbled on a book that passed from my teacher to me and from me to him. The third chapter of Richard's book is about the importance of considering Arnold's career as a school inspector—it is a direct extension of David Osborne's work.

It is appropriate, even essential, that Richard and I would tell the "footnote" story differently. One is a teacher's story; the other is a story of scholarship and writing, of discovery and initiative, where the work is Richard's and not mine and not David Osborne's. I'm not concerned with who has the better memory; I am concerned with the necessity of memorial, and there is no dearer memorial than to see a student write himself (or herself) into the narrative of scholarship. And in the narrative of scholarship, the teacher must disappear and become silent. In his dedication to my copy of his book, Richard wrote: "For Dave, my mentor, my most trusted advisor, and my dear friend, who made this book and my unlikely academic career possible by teaching me how to invent a place for myself in the community." His was the act of invention, and Richard, in remembering me so kindly, is echoing the title of an essay of mine, "Inventing the University," an essay that talks about learning in something like these terms. Richard will also know that my method in this talk is his, one thing next to another, inspired by the remarkable (Arnold would say "beautiful") essays in his book *Writing at the End of the World*.

The first time I read Walt Whitman was at Ohio Wesleyan in a junior seminar. I was sitting next to Ben Spencer in a small room with a round table. While he was talking, I was watching his face and trying in my mind to compose a poem (which I'm afraid I often did in lieu of taking notes). This was going to be a poem about his thick skin, which was coarse and freckled and whiskered and folded as it broke over his tight shirt collar. ("Elephantine" was the word I was stuck on, and I was trying to think about how to make it honorific.) I was captured by Ben Spencer's voice when he read and spoke, by the look of his skin and the hairs sticking out of his ears, features I had not yet seen in my own father and that, of course, I now see in the morning when I look into the mirror to shave—or that I see if I have my glasses handy.

He read,

> I teach straying from me, yet who can stray from me?
> I follow you whoever you are from the present hour,
> My words itch at your ears till you understand them.
>
> I do not say these things for a dollar, or to fill up the time
>   while I wait for a boat;
> (It is you talking just as much as myself, I act as the tongue of you,
> Tied in your mouth, in mine it begins to be loosen'd.)

And in the famous final lines of *Song of Myself*, Whitman says:

You will hardly know who I am or what I mean,
But I shall be good health to you nevertheless,
And filter and fibre your blood.

Failing to fetch me at first keep encouraged,
Missing me one place search another,
I stop somewhere waiting for you.

I do not say these things for a dollar, or to fill up the time while I wait for a boat. For me and for many, more than I could know or number, David Osborne has been good health and filter and fibre, central to me to the order of ideas. I think of him when I think of the desire for the best that is thought and known. I wish everyone the opportunity of such teachers.

* As I was preparing this collection, I received the news that Tony Hoagland died at age sixty-four of pancreatic cancer. For several years, I used *What Narcissism Means to Me* as the opening text in my first-year composition course. It spoke to students in ways that made them smarter and funnier and bolder and more interesting. It opened up possibilities and it always worked, week after week, as a prompt or a reminder of what it means to be alive in the world.

CHAPTER TWO

Teacher Teacher

It is with some of the canniness of his commitment to what he terms "ulteriority" that Frost refrains from remarking on the conventional representation of the oven bird's characteristic call: "*Teacher, teacher*." Frost himself is such a teacher to teachers, and so is Poirier, whose splendid book represents the work of knowing at its highest and most unlabored intensity.

—John Hollander, foreword to *Robert Frost: The Work of Knowing* by Richard Poirier

It is Fall, 2010, and I'm headed toward the final weeks of our required first-year writing course. I have received a paper I've read many times before, and I am preparing to teach it in class. I will distribute a copy to my students; I will read it out loud, ask an opening question and organize the discussion.

If you have taught this course, you've received this paper. It is a standard theme, student writing—the writing produced from a certain well-defined (and overdetermined) cultural and institutional space. In this version, the student was asked to think about himself as a representative case and to write about the forces that shaped a young person's life here and now, in the United States in 2010. The prompt was framed by a chapter from K. Anthony Appiah's "Race, Culture, Identity: Misunderstood Connections" (in *Color Conscious*).

The writer of this paper had come to college in the fall of 2010 after serving in the Third Ranger Battalion as part of the US Army Special Operations Command. Although everyone in the class knew that he had been in the armed services, no one knew the details. This was the first and only personal essay I had assigned; his essay was eagerly anticipated and eagerly read. When it came time for class discussion, however, there was only one paragraph that seemed to command attention:

> We were on a mission in Afghanistan, and while we were setting into position we began taking fire. This was not uncommon for Afghanistan, because the people there are much more aggressive than in Iraq. Usually the gun fights last only a few minutes, but this one lasted eight hours, during which we took three casualties. One casualty had a gunshot wound to the shoulder, and one had a gunshot wound to the foot. These two only spent a few days in the hospital. The third casualty, Matthew Bradford Smith, had a gunshot wound to the leg which severed his femoral artery. This wound would ultimately lead to his death eight days later. This was by far the most difficult time of my life, but I think I have become a better man because of it. After learning to deal with pain that extreme, I can easily say that there is not a situation that I can't handle. Problems that seemed so difficult before are now easily solved. It is a horrible way to learn a lesson, but it is important to learn from every situation in life no matter how good or bad it is.

When I asked the class, "What is it that makes this passage notable, remarkable?," the students wanted to talk about the quality of the sentences. The prose (they said) was calm, confident, understated; you felt the authority of the writer; there was, they said, the ring of truth. The sentences, that is, came from within the experience; the speaker was both in the story and on the page. Someone mentioned Hemingway. The best sentence, by acclaim, was the one that named the central character: "The third casualty, Matthew Bradford Smith, had a gunshot wound to the leg which severed his femoral artery."

I asked what other sentences they could find that had a similar charge. And they pointed to the first sentence and the phrase, "setting into position," a phrase that is not an ordinary one. It belonged to a special or particular world of experience. And they pointed to the sentence about the differences between firefights in Iraq and Afghanistan.

No one wanted to talk about the sentences that followed. It was my job to bring them forward and to make them a focus of instruction, which I have learned to do by asking students how and why they might be revised. "This was by far the most difficult time of my life, but I think I have become a better man because of it. After learning to deal with pain that extreme, I can easily say that there is not a situation that I can't handle. Problems that seemed so difficult before are now easily solved. It is a horrible way to learn a lesson, but it is important to learn from every situation in life no matter how good or bad it is."

The simplest thing to say of this moment in my student's paper is that it marks a break from the previous sentences—there is a shift in tone and intent; the essay shifts from narrative to argument (an argument about a Lesson in Life). The prose becomes flat and predictable, rehearsed: "It is a horrible way to learn a lesson, but it is important to learn from every situation in life. . . ." At this moment the writer offers a sentence that could be the key sentence in any number of essays telling any number of stories in any number of contexts and at many moments in history: My Parent's Divorce, My Automobile Accident, My Summer Job, My Sports Injury, Not Making the Cut for the Student Musical, the End of a Romance. I learned a lesson and I'm a better person because of it.

I wanted to teach my students to ask a different kind of question—not "What does this story say?" but "What does it do?" Not "What lesson can we learn" from this text? but "How might this text be revised?" I wanted to call attention to the drama enacted in the prose. I wanted to ask: What does it mean to be a writer in the midst of such sentences?

I learned to ask these questions as a graduate student at Rutgers. I went from Ohio Wesleyan University to Rutgers and then, with a new PhD from Rutgers, to the University of Pittsburgh (turning down a job as a Victorianist at Boston University along the way). I went from a dissertation on Thomas Hardy to a career in Composition and Rhetoric, a trajectory that seemed baffling to many of my friends and teachers but that seemed sensible to me then and seems perfectly sensible to me now. (It is worth noting that a remarkable number of graduate students from my cohort at Rutgers went on to have influential careers in Composition and Rhetoric: Don McQuade, Linda Flower, Pat Bizzell, Bruce Herzberg, and Greg Waters, among others.)

Let Rutgers and Pittsburgh stand as placeholders. I want to think about a line of force in the teaching of writing that begins with the creation of English studies at Cambridge University in England in the 1920s and that connects a number of other institutions—including Amherst, Harvard, Rutgers, and Pittsburgh. The line I want to draw links people and places that are not a part of the usual accounts of the history of Composition in the United States.

I rely on the phrase "line of force" because I am not setting out to write intellectual history or to tell a story of influence. I want, rather, to trace a set of common concerns, concerns carried by an odd, deep, and persistent vocabulary, a set of terms that enabled work at different institutions at different moments in time—and, in particular, as it enabled certain forms of teaching.

I take the phrase from the opening sentences of Richard Poirier's surprising essay "Learning from the Beatles" (from *The Performing Self*):

> I am proposing that a line of force in literature beginning with some American works of the last century and passing through Eliot and Joyce to the present has offered a radical challenge to customary ways of thinking about expression in and out of the arts. And I am further proposing that because this challenge hasn't been sufficiently recognized, criticism especially as practiced in the university, where it should be most exploratory,

simply fails to give an adequate reading to some of the very texts it cares most about, and shows almost no capacity to cope with what are considered less distinguished ones placed under the heading of popular culture: in films, advertising, TV entertainment, the music of the young, or dance.

And the voice in my head adds, *or student writing*. Damn it. Student writing should be part of this list. *Because this challenge hasn't been sufficiently recognized, criticism, as practiced in the university, where it should be most exploratory, shows almost no capacity to cope with student writing—or to the teaching of writing.* It is not a huge leap to include student writing as one of the less distinguished genres—one more genre to which criticism must learn to attend.

This is how I read Poirier then (and how I continue to read him now), as if we were talking about the same things, sharing the same concerns, arriving at similar conclusions. I am aware that this way of reading does violence to his prose.

Poirier was my first and, in many ways, my only writing teacher. I took his required first-year seminar, Introduction to Graduate Studies, and, because I found him to be such a commanding presence, I turned to his writing—as though I might, myself, find a way of inhabiting these remarkable sentences: *A World Elsewhere: The Place of Style in American Literature* and the essays that later became *The Performing Self: Compositions and Decompositions in the Languages of Contemporary Life.*

I was taken first of all by the prose, which demonstrated as well as argued that writing was an *action*, "an activity, an agitated, often dislocating effort to appropriate and change the reality it confronts." At its most alive, he said, "writing exemplifies the *kind* of effort that can and needs to be made by anyone who proposes to make more than submissive sense of the world as it now is."

This was a concern Poirier brought to the work of Mailer, Pynchon, Eliot, or Frost, but it was also applied to the regular short papers we wrote for his course. On mine, he would often write in the margins, "Don't do that." He was teaching me to see a sentence as a gesture, as indicating a way of being alive in the world—one that I would do best to treat with suspicion. And I knew exactly what he meant. They marked moments when I was most trying to be a good graduate student, a would-be professional, going on and giving in as I moved confidently toward an inevitably rounded conclusion.

I had to chuckle when I read through the remarks collected in the memorial edition of *Raritan*. Jackson Lears had asked contributors for comments on Poirier's role as an editor. Mark Edmundson wrote: "He was very formidable and at the start a little scary. . . . He pushed me, early on, to stop writing like an assistant professor. Then, in time, he nudged me away from a style that he thought too pop. He was a great stylist himself and he understood, I think, that developing a style was about developing a sense of yourself—who you were and what you might be and do." That is what I heard Poirier saying to me: "Don't write like a graduate student." Don't do that. Don't be that person. He characterized my prose by asking me to consider its central character—some version of myself as a young intellectual. (*Who do you become when you talk that way? Who do I become, your reader, if I take you seriously?*)

These are questions I carried to the margins of my own students' papers, a pedagogical move I also learned through the example of William E. Coles Jr., one of the other great teachers in my career, who is connected to Poirier through the shared experience of teaching writing to first-year students at Amherst College, in a course developed by Theodore Baird. "Stop writing like an assistant professor." Don't be disciplined by the discipline. Find a way to be present rather than absent inside your sentences, within the genres of academic work.

Coles would say to his first-year students, "Stop writing like the one-thousand-year-old man, like the Jolly Green Giant; don't be such a phony." I. A. Richards once characterized the voice he heard in a student paper as the voice of "our expert on the real world." For all these teachers, the first and most important pedagogical move was to characterize the prose, to assign it a voice, and, through that voice, to position it in a recognizable social world, one that could be considered and revised.

I felt that I had gained access to a profession by questions such as these, questions that I took as guides for revision. At the time it did not feel like surrender. It was inspiring to feel that my own sentences could define a project, a field of work, even a career. At the end of *Robert Frost: The Work of Knowing*, Poirier calls upon Thoreau to make this point about a writer and his field:

> How does anyone "know beans"? More perplexing still, how does anyone know that he knows them? This is a question set and answered by Thoreau and, with more subtlety and less show-off wit, by Frost in his poems of work and in the work of his poems. The answer is that you "know" a thing and know that you know it only when "work" begins to yield a language that puts you and something else, like a field, at a point of vibrant intersection.

At my best, I felt like I had entered, at least briefly, such a point of "vibrant intersection." In my teaching, I often use this passage as a headnote to a writing assignment. I also like to use these sentences from Stanley Cavell: "I recognize words as mine when I see that I have to forgo them to use them. Pawn them and redeem them to own them."

I have been writing about Poirier as a writing teacher, mine. There is, however, a pedagogical imperative throughout his work, one whose object it is very hard to name or to define without using a word like composition. To make this point, I will be relying on only two of his books, both from the 1970s—the book on Frost, *Robert Frost: The Work of Knowing* (1977) and *The Performing Self* (1971).

In the era of de Man and Derrida, the era of big statements and specialized vocabularies, Poirier was an anomaly. He wrote in an ordinary language—few endnotes, if any; few references to critics or scholars—and he insisted that his subject, too, was ordinary, everyday. He insisted that his subjects were reading and writing, small *r* and small *w*, rather than Literature and Criticism, capital *L* and capital *C*. It was as though these big words belonged to a discourse he could never quite share or never fully enter, at least not seriously, not willingly.

As I read his work, and I say this with admiration, he had one fundamental point to make about reading and writing, reading and writing as a form of action, as performance, and he made this point over and over again by means of dazzling demonstrations, readings of key passages from key texts, texts that engaged, enlarged, and repaid his attention, and he wrote these readings out as performances of his own, where the admiration for the work he was presenting was matched by the energies and odd rhythms in his prose. He provides a series of dazzling readings, all meant to demonstrate what it meant to be alive as a writer (or dancer or composer or singer or teacher), and these were applied to a quite daunting range of materials, a range that continued to increase until the end of his life, and that moved beyond classic literary texts to include a variety of forms of high and popular culture, from the Beatles to Bette Midler.

His work suggests that this is the only way to teach the work of knowing, by setting out to do it again and again, by providing demonstrations to show that it can still be done and that the need is as urgent as ever. The struggle to be present in language, to know that you have known something, requires repetition, the same thing over and over but with a difference and a continued sense of purpose. It is the application, or the constant struggle, that keeps the method alive and in circulation.

Poirier would often turn to the gym for his metaphors—talking about muscle memory achieved through exercise and repetition. This lesson, he says, "is something athletes know as well as laborers of a certain kind. To do any job well requires the capacity to concentrate on the labor with a full and simultaneous awareness of the different orders of experience that get brought into play." He returns several times to Frost's articulation of this poised moment—where inside a sentence something can be made to happen:

Every single poem written regular is a symbol small or great of the way the will has to pitch into commitments deeper and deeper to a rounded conclusion and then be judged for whether any original intention it had has been strongly spent or weakly lost; be it in art, politics, school, church, business, love, or marriage—in a piece of work or in a career. Strongly spent is synonymous with kept.

And Poirier translates Frost in these terms:

Poetry is not life, but the performance in the writing of it can be an image of the proper conduct of life. The exercise of the will *in* poetry, the *writing* of a poem, is analogous to any attempted exercise of will in whatever else one tries to do. This position is not asserted, since the whole point, after all, is that nothing can be carried merely by assertion. One can only "pitch" in "deeper and deeper," and in this passage itself there is a demonstration rather than simply a claim of the validity of what is being said. The validation is implicit in his inclusive suppleness of voice. As in similar moments in Thoreau, the voice here manages to show its facility in the tones and nuances—like the submerged metaphors of sex and love-making, of farming and business—that belong to the tones, the argots of occupations outside poetry.

And this was the reason for teaching Frost—to learn to hear (and to value and to produce) such tones and nuances. These were the fundamental lessons in reading and writing. How does it sound? Where does it place me? Where do I stand? Where and how do I locate myself in relation to this way of speaking or writing?

Frost provided the spirit and the occasion for the training one needed to stay alive in language, to be wary of its false securities and to work toward something other than routine (or submissive) understandings of matters concerning human life:

> Frost seems to me of vital interest and consequence because his ultimate subject is the interpretive process itself. He "plays" with possibilities for interpretation in a poetry that seems "obvious" only because it is all the while also concerned with the interpretations of what, in the most ordinary sense, are the "signs" of life itself, particular and mundane signs which nonetheless hint at possibilities that continually elude us.

His reiterations about the limits of metaphor and the boundaries of form are evidences not of fastidiousness or fear—though he shows instances of both—so much as an effort to promote in writing and in reading an *inquisitiveness* about what cannot quite be signified.

I love what happens to a word like "inquisitiveness" in a sentence like this. On the one hand there is a drama unfolding here of biblical dimension—something vital is at stake, life itself perhaps; there is the occasion for fear. But in the end it is not a matter of superhuman achievement. The end falls to basic human intellectual capabilities, and to a very ordinary quality, something like "inquisitiveness," to be in the game.

If you think of the moment of theory in English studies, you can quickly call up any number of very technical descriptions to demonstrate that only a select few can be granted anything like critical awareness. For me, the importance of Poirier's work is that it always located critical, intellectual work in the broadest possible arena, available to everyone or anyone who will do the work and who will learn to be inquisitive.

Still, it takes an effort of will to bring these passages to the work of student writers in a composition course. Even though he insists, as he does above, on a pairing of writing and reading, the classroom he imagines is one where students learn by reading. This is from the opening to *The Work of Knowing*:

> To some extent any poem is an act of interpretation, an inquiry into the resources of the language it can make available to itself. Reading is an analogous act calling on its own literary resources which may, at times, be greater or less than the poem's.

It is not that this is an odd twist—that you learn to write by reading. That the "expenditure in the writer" could generate a "corresponding energy in a reader," and that this energy would carry over again to the student who will be writing. In some ways, it was commonplace in the 1970s to think that the reading of literature would have inevitable and beneficial effects on student writing. This is a pedagogy with a long history.

Poirier's argument, however, stands well outside the commonplaces about the value of literary study in the 1970s. Each of his books insists upon this. His is not a trickle-down theory, nor is it a form of the "new criticism." He argues for a very specific and determined form of work, with certain kinds of texts and with very local rewards or consequences. His attention is to the sentence and to style—and these were not the usual points of reference when first-year writing courses were built around a standard set of literary texts.

Poirier's 1970 collection of essays, *The Performing Self,* takes as one of its subjects the undergraduate curriculum in English. He challenges a reader to turn to and to think about a scene of instruction represented not solely on the page but also in a college classroom. In its final sentence he calls for a "new curriculum," one that can answer to the energies he describes in the book's preface.

Writing is a form of energy not accountable to the orderings anyone makes of it and specifically not accountable to the liberal humanitarian values most readers want to find there. . . . Energy which cannot arrange itself within the existing order of things, and the consequent fear of it which takes the form of repressive analysis—these are what make the literary and academic issues I shall be discussing inseparable from larger cultural and political ones.

Writing is a form of energy that, at its best, is resistant, uncomfortable, out of the mold. This is the key to understanding the relations between writing and schooling, where the discomfort, the mismatch, is the condition of the classroom and the starting point for instruction. A similar argument was being worked out in the late 1970s in the Composition community. I am thinking, for example, of the work of Richard Ohmann. (*English in America* was published in 1976. Ohmann was part of the group working with Brower and Poirier at Harvard. Mina Shaughnessy's *Errors and Expectations* was published in 1977.)

And as he is writing about a new curriculum, he is unable to avoid the fact of student writing. This pressure comes to a head in the essay "What is English Studies, and If You Know What That Is, What is English Literature?" This essay has been a touchstone for me. I've taught it and returned to it many times. In it, Poirier asks this question:

What, then, is anyone to do who thinks of himself as a custodian not so much of language in the abstract but even of his own language? How can he begin to dislocate language into his own meaning?

I think it is important to hear the word "anyone" in that opening sentence: What, then, is *anyone* to do who thinks of himself as a custodian of his own language? The case is not being made only on behalf of geniuses or those of proven critical sophistication; it not being made only on behalf of graduate students or English majors.

(I remember Poirier once asked us to prepare a writing assignment, something we would use in teaching *Antony and Cleopatra*. And I asked, But what about the audience? Was this to be an assignment for a freshman English class, a class for English majors, a graduate seminar? And Poirier answered, "What difference would it make?")

The argument pertains to *anyone* who hopes to be a custodian of his (or her) own language. And I think it is important to hear the word *custodian*, as it calls up vocations both high and low. He then turns to writing as a matter of technique: "How can he begin to dislocate language into his own meaning?" And then he moves to his conclusion—where he can't *not* speak to the broad concerns of an education that takes seriously the problems of writing.

> Locating, then watching, then describing and participating in this struggle [the struggle for verbal consciousness] as it takes place in the writings of any period could be the most exciting and promising direction of English studies. It points to where language and history truly meet. Literary study can thus be made relevant to life not as a mere supplier of images or visions, but as an activity; it can create capacities through exercise with the language of literature that can then be applied to the language of politics and power, the language of daily life.

Poirier goes on, driven I think by the necessary indeterminacy of his key terms "capacities" and "exercise," to imagine again a pedagogical encounter:

> It is simply terribly hard to do this, however—to make this shift of muscularity of mind and spirit from one allegedly elevated mode of expression, where the muscles can be most

conveniently developed, to another mode of expression both more inaccessible and considered so ordinary, so natural as to be beyond inquiry. And yet in this transfer of activity, and the reciprocations that follow from it, is the promise of some genuine interplay between different and multiplying cultural traditions.

Including, I would add, the difficult interplay between the work of students and the expectations of the academy.

I'm going to compress the final argument by working with just short passages:

> If English studies is not in command of a field of knowledge it can be in command of a field of energy. . . . English studies cannot be the body of English literature but it can be at one with its spirit: of struggling, or wrestling with words and meanings. . . . It can further develop ways of treating *all* writing and *all* reading as analogous acts, as simultaneously developing performances, some of which will deaden, some of which will quicken us. [*The emphasis is in the original, and it is essential to the argument, since Poirier is worried that readers will be mentally editing out certain acts of writing and reading as beneath or beyond the range of reference.*] Once on its way, this activity can be applied to performances other than those occurring in language—to dance and sports, as much as to film or popular music. English studies must come to grips with the different languages of popular culture, with newspapers, political speeches, advertising, conversation, the conduct of the classroom itself. Until proven otherwise, none of these need be treated as if it were necessarily simpler than any other or than literature. The same hard questions for all.

Why is there no more direct reference to student writing? Composition becomes a necessary term in this essay, and yet the course that carries that name is unacknowledged. The same hard questions for all.

Poirier was closely involved with Humanities 6 at Harvard (he writes about this, and about the course at Amherst in *Poetry and Pragmatism*), and this course was defined by a regular sequence of writing assignments, "exercises" they were called. Why is it so difficult for Poirier to represent students as writers—and not just as readers? Or to imagine that students could learn these lessons by writing poems or by writing prose? It is not as though composition (or creative writing) were unthinkable as courses in an undergraduate curriculum in the 1970s. They may have been unmentionable. But I don't see (or hear) Poirier expressing such disdain.

Why is composition absent? One simple answer, I think, is that Poirier was unwilling to let his subject be co-opted by the emerging professional field of Composition, Composition with a capital *C* and with its own emerging account of what writing is, how it relates to the traditions of literature, who writers are, what they do, and how they learn. Remember, Poirier is equally determined to distance himself from Literature with a capital *L*. He doesn't want to be part of that institutional location, either. I am inclined to say that he is determined to find a language that will preserve some form of language instruction in the lower division, to preserve it as an area of primary concern and yet still not divide English studies into Literature and Composition. He is imagining something different, something with Performance in its title.

And "composition," in fact, becomes a necessary term to articulate this vision of the possibilities of English:

> We ourselves, each of us [*anyone*], insofar as we are composed
> in and by language, should be as much the subject of literary
> studies as is any literary work similarly composed. The con-
> frontation of these two kinds of composition should be the
> substance of our work. It is murderously hard work, however,
> except for those who take for granted the self known as the
> reader or for those satisfied with the almost invariably slapdash

compositions of a self put together for any given discussion of political relevance. It's terribly difficult to find out who one is during an act of reading or to help a student find out who he or she is. And perhaps it is harder now than ever before.

It is terribly difficult to find out who one is during an act of reading or to help a student find out who he or she is. I have wanted to fill in the blanks in order to put *writing* into this sentence. But I don't have to. Listen, rather, to this. It should sound familiar:

> Every year I make a new sequence of Assignments, dealing with a new and different problem, so that for all concerned, teacher and student, this is a new course, a fresh progression in thought and expression, a gradual building up of a common vocabulary, a more precise definition of terms. [And] . . . though I have never repeated an Assignment, every Assignment I have ever worked with, every question I have ever asked, involves the same issues: Where and how with this problem do you locate yourself? To what extent and in what ways is that self definable in language? What is this self to judge from the language shaping it? What has this self to do with you?

Style, writing, composing, the self—these are the terms this teacher is trying to bring into play as the key terms of a writing class.

The document goes on in the same fashion (struggling to say what it is difficult for a teacher to say):

> I wish to make clear that the self I am speaking of here, and the one with which we will be concerned in the classroom, is a literary self, not a mock or false self, but a stylistic self, the self construable from the way words fall on a page. The other self,

the identity of a student, is something with which I as a teacher can have nothing to do, not if I intend to remain a teacher. That there is a relation between these two selves, between writing and thinking, intellect and being, a confusing, complicated, and involving relation indeed—this is undeniable. This relation, in fact, is the center of both the [composition] course as a course and the course as more than that. . . . Ideally, hopefully, primarily, our concern is with words: not with thinking, but with a language about thinking: not with people or selves but with languages about people and selves.

This is from a course description addressed to students taking a first-year composition course. I've taken it from Bill Coles's 1978 book, *The Plural I*, a book that provides a narrative account of a first-year writing course at Case Institute of Technology (now Case Western Reserve University) in the 1960s. Here is its opening:

The subject, the content, or however you want to describe it, of this course is writing. Writing is an action. It is something you do. It is not something you know about except in the same more or less ineffective way you know about health, or you know about the symphony. You do know, for example, that Good Writing should be Clear, Coherent, and somehow Pleasing to a reader. But how to make your writing clear, coherent, and pleasing is another matter altogether.

And here is an excerpt from a course description Poirier prepared for Harvard's Humanities 6 in the 1960s:

This course, we might recall, is an 'action,' not a body of 'material' to be 'covered.' The action of the first half-year is learning how to read and how to communicate the experience of reading through writing. Our whole aim is to secure a higher level of attention to works of literature, to get the student to confront *this* particular work and to discover the satisfaction that comes from attending. There is no sacred method (as students suppose) for achieving this level of attention.

I present these passages to bring forward the echoes between Coles's and Poirier's prose, and not just in the argument that writing is an action, or that what is at stake is the "self," a self that can be found only in sentences, providing a momentary stay against confusion, but I'm also hoping that you see the similarities in the rhythms and style, the use of capital letters, the way the language turns back on itself and against the usual ways of thinking and talking. Even the titles rhyme: *The Performing Self* (1971); *The Plural I* (1978). (And both echo the title of Lionel Trilling's 1955 collection of essays, *The Opposing Self: Nine Essays in Criticism.*)

I want to be clear. I am not suggesting that Coles learned from, drew upon, or was in any way indebted to Poirier or to Poirier's book. I doubt that he read it, and I think I would have known. I knew Bill Coles well in the 1970s. I was his first hire at the University of Pittsburgh, in 1975. I went there to be his Assistant Director of Composition. We worked closely together for about six years and, after that, we remained colleagues.

I can remember vividly how odd it was in that first year. Although we had no apparent connection, it was as though we shared a common mission and a common language. Bill thought of himself as a maverick, self-made; I thought of myself as clueless, completely unprepared for the job I had taken, and yet we shared a language and a focus that made our work more than collegial. I don't know how else to describe it. We were secret sharers, part of a close circle; when it came to teaching or reading a student paper, to teacher training or curriculum design, there was some deep connection that often eliminated any need for warm-up or for explanation, even exposition.

Coles didn't talk about books like *The Performing Self*; he didn't work that way. The sources he claimed as reference points were always odd and surprising—and determinedly outside the range of what a Professor of Composition was supposed to be reading. He found the professional literature on Composition almost impossible to read or to admire, but whatever he read, he read with composition on his mind, and so books that made no obvious connection were read in such a way that they became crucial points of reference *about* teaching—if only you were open enough to make the connection, to understand that the sentences might speak to you. (One such book, I remember, was Vicki Hearne's *Adam's Task: Calling Animals by Name*, 1986, a chapter of which had been published by Poirier in *Raritan* in 1982.)

Poirier and Coles were part of a circle whose circumference I don't quite know how to draw but whose center point was Amherst, in particular a freshman writing course, English 1-2, directed by Theodore Baird, and a sophomore reading course, English 19-20, which provided (through Reuben Brower) a model for Humanities 6 at Harvard. These courses provided a powerful, definitive, and sometimes troubling experience for teachers and students.

Amherst remained a crucial point of reference for Coles throughout his career. The course description I cited earlier was based on a course description developed over time by Amherst faculty. Coles says, "Few teachers have had the experience of seeing how either the students' writing or the activity of working with it can be made into something to be believed in." He goes on:

> I had been so privileged. I was fresh from having taught five years at Amherst College where, in working with Professor Theodore Baird, I had experienced an approach to the teaching of writing that I had seen enable teachers to find themselves as teachers. The approach—it sounds so simple—was one based on making the students' writing (and not something else), and the students' writing as a form of language using, the center of the course.

Recall for a moment Humanities 6, where students' reading, and not something else, was to be the subject of the course. I should take a moment to gloss the parenthetical "and not something else" as it functions in *The Plural I*. The reference is deliberately vague, since composition in the 1970s was searching for content, something to write about, but among its references is the composition course that centered on a collection of literary texts.

My colleague Mariolina Salvatori uses Coles to represent the general argument that literature in the 1970s and 1980s was not considered an appropriate subject for a composition course, that "students in writing courses had been harmed by a literature-centered pedagogy." Throughout his career Coles argued that the primary text of a composition course had to be the writing of its students. In this sense, anything that would take time from student writing, like the weekly discussion of a novel or a poem, was forbidden. As he was developing a composition program at Pitt, he was correct in arguing that faculty, including graduating assistants, knew how to fill up a class period discussing a poem by Frost. They didn't know how to use a poem by Frost as a lesson in composition. And they did not know how to talk about a student paper (how to give it attention, how to value it), and their preparation as writing teachers required that they learn to do so.

At the same time, Coles was proposing what you would have to call a literature-centered pedagogy, if by that you mean a pedagogy that insisted on a close attention to language and whose values were derived from literary criticism in the Cambridge tradition (which is different from the New Criticism). The course in *The Plural I* featured assigned readings, usually (but not always) short passages. Sometimes they are used to call up a way of speaking (a discursive field), and students are asked: "What happens if you talk like that? Where do you end up?" But sometimes they are offered as models to emulate or as cruxes to represent fundamental writing problems. A long passage by Darwin functions as the former; an extended passage from Salinger provides the latter.

The key terms in the analysis of writing were voice (or tone), metaphor, and stock response. As such, they extend or put into play the key terms of the Cambridge project (as first articulated by I. A. Richards, one of Brower's teachers, as F. R. Leavis had been one of Poirier's). This attention to tone was powerfully inflected (redirected) by the presence of Robert Frost at Amherst. Frost, too, is an important presence in the line I am tracing. In the course at the center of *The Plural I*, students learn to see that words or phrases that they take as *true*, fixed and transparent, are, in fact, slippery and metaphorical in their relation to the world. This was the lasting point made by Frost in his lecture to the students at Amherst, "Education by Poetry."

> What I am pointing out is that unless you are at home in the metaphor, unless you have had your proper poetical education in the metaphor, you are not safe anywhere. Because you are not at ease with figurative values: you don't know the metaphor in its strength and its weakness. You don't know how far you may expect to ride it and when it may break down with you. You are not safe in science; you are not safe in history.

And students learn to judge character (which, in this pedagogy, is evident at the level of the sentence) by attending to voice. Here is Frost:

> The ear is the only true writer and the only true reader. I have known people who could read without hearing the sentence sounds and they were the fastest readers. Eye readers we call them. They get the meaning by glances. But they are bad readers because they miss the best part of what a good writer puts into his work.

Coles was offering, to use Frost's terms, a "proper poetical education." And the point of this education is to find a way of becoming alive inside sentences—to escape or deflect what Coles refers to as "themewriting," the usual stuff—empty, routine, submissive, thoughtless, inattentive, and adrift, content to repeat the standard commonplaces:

> Did "experience," shaped in the terminology those writers had used, really continue to exist in some throbbing human fullness somewhere outside that language, in contradistinction to that language? And to go through life Themewriting one's experience into bloodless abstractions—we had a swell time; it was a great trip; she was really cool—was to end up with how much of life having dibbled through one's fingers? Yes, the habit of Themewriting was a choice, I concluded class by saying. But maybe not always a free one, and maybe not one that remained open forever.

Coles carried a composition course from Amherst to (eventually) Pittsburgh. Poirier, with Brower, was part of a group to carry an introductory literature course to Harvard. Poirier wrote about his experience at Amherst in "Reading Pragmatically" (in *Poetry and Pragmatism*).

The essay argues that the creation of a course or a curriculum, something sustained and developed across time, a project that includes the cooperation and training of a staff, can be serious critical work, real and lasting scholarship. Theory can be elaborated in practice, in the argument of a course, including a lower division general education course. In reference to Amherst, Poirier argued that generations of teachers had been teaching forms of linguistic skepticism long before the postmodernist, critical revolution:

> . . . certain kinds of intense close reading were being peda-gogically advanced, well before the post–World War II period, which without defining themselves theoretically—at the time that would have been thought inappropriate in undergraduate

classrooms—or calling themselves skeptical, managed to inculcate in more than a few teachers and students a habit of enjoying the way words undo and redo themselves to the benefit of social as well as literary practice. This latter development was fairly frequent in the more enterprising small colleges, where intimate and intense workshop teaching most frequently occurs. On this occasion I have in mind my own experiences as an undergraduate after World War II at Amherst College and in an undergraduate course I later helped teach at Harvard called "Humanities 6: The Interpretation of Literature."

Because this tradition took seriously the work of students, what students could *do* with texts, it could not finesse the "vexed question of self-presence in writing and reading." And he continues, citing Emerson (since, he insists, this is a US, and not a French, pedagogical tradition):

> For Emerson, writing and reading do not, merely because of the deconstructive tendencies inherent in language, dissolve human presence; human presence comes into existence *in* writing and reading thanks to these traceable actions by which, through troping, deconstructive tendencies are acknowledged and contravened. There exists a crude and over-emphatic perception of the assumed antagonism between deconstruction in language, on the one hand, and, on the other, the possible shaping, in language of Emersonian selves.

Or plural *I*'s. Earlier in this essay Poirier says, "Reading is nothing if not personal. It ought to get down ultimately to a struggle between what you want to make of a text and what it wants to make of itself and of you."

My point is a simple one. Even though these two important books are seldom, almost never read together, they speak to each other. *The*

Plural I. The Performing Self. They belong in the same circle. They are at home together. And because of the odd coincidences of my graduate training, I quickly felt at home with them. (I know. I am a student of Frost. Home can make you crazy, send you out into the woods at night.) They share a language and a style. They do not turn to or rely upon a specialized vocabulary: tagmemics or topoi, clinamen or kenosis. They use ordinary language to do critical work, something beyond the ordinary. And they believe this critical project can be taught to others, to anyone, including the young.

I want to take a moment with *The Plural I*, a book that is now seldom read and seldom taught.

The Plural I is a narrative account of a first-year writing course, complete with copies of student papers. It is organized by means of the writing assignments that defined the course—two each week in a fifteen-week semester—and a narrative re-creation of the classroom discussions prompted by the presentation of two or three student papers, hard copies via mimeo or xerox. The assignments define a sequence ("a fresh progression in thought and expression") where a "nominal subject" (in this case an exploration of the difference between an amateur and a professional—the real subject, of course, was language and its users), where a nominal subject is investigated from one angle and then another but always through close readings of the students' papers. The sequence is both "repetitive and incremental."

The first six assignments ask students to think along with two key terms, *amateur* and *professional.* The course begins with questions of definition in order to call attention to the problem of meaning—meanings don't reside in words, words are put into play by writers trying to say something. They struggle to communicate, to make the words meaningful to themselves and to others. The better the writer, the more self-conscious the struggle. And so the opening assignment begins not by asking students for a definition, "What is an amateur?," but by giving them something said (words already in play) and by asking (always) "Where and how do you locate yourself with this way of speaking?" "To what extent and in what ways is that self definable in language?" And, crucially, "What has this self to do with you?"

In this course, papers are reproduced for each class and students learn to give a close, critical reading to the language on the page. At first it is quite simple. *Who is speaking here? Who do you have to be to take this form of address seriously?* The discussion characterizes students as the Jolly Green Giant, the one-thousand-year-old man; writing that is routine or empty, submissive, is called "Themewriting" with a capital *T*. As the semester goes along, the forms of close reading become much more subtle, the critical positions much more complicated and compelling.

The first paper presented for discussion opens as follows—and a single sentence is enough to recognize the paper and its version of knowledge. It is the standard opening of a first-year writing class. "The question of the amateur's place in a society of professionals is one that has greatly been changed by the scientific and cultural revolutions of the nineteenth and twentieth centuries."

In introducing the discussion in class (which is represented in the book through dialogue), Coles says:

> I began, as I generally do, with the question of voice, not as a way of suggesting that writing is speech, but to get students used to the idea that sensitivity to words on a page is analogous to one's response to the tonal variations of the spoken word—a response that for all of us, whatever difficulty we may have in describing how we hear what we do, is immediate and full. The concept of voice, then, involving as it does the *feel* of words, can, after a time, become an appropriate metaphor for the life of writing—or the lack of it.
>
> What sort of voice speaks in this first paper? I asked after reading it aloud with the students. How do you characterize it? What's your response to what you hear?

I don't have time to work through the discussion in detail, but I recommend this book to anyone who teaches writing (or who "thinks of himself as a custodian not so much of language in the abstract but even of his own language"). Here is Coles's summary of the outcome:

> None of the students with this first writing assignment behaved any differently from what I expected. Triumphs of self-obliteration the papers were, put-up jobs every one of them, and as much of a bore to read as they must have been to write. I found myself being talked to as though I were a rube ("Now it may, perhaps, by thought by my reader . . ."), unoffendable ("It has probably never been a matter of concern to the reader . . .") or a confederate, someone in on the joke of why none of it mattered ("of course, we, in a college classroom, can hardly hope to settle the question of . . ."). No observation was too trivial to escape oratorical pronouncement ("It is unfair to call the amateur a 'clumsy bastard!'"); no moral stance too obvious to assume ("After all, professionals are not necessarily good people"). So far as the proposition was concerned, the students handled it in the way that a Themewriter traditionally handles the Themetopic, as a moral issue (on about the level needed to condemn the man-eating shark), which is to say inside a moral vacuum from which all living concerns are carefully excluded. . . . There wasn't one student who convinced me that he had a modicum of interest in anything he was saying.

In *The Plural I*, the focus is on what happens in the writing, on what the language does. If a student is asked, for example, to "describe a situation . . . in which someone gave you what you consider to be very good advice," the final question on the assignment sheet is this, "To judge from the way you have written about it, what exactly is good advice." The discussion of the papers follows the forms of (and motives for) close reading presented, say, Poirier's readings of poems by Frost or in Brower's textbook, *Fields of Light*. Let me provide a brief example.

In the first half of the course described in *The Plural I*, the discussion often turns to cliché, but discussion moves fairly quickly beyond the simple policing of commonplaces. In writing about himself as, perhaps, an "amateur" lover, one student writes:

> It was a cool night, the stars were peeping through the trees, and the night air was holding its breath expectantly. There we were, just the two of us, standing at her front door. She had her hands behind her back and leaned forward encouragingly. I kept my hands behind my back and leaned backwards. . . .

The class found this to be only one more formula paper, until one student says,

> Sure this is trite, but the point is the guy knows that. Here's a simple scene, night air and her waiting and all the rest. The point is that the guy knows what he's supposed to do, but he can't make it. He can't make the scene. That's why he's an amateur. I think he's using the triteness in the paper on purpose.

And Coles, represented in the narrative through the figure of the teacher, says,

> I did too and said so. And I went on to say that it was precisely the quality of "using" the writer's consciousness of a cliché as a cliché, which for me created the illusion of character. The clichés the writer uses he transforms syntactically into an

expression of a convention which is broken again and again by his character's inability to fill it.

(This discussion of cliché echoes quite closely I. A. Richard's defense of Gray's "Elegy Written in a Country Churchyard" in *Practical Criticism*.)

After presenting the discussion of other student papers, Coles ends the account of this class with:

> The students were hearteningly quick to see that in neither instance had the writers begun to do anything like justice to their own tonal complexity. The character of paper two was more than a phony just as that of paper three was more than inept. It was the first example of writing we had shared which created the illusion of something like human beings involved in human experience.

Later in the course (and later in the book) Coles refers to this as a recurring problem, the fundamental writing problem that motivates the pedagogy of this course:

> A great many students seemed for some reason to resent the suggestion that the self might be seen as other than one, entire, and whole. But in order to preserve the notion of the self as irreducible, and as a consequence to have to develop some alternative metaphor for "people," the students either ground out allegories on the nervous system (my logic told my emotions; my conscience told my reason) or leeched onto the vocabularies of language systems with which they had only minimal familiarity (my id told my ego). The difficulty in both cases was that the students had nowhere to go in explaining themselves.

. . . Again, I was facing a set of papers most of which were only one sentence deep. Again the problem, though I wasn't about to talk this way in class, was one that involved an inadequate understanding of language as metaphor.

At the time of its publication, in the late 1970s, when composition was beginning to develop a set of methods, a literature, a constellation of stars, *The Plural I* proved to be largely unreadable. Those who reviewed it or wrote about it (or spoke about it at meetings) pretty much missed the point. For one thing, the book requires a sophisticated ear. And it assumes that a reader will give time and attention to the student writing. You can't skip over the student papers. They are not just illustration; they are where the action is, and so you have to read closely and with particular attention to tone and voice.

It was also a book that blurred genres. *The Plural I* is both fiction and report. It is narrative nonfiction, or "creative nonfiction," a genre that is now part of the stock and trade of every MFA program, but in the 1970s, when composition was turning to ethnography, looking for positive, "scientific" access to student learning via descriptive accounts of scenes of instruction, its audience was poorly prepared and predisposed to file the book outside the categories of scholarship. He was misread, and the book was characterized, perhaps inevitably, as either touchy-feely or as a narcissist's memoir. Its subtle and challenging account of language use was reduced to a single (and reductive) term, "expressivism."

Let me return to the student paper that opened this essay. Below is the revised conclusion of the firefight paragraph. It was completed as a formal assignment three weeks after the first draft. Revision is a fundamental part of the course I teach, not something that is offered for extra credit. It is, in my department, how students learn to write. The point is not to correct a first draft but to take it on to its next step. Our students learn to write by learning to work on their own writing, by revising:

> The third casualty, Matthew Bradford Smith, had a gunshot wound to the leg which severed his femoral artery. This wound would ultimately lead to his death eight days later. We held an informal ceremony for him in Afghanistan; only the people who escorted his corpse home got to go to the funeral. The picture of the soldier kneeling in front of the boots and helmet of another soldier is a cool decoration until it's you on a knee in front of your friend's boots. [*In the margin, I wrote: "What if this paragraph ended end here?" What would be lost? What would be gained?*] As I stood up from in front of his memorial, I tried with all my might to hide that I was crying until I saw the entire formation of guys that I worked with in tears. Only two of the guys really stood out to me, my boss Taylor and my best friend Ray. . . . You couldn't defeat them at anything, and yet there they stand in tears. I have been mad at people and held grudges, but until this day, I can say with complete confidence that I have never known hate or misery. Today I find it difficult to get truly angry at someone, and I don't think I've had any grudges since about three months after his death.

I admire this sentence: "The picture of the soldier kneeling in front of the boots and helmet of another soldier is a cool decoration until it's you on a knee in front of your friend's boots." This is the sentence I would use to define the act (and the importance) of revision in student writing—and it is a sentence I would use to define revision as an act of ordinary language criticism, doing what you can with that which is available. The writer rejects (by deploying) the explanatory power of the standard image of the soldier kneeling in front of the boots and helmet of a fallen comrade. He has to forgo the language to use the language.

And at moments like this, the language shudders or fails, the writer is at a loss, which is why I find a particular force and appropriateness in the awkward use of the word "cool." What other word could you use in this sentence if the sentence is moving toward a word like "decoration"? "Cool" is marked as simultaneously ironic and sincere. And the work done by this sentence is why, if I had complete editorial control (which I did not), I would have cut the paragraph from this point on. The writing that follows is initially rough, at least at the beginning (the passages about Ray), but then it becomes smooth and set, comfortable again in a context where comfort is not necessary of value. These sentences volunteer themselves. They are drawn from the available stock—from the tool kit marked "lessons on life."

This, I think, is one of the things a writing course can do—it can provoke and then call attention to moments like this. A revision like this one is a way of making sense present, where sense is always a matter of struggle or contention. I do not expect a student writer to reinvent the narrative of war, to do what our very best writers struggle to do. And I don't insist that the problem in the essay is the problem of American foreign policy, a willed blindness. This is a writing course. I'm interested in what students can do with sentences; I don't require a pledge of allegiance or a forced confession.

In "What is English Studies," Poirier said:

Literary study might well consist of such "lessons" in how to meet and to know words under different kinds of social and historical stress. The point would be that any given expression in words has to be confronted as if it were meant pointedly, personally for you, meant as a violation, pleasurable or otherwise, of the self you'd put together before this shape of words entered into it and before the self in turn, with all its biases, cautions, histories, moved reciprocally back into those words. Literary study should show how, in this engagement, words can sicken and befoul, heal and uplift us, and how precarious and momentary each such induced state can be. A class can watch how words suddenly get snatched from our possession and are so recast that we don't want to possess them any more. This active way of responding to language and to the structures of imagination that are made from it is not, alas, what goes on in the classrooms of our colleges and universities. . . .

"An active way of responding to language and to the structures of imagination that are made from it." What better place to do this than the required composition course?

I have been doing my best to teach this course for the past forty-plus years. I should be clear. This is not an easy course to teach. There are weekly papers to read, and to read closely. (Although the weekly cycle includes revisions, and I find I often look forward to what might come next, at least when a course is going well.) You have to take care with the assignments and the readings. (If you can't engage your best students at their best, it will be a long semester.) The best moments can seem slight in retrospect—or when you describe them to colleagues. And no one enjoys the constant questioning, on either side of the desk. A good teacher learns how and when to praise and to encourage. But if criticism matters, the writing becomes harder, not easier. That is the hard truth of a writing class, and an even harder truth in a required course for first-year students.

I see myself as part of a tradition of teaching that refused to make a fundamental distinction between reading and writing, Literature and Composition, and this has made me increasingly odd, sometimes illegible, in professional circles (and in my own department), where literature and composition have become separate fields of research and teaching. And so it has been a deep pleasure (and continued encouragement) to read around in that course's long history, a history that came into focus for me in the 1970s, when I began to teach at Rutgers and in Pittsburgh.

CHAPTER THREE

student mistakes as sites of engagement — Ruben

"Inventing the University" at 25

An Interview with John Schilb, Editor, *College English*

Editor's Note: 2010 saw the twenty-fifth anniversary of perhaps the most often cited and discussed essay in composition
studies: David Bartholomae's "Inventing the University."
With this event in mind, I invited Bartholomae to reflect on
the essay's background, subsequent reception, and continued
impact. As you will see, he graciously complied. The following
interview is a series of email exchanges between us during the
spring of 2010, while Bartholomae was on sabbatical in Spain.

— John Schilb

John Schilb (JS): Personally, I find it hard to believe that "Inventing
the University" was first published as long ago as 1985. Its observations and suggestions come across as fresh and as thought-provoking
as ever, whether or not one agrees with each. Indeed, as you know,
the essay is still anthologized in all sorts of venues, and it remains a
staple of composition theory courses. Nevertheless, ruminating on the
essay's birth seems worthwhile, if only to dispel the impression—held,
I think, by several of its present readers—that you wrote it yesterday
and that it reflects everything about your latest thinking.

So, let me begin with some questions about the essay's original
circumstances. "Inventing the University" first appeared in a 1985
Guilford Press collection edited by Mike Rose and entitled *When a
Writer Can't Write: Studies in Writer's Block and Other Composing-Process*

Problems. In his preface to the book, Rose says that "[t]he authors and I worked closely together on this volume. For nearly two years we wrestled with the issues and with ways to present our theories and our findings." He even uses the word "collaboration." As you worked on your essay, did you see yourself as very much participating in a collective project? Or were you more independent than Rose implies? The book's subtitle gives priority to "writer's block," which is something that Rose himself was notably studying back then. Did you see your own essay as bearing on this, or did you associate it with another kind of "composing process problem"?

David Bartholomae (DB): I wrote the essay in the spring of 1983, and that was, indeed, a long time ago. At the beginning of the 1982–1983 academic year, I was at one of those wonderful, hinge-like moments in time. I had established the beginnings of a career, received tenure, applied for and won a year-long Fulbright lectureship (in American literature) at the University of Deusto, in Bilbao, Spain. I was eager for the breathing space; I wanted to stop, take stock, and think about what I had done and what I might do next. I had a set of fundamental concerns, but I didn't want to keep doing the same thing over and over again.

(As I write my answers to your questions now, in spring 2010, I am back in the same place, living in the same town on the north coast of Spain, engaged as a visiting scholar at the University of Deusto, and on a year's leave. I have just completed 14 years as a department chair; I was eager for the breathing space and the chance to stop, take stock, and think about what I might do next.)

Before "Inventing the University," the work that I had done drew upon research in cognitive psychology, and I could properly have been called a "cognitivist." (In 1985, I also published an essay on sentence-combining.) It was in that frame, I believe, that Mike asked me to contribute to *When a Writer Can't Write*. I had published "The Study of Error," which used methods drawn from cognitivist work on math and second language learning. On the basis of that essay, I was asked to join the University of Pittsburgh's Learning Research

Cognitive Studies [handwritten annotation]

and Development Center, a federally funded center for educational
research, one leading the way at the time in cognitive studies—both
experimental studies of learning and theoretical work on learning and
cognition. This put me in contact with a range of established scholars, all of whom continue to be important points of reference at, for
example, the annual meeting of AERA (the American Educational
Research Association): Bob Glazer, Lauren Resnick, Alan Lesgold,
Chuck Perfetti, Isabel Beck and James Voss. I learned much from
their work; I was involved in several funded projects on writing and
learning, including a project trying to derive a "grammar" of error
in student writing, one that could be turned into software so that a
computer could recognize patterns of error in an individual text. With
this, the computer could "teach" proofreading and correction.

Lit Theory [handwritten annotation]

At the same time, my department was deeply invested in literary
theory. We had leading theorists on campus; the *boundary 2* collective sponsored regular colloquia; and colleagues across our programs
in film, literature, composition, and creative writing were thinking
about the implications for teaching. (Patrick Brantlinger, in *Crusoe's
Footprints: Cultural Studies in Britain and America*, identified our department as one of the first to develop a cultural studies curriculum.) I
couldn't say that I was equally engaged with the theoretical project—I
was a WPA (Writing Program Administrator) and didn't have the
time—but I was doing my best to keep up with the reading and to be
a part of the conversation. Like many at the time, I was very much
engaged with Barthes, Foucault, and Derrida. I was trying to focus
on their work rather than the commentaries. I wrote a long paper
on Roland Barthes and another on *Of Grammatology*. Neither was
ever published, although I gave a section of the Derrida essay at an
MLA convention in the early '80s. (It was a night session, 8:00 on a
Friday night; the panel was made up of Don McQuade, me and, I
think, Joe Trimmer. We had an audience of about five, including our
spouses.) I published a piece of the Barthes essay in *Letras de Deusto*
during my year as a Fulbright lecturer; it drew upon a lecture I gave
at the time on autobiography, at that point still a fairly limited genre
in Spain (although not in Latin America). I never felt I had enough

command of what I was saying to send the big essays out to journals in advance of my tenure review. Besides, I didn't really want to write *about* Derrida or Barthes or Foucault, but to put them to work, to imagine the discursive world of students in their terms. (I'd like to believe that "Inventing," and my later work, helped the transition at LRDC toward thinking about "situated" cognition.)

Mike was looking for an essay from a cognitivist. I sent him something very different.

In this sense, I was not a part of the collaboration he refers to in his "Introduction." I think I my essay came late, I was out of the country and out of the loop, and what I wrote seemed to have little to do with the core concerns of the volume. I didn't set out to be different, but by the time I wrote the essay I was thinking differently. I can remember the pleasure and the energy I found in the essay once I started to work on it. And so I did what we all do in such a situation: I sent what I had. I think Mike was initially flummoxed. It was a big jump from mental blocks to the prison house of language! I know that we wrote back and forth about the essay. Whatever dissonance I had created, however, couldn't be revised away. It was just a question of whether he wanted the essay in the collection or not. Mike was, as he always is, open and generous and curious and thoughtful. I know that he was interested in what I was doing and saw its importance—and so, in the end, my essay was part of the book.

JS: Previewing your essay in his introduction to *When a Writer Can't Write*, Rose says that you rely "on textual analysis informed by recent Continental literary theory." Would you say more about this? As I recall, most scholarship that conceivably fell under the rubric of "composition theory" back then was based on the author's classroom experiences or on smaller, face-to-face interactions with particular students. The essay draws upon your review of 500 student essays, which were used to determine where the authors would be placed in the University of Pittsburgh's first-year writing sequence. When you first pored through these essays, were you thinking about Foucault? Or were you examining them without assuming that you would be writing a piece about them?

DB: The 500 essays! I carried them with me on the plane. They were essential to my sabbatical project. I initially thought I would be writing something similar to "The Study of Error." From that frame of reference, the quality of the work depended upon the quality of the sample. If you were going to generalize, you needed a sufficient and representative sample, like in a laboratory or in a survey. As you've noted in your own writing, those of us who were trained as graduate students to read, to study, and to write about literary texts were struggling to find a way of doing "research" in our new area of employment, composition. And it wasn't immediately evident that there were points of connection.

In her essay on research in composition and the rhetoric for the 1992 MLA volume *Introduction to Scholarship in Modern Languages and Literatures*, Andrea Lunsford tells a representative story, a story of origins, one that has been often told in different ways by different people. In her version, she had completed an MA at a Southern university (I don't remember which), with a thesis on Faulkner, and she was teaching at a community college, teaching students whom we later came to call "basic writers." She was struggling to find a way of working with the problems she found in her students' prose. Nothing in her graduate education in literature would serve. She read Ed Corbett's *Classical Rhetoric for the Modern Student*; she saw that the texts of classical rhetoric gave her a way of thinking about writing and learning, and she went to Ohio State for her PhD. She found a way of connecting her teaching and research.

But think about it for a minute. Surely Faulkner, and those writing about Faulkner at the time, had plenty to say about race, class, writing, and the competing languages of the American South. In fact, although I haven't done the reading to say this with authority, I'd wager that the three major books written on Faulkner in the 1970s could be said to have *more* relevance to attempts to understand and to value the writing of her students, to think about the relationship of standard to nonstandard American English, and, therefore, to think about the problems of such a classroom than Aristotle's *Rhetoric*. Faulkner's novels surely would. This is not a statement about Andrea but about

English as a field of study, then and (to a certain degree) now. There was no way of thinking about the study of English literature that would enable a young scholar to make a connection between the study of Faulkner and a composition classroom, between Faulkner's writing and the writing of students in a first-year composition course. In fact, it would have been laughable to put Faulkner and composition in the same sentence.

In the fall of 1982, once we settled into Bilbao, I was teaching American literature, preparing a lecture on Emerson for a conference of the European American studies group, and I was reading or rereading Foucault: *The Order of Things*, *The Archeology of Knowledge*, "The Discourse on Language" (which provided the epigraph for "Inventing"), *Discipline and Punish*, and the collection *Language, Counter-Memory, Practice: Selected Essays and Interviews*. I was reading him, as I read all the French theorists, in translation, but I was taken by the prose and what it was able to do, its gestures against the normal or inevitable shape of the sentence or the paragraph, the essay or chapter. The same was true with Barthes and Derrida, but in Barthes and Foucault there was also this fascination with detail—with the ordinary, with documents, letters, images, anecdotes, with the "archive." Foucault went to the archive looking to document systematic, institutional networks of power, but always with an eye for the odd detail, for evidence of human resistance or performance beyond, despite, or in excess of the normal, something outside the rules or beyond what could be said or understood. That was the duty of the scholar, he said, to pay this kind of attention. And from this vantage point, working from these details, he showed how you could think your way back to the discursive context, the energies it channeled and the energies it resisted.

And, to put it simply, I wanted to do that. Although it sounds a little glib in retrospect, the 500 essays went from serving as a representative sample, where I would count or chart patterns in the student writing, to serving as an archive, where I would look for the crucial (but otherwise incomprehensible) detail. And so I read differently and, as I said earlier, I can still remember how much fun it was, what pleasure I had in reading through a stack of essays that I would otherwise have read dutifully.

Bill Coles, who hired me and who was my first composition teacher, always insisted that the proper preparation in composition was to learn to read student writing, to read it with care and attention for ✳ what it did (as opposed to what it said). This, he said, was not easy and it was not taught to us in graduate school. You had to learn to do it. That was how he would evaluate a teacher. He'd ask, What did this teacher notice in a student essay? What became interesting or important through that noticing? And, as a consequence, what should the student and the teacher do next?

I had spent six years working with Bill; I learned from him how and why to pay attention to student prose; I am, as I've said in other settings, eternally grateful. Foucault, for me, made this attention to student writing part of something bigger than a moment between a student and a teacher in a classroom. In saying that, I know that I am misrepresenting Bill's work, which was always about more than a moment between a student and a teacher. What Bill called "theme-writing" was a quick reference to the ways in which a writer was overcome by the discursive orders of his or her time and place. I understood this, at some level. Still, as I was figuring these things out at the time, reading Foucault, for me, set the drama of writing against a larger screen. And, I need to add, Foucault gave me a way of having a place in the conversations going on between colleagues in my department. I wanted to be at that table, and I wanted to have something to say.

JS: Can you say more about how Foucault helped you analyze student writing?

DB: In 1984, when Foucault died, Edward Said wrote an eloquent and brilliant memorial essay for *Raritan*, which I read when it came out that fall term, a year after the sabbatical leave and when "Inventing" was out of my hands. Said is a wonderful writer; in this essay he was able to do what seemed impossible, to summarize Foucault's prodigious career with apparent ease, and to note its worth. He said, "A [. . .] striking irony is that 'the philosopher of the death of man,' as Foucault is sometimes called, should seem to be, at the time of his own death, the very example of what a truly remarkable, unmistakably eccentric, and individual thing a human life really is." Said also said,

> Instead of seeing everything in culture and society as ultimately emanating from either a sort of unchanging Cartesian ego or a heroic solitary artist, Foucault proposed the much juster notion that all work, like social life itself, is collective. The principal task therefore is to circumvent or break down the ideological biases that prevent us from saying that what enables a doctor to practice medicine or a historian to write history is not mainly a set of individual gifts, but an ability to follow rules that are taken for granted as an unconscious a priori by all professionals. More than anyone before him Foucault specified rules for those rules, and even more impressively, he showed how over long periods of time the rules became epistemological enforcers of what (as well as how) people thought, lived and spoke. If he was less interested in how the rules could be changed, it was perhaps because as a first discoverer of their enormously detailed power he wanted everyone to be aware of what disciplines, discourses, epistemes, and statements were *really* all about, without illusion.

I wrote this passage out at the time. It has been with me in one way or another ever since, and I have used it often in seminars or lectures. It gives me a way of saying what I wanted to be able to do. In "Inventing" I wanted to describe what writing and schooling were *really* all about, without illusion. It has been odd for me to hear myself described as someone who was advocating imitation or submission or indoctrination as desirable goals or as ends in themselves. I was trying to speak from within a Foucauldian interpretive project, as I understood its key terms and goals. I was trying to give teachers and students a sense of the landscape, of the real politics of institutional work. I hoped that in my attention to the students' prose I would show what I valued, and that I valued the work of the individual in such a setting—or at least certain forms of individual work in such a setting.

In this sense, "Inventing" enacts its argument. I was trying to write my way into a critical project that I certainly did not invent. It was a way for me to learn to do something I wanted to do but could not do yet, and could not do on my own. It did not feel like possession; it felt like a breaking through, and it felt like my work.

I have just finished reading a new book by a friend and former colleague, the poet Ben Lerner, *Mean Free Path*. It is formally challenging; the narrative is engaging; the argument is rich and dense; and it is an impressive piece of work. Within stanzas, sentences cross and interrupt each other; there are unmarked parentheticals and, as the book says, "appropriate delays" as sentences collide "along the paths of reference." It is a book-length love poem about the difficulty (or impossibility) of writing a love poem at this time and in this place. At one point, it says

I admire the use of felt
Theory, like swimming in a storm, but object
To antirepresentational bias in an era of
You're not listening. I'm sorry.

I think of "Inventing" as an exercise in "felt theory." I was not writing *about* Foucault or translating Foucault for an audience unprepared or unwilling to read him on its own. I wanted to do something in his spirit, to extend his project to a set of materials (initially those 500 essays) that mattered to me. I wanted to do it, and Mike's request for an essay was the prompt that set things in motion.

JS: For the placement essay, the specific prompt that the students were responding to was this: "Describe a time when you did something you felt to be creative. Then, on the basis of the incident you have described, go on to draw some general conclusions about 'creativity.'" To me, this seems a Bill Coles-type of assignment, the kind often given in the Amherst College writing program where he had taught before coming to the University of Pittsburgh. Yet, while many of Coles's assignments and many in the Amherst program asked students to respond to small passages from texts by others, my impression is that you've been much more interested in having students write about their reading—especially their reading of long essays and full-length books. So, as I look back now on "Inventing," I'm struck that this career-long interest of yours isn't explicitly there in the essay, except perhaps in your brief discussion of your own students' relationship to the discourse of literary criticism.

By contrast, some of the other pieces that you were writing at the time did attend a lot to reading even as they echoed and sometimes even repeated remarks you made in "Inventing" about students' efforts to compose. When you were working on "Inventing," did you sense what I sense—i.e., that the David Bartholomae who's long been oc-cupied with student *reading* isn't on display?

DB: I don't think it *was* a Bill Coles-type assignment, or an Am-herst assignment. Those assignments were much trickier and always brought attention around to the instability of language. They would find a way of asking: how is this word, "creativity," a slippery word? [W]hat else does it mean in this context? In other contexts? How is its definition beyond your control? Where does the metaphor break down? What does it mean to use this word thoughtfully, with care?

And the Amherst assignments always brought attention to the writer as someone making something or doing something with lan-guage—not just channeling it. The assignments would offer a brief passage and highlight a particular word, like "creativity," and then ask, "Where do you locate yourself in relation to this way of speaking and thinking?" Long before Foucault, these teachers were asking students to think about how and where a particular way of speaking "located" them discursively.

The assignment in our placement test (and this was long ago) was much simpler and more appropriate for the occasion—100-plus kids sitting in a hot room during summer orientation, with 45 minutes to write an essay. This is not a happy occasion, but it can be representative of writing and schooling, which is how we understood the essays they wrote when we used them as a device for sorting students toward one course or another. The assignments we wrote for our courses were quite different, and they were conceived as part of a sequence, or (as we said) a semester-long intellectual project.

But your question was about reading, and why reading is not part of the argument in "Inventing the University" when reading has always been a part of my teaching and my thinking about the teaching of writing. The short answer is that "Inventing" was focused on that particular set of student papers and their context. It assumed that students would be reading in the literature of the various areas of study they would encounter in the course of a 4 or 5 year undergraduate education. It assumed that the texts they read were the outward and visible signs of tradition and authority, of knowledge and power. The pedagogical question, then, was what students could do with what they read—how and where they might "locate" themselves in relation to those texts (or where and how they might be located by the work their teachers set for them). But I did not take up the pedagogical question in any detail in "Inventing."

We recently completed a two-year study of writing in the undergraduate curriculum on my campus. (A version of this report, "The Pittsburgh Study of Writing," can be found in *The Best of the Independent Rhetoric and Composition Journals 2011*.) I was pleased to see the care and attention my colleagues across the disciplines gave to the ways they engaged students, as writers, with what they read and studied. Attention was paid to the assigned texts as acts of writing, not just as repositories of "content," and their assignments directed students to think about what they might *do* with these texts—what they had to add, where their own research and thinking came into play, and what they could learn, as writers, from their reading. I know much more now than I did then about writing in the disciplines, but I think my original assumption was correct—that reading and writing are fundamental in producing majors (or the curricular version of "disciplined" subjects). In my own teaching, to make this challenge visible, I like to use the block quotation to represent the problem that students confront when they must locate themselves in relation to the words and ideas of others. How does a writer choose this piece of text? How is it introduced? How are others prepared to read it? What comes after the block quotation, in the space that is now left for the writer to fill? (I like to ask students to do something stylistically in the writing that follows as a wink of the eye, to provide an allusion or homage to what was happening in the source text.)

But you are right, all of this is in the background, not the foreground of the essay. I was certainly thinking at the time about the uses of reading in the teaching of writing, but I was writing about this elsewhere.

JS: In retrospect, it strikes me as a rather bold decision to entitle your essay simply "Inventing the University." Very few articles in our field these days are so succinct. You don't even have a colon there! Why did you want to make *inventing* such a key term in this piece? To what extent did you see yourself as breaking with certain traditional ways of defining the term?

DB: The title came to me from the opening sentence, which was where the essay began. (This is not a usual practice for me, I should add.) "Every time a student sits down to write for us, he has to invent the university for the occasion—invent the university, that is, or a branch of it, like history or anthropology or economics or English." I thought the phrase made a strong statement and provided the governing metaphor for all that followed.

I know that I was determined *not* to use scare quotes with either "invent" or "university." I assumed the reference would be read as ironic, whether I bracketed the words or not, but I didn't want to invite or insist on or authorize this distance between practice and expectation, or between the institution and the individual. So I wrote it straight, knowing that the construction was odd.

It is also true, as you suggest, that I wanted to allude to rhetorical invention as it was then being imagined and practiced, particularly invention as "pre-writing," and I wanted to push against the poverty or the anti-intellectualism of much that was driving the "process" movement in the field.

More than anything else, though, I wanted to honor the moment when a student sits down to write for us, to take seriously the challenge and the opportunity, and to recognize, as I think I do in the readings of the student papers (and papers written under such dreadful conditions) that serious intellectual effort is possible, that there are real individual achievements, even under such conditions, that we often get more than we deserve, and that these writers deserve our respect and attention. As I said [earlier], I think it is our job to make the achievement in such moments visible and to provide reasons to speak about students' work without hanging scare quotes around the words that matter.

Perhaps this is a moment to return to Amherst. The other book that was important to me at the time I was writing "Inventing the University" was Richard Poirier's *The Performing Self: Compositions and Decompositions in the Languages of Contemporary Life.* The first edition appeared in 1971, while I was in graduate school and studying with Poirier. It was reissued (with a preface by Edward Said) in 1992. I taught it in 1980 or 1981 in a graduate seminar on Contemporary Rhetoric. I think it has much to say to composition. It did not make a direct appearance in "Inventing," although it has in other things I have written. It was a book I tried to promote, but Poirier was not a theorist, at least not of the type that drew crowds in the 1980s; he often wrote about literary texts and they seemed remote from the concerns of CCCC. Poirier was teaching at Amherst in the key years of Ted Baird and Robert Frost; he went to Harvard with Reuben Brower, where he was engaged with the first-year course, Humanities 6. (Poirier passed away last summer. I learned of his death while on the plane to Bilbao, when I was shocked to find Bruce Weber's obituary of him in the *New York Times*.)

I would say that *The Performing Self* is about invention, about the possibilities of being intellectually alive and present, usually momentarily, in the turn of a sentence, or the shape of a paragraph, or the sudden (if passing) presence of voice. Poirier uses a phrase from D. H. Lawrence as a point of reference, the "struggle for verbal consciousness." And he says: "Locating, then watching, then describing and participating in this struggle as it takes place in the writings of any period could be the most exciting and promising direction of English studies. It points to where language and history truly meet."

And he adds, with an eye, I think, toward the realities and the possibilities of student writing:

> Literary study can thus be made relevant to life not as a mere supplier of images or visions, but as an activity; it can create capacities through exercise with the language of literature that can then be applied to the language of politics and power, the language of daily life. It's simply terribly hard to do this, however—to make this shift of muscularity of mind and spirit from one allegedly elevated mode of expression, where the muscles can be most conveniently developed, to another mode of expression both more inaccessible and considered so ordinary, so natural as to be beyond inquiry. And yet in this transfer of activity, and in the reciprocations that would follow from it, is the promise of some genuine interplay between different and multiplying cultural traditions.

The Performing Self is a book that celebrates writing rather than literature (or the institutions of literature). (This was how I taught the book in the graduate seminar, as a way of thinking about invention. I used two books, *The Performing Self* and Edward Said's *Beginnings*, to provide a counterpoint to the more official literature.) And I was reading 500 placement essays, all the writers announcing their originality in the same terms, and I was looking for moments when something else was happening. These students were not going to provide new ways of thinking or speaking about "creativity," but there were, I wanted to believe, moments that could be said to be signature moments, when something was happening that you would want to identify as the work of this particular writer, for better or for worse—when something wasn't completely pre-written.

The Performing Self provided extended and eloquent examples of such reading, grounded in the argument that writing, even as evidenced by the very best writers we have, is a struggle with language, a struggle to make it work. The book is a collection of essays, many of them describing moments of such achievement (moments rather than masterpieces) and doing so in reference to the work of canonical writers (Eliot or Frost), contemporary writers (Norman Mailer or Thomas Pynchon), and figures from popular culture (the Beatles and the Rolling Stones). The *New York Times* obituary for Poirier quotes him saying this about Mailer: "[H]is writing exemplifies the *kind* of effort that can and needs to be made by anyone who proposes to make more than submissive sense of the world as it is now."

Although *The Performing Self* never names composition as a field, it assumes that "composition" is something we come to understand by reading and by learning through the example of other writers. It argues that a certain form of close reading (although not the close reading of the New Criticism) is the essential lesson for any writer/reader/thinker. The book repeatedly insists that such efforts can be the work of *anyone*, anyone who wants to "make more than submissive sense of the world as it is now." In one of the essays, "What Is English Studies, and If You Know What That Is, What Is English Literature?," Poirier imagines a field of English studies directed to the promotion of such acts of reading and writing. This is not, he insists, the same thing as promoting literature. He says:

> English studies cannot be the body of English literature but it can be at one with its spirit; of struggling, or wrestling with words and meaning. Otherwise English studies may go one of two ways: it can shrink, in a manner possibly as invigorating as that which accompanied the retrenchment of Classics

departments; or it can become distended by claims to a relevance merely topical. Alternatively, it can take a positive new step. It can further develop ways of treating all writing and reading as analogous acts, as simultaneously developing performances, some of which will deaden, some of which will quicken us.

Deaden and quicken. Poirier makes this a game with high stakes. I would hear the same kind of King James cadences when Bill Coles would talk about writing. Long before I had any sense of English 1-2 at Amherst, long before I knew that Coles and Poirier had been part of the same program of teaching, I knew that there was a connectedness, ways of thinking all at once about reading and writing and literature and composition, and that their work provided a language to make this thinking possible.

JS: Near the end of "Inventing," you say this: "The challenge to researchers, it seems to me, is to turn their attention again to products, to student writing, since the drama in a student's essay, as he or she struggles with and against the languages of our contemporary life, is as intense and telling as the drama of an essay's mental preparation or physical production. A written text, too, can be a compelling model of the 'composing process' once we conceive of a writer as at work within a text and simultaneously, then within a society, a history, and a culture." It sounds as if you were worried that, given our field's burgeoning interest in "writing as a process," a necessary attention to writing as a *product* was in danger of fading. Am I right in thinking that you were even being somewhat polemical here?

DB: "The languages of contemporary life!" That's from the subtitle of *The Performing Self.* I had forgotten that I used (or channeled) the phrase! I haven't reread "Inventing" since the time it left my desk; you are helping me to remember details. So I guess Richard Poirier *is* quoted in "Inventing," even if he doesn't get a proper citation.

Was I arguing for an attention to the product at a time when people were discovering writing as a process? Yes. To be sure. It is hard to think back to that moment. It was very tempting to empty writing of language and meaning, to get rid of all the problems of reference and signification, and to concentrate on behaviors. It would be wrong to say that this was the aim or outcome of the best or the most important work at the time, like Linda Flower's work and the work of her colleagues and coauthors. But I think it is accurate to say that this was the temptation.

I can hear in the passage you cite [earlier] an attempt to argue that the page is not fixed and static, two-dimensional, but that the page (and not the brain) is where the action is, the drama, if you assume that writers are struggling, inside sentences, with the forces of history and convention that want to determine what will be said. (You can hear Poirier in "Inventing" but also Harold Bloom, whose *The Anxiety of Influence*, another book from the '70s, had also captured my attention). I thought we needed to return attention to the page, but with a difference.

The pedagogical outcome of this thinking is usually represented by references to Jim Berlin or others who were promoting a critical pedagogy. (Where one course in the first year was to overcome a lifetime of training in the American way—and prevent students from buying designer jeans.) My own feeling was (and is) that revision is the primary tool in a critical pedagogy. In a strict materialist sense, the one thing we can change in a writing class is sentences. If revision is seen as something other than fixing up a paper or shoring up an argument (getting rid of the contradictions by pretending they don't exist), it can be a way of enacting critique. A revision can, say, feature the contractions rather than hide them.

I've told the story elsewhere, so I'll do it quickly here. Long ago, I taught a first-year composition course based around Mary Louise Pratt's *Imperial Eyes: Travel Writing and Transculturation*. One of the assignments had students writing and revising a travel narrative, and the students tended to write missionary narratives. One student wrote about the positive effects of a church group service project in St. Croix, where the natives learned to appreciate the American way. She was a excellent student and the paper went through several Pratt-inspired drafts, where she brought in the voices of the natives, where she included research she had done on the history of the United States in St. Croix, where she worked with the idea of transculturation (and made reference to "imperial eyes"), and where the text was broken into numbered and sometimes competing sections (like 13 ways of looking at St. Croix), but she couldn't or wouldn't change her final paragraph—a deeply predictable view of the island and its grateful natives waving good-bye to the writer and her friends.

Was the essay a critical exercise? I would say yes. The writing was significantly different and, however clichéd the conclusion, the differences were important. She had learned something that she could only have learned as a writer revising, that sentences are flexible.

JS: Earlier in this interview, you referred to Foucault's "project," and I think that has always been an important term for you. At one point in "Inventing," for example, you say ruefully that "education has failed to involve students in scholarly projects, projects that allow students to act as though they were colleagues in an academic enterprise." I get the sense that for you, the term "project" has long had a special glow. Can you say more about what you mean by a "project"? Do you still feel that the academy doesn't encourage students to undertake "projects" enough?

DB: Yikes! Yes, I think the term "project" has had a long glow for me! It is a term I use all of the time, probably now somewhat thoughtlessly. Initially it was part of a desire to use a language that would include (rather than exclude) students in the work that we value in the academy. We had created a curriculum where reading and writing assignments were sequenced, so that students worked on a semester-long project, thinking from one essay to the next, rather than writing discrete essays, this topic one week, another the next. We would choose readings and assignments that seemed to speak back and forth, one to another, but somewhat vaguely, so students could define a specific topic and direction on their own. We didn't want everyone writing the same papers—both for their sakes and for ours.

In the last 20 years I have traveled a good bit from campus to campus, either as a speaker or doing program or department evaluations. I think in general that the academy now does encourage projects more than before, and I think the faculty is more willing to see students as capable of serious intellectual engagement.

JS: I suspect that one reason for our field's continuing interest in your essay has to do with its role in graduate courses. I have repeatedly found that when graduate students read "Inventing the University" in a seminar, they find themselves immediately applying it to their own situations: that is, their own efforts to become more adept at scholarly discourse. Have you found this to be the case?

DB: I have never taught the essay. As a rule, I seldom teach my own work, either to graduate students or to undergraduates. I will get letters or emails from graduate students on other campuses, usually asking me about influences, about work of mine that followed "Inventing," about what I was reading at the time—or what I am reading now.

In the essay, I tell the story of a moment in my own graduate education, when a professor, Fred Main, gave us (with a sense of irony) the following prompt to use if ever we were stuck for something to say: "While most readers of _____ have said _____, a close and careful reading shows that _____." This was memorable for me (I was from Ohio and not accustomed to irony) because it took what felt like an existential problem and made it a writing problem, one that could be addressed formally. It wasn't that I needed something to say; it was that I needed to create a space on the page that called forth a figure who had something to say. I could work on that. Gerald Graff and Cathy Birkenstein have said that this example was useful to them as they thought their way toward *They Say/I Say: The Moves That Matter in Academic Writing*, a book I admire.

The graduate students I work with are much more confident than I was at that stage of my career, more confident and with a greater sense of focus and direction. For better or for worse, I think this is a product of the teaching of theory in English, that and the elimination of old-style comprehensive exams. I find, in fact, that I am constantly trying to get graduate students to read *outside* their reading lists, to look for books that could be important to them but that don't directly address their topic. I think there is an advantage to bringing to the table something unexpected or askew. The writing lessons I provide at the graduate level are pretty specific to the individuals, since these folks write very well. In general, I try to push students toward ordinary language and away from insistent citation. If I find someone to be stuck, I will suggest that they return to the scholarly book that meant the most to them, that most excited them as readers, and to take it as a model, to say: I want to do *that* in my dissertation. Most of the graduate students I've worked with, however, have been very self-directed. I can help to get things started, I can be a close and careful and critical reader, I can provide some basic career advice, but as far as the projects are concerned, I just hang on and enjoy the ride and say whoa every now and then.

I think our position in relation to undergraduates is very different. At Pitt, we have three courses that provide the "spine" to our literature major: Introduction to Critical Reading, Junior Seminar, and Senior Seminar. Around them are clusters of period, genre, and theory courses. These three courses have limited enrollments and expect a substantial amount of writing. The first course, Introduction to Critical Reading, has students working with secondary sources as well as providing close readings of primary texts. I teach it as a kind of *Ways of Reading* course, where there are two primary concerns: the appropriate use of the words of others and the move beyond summary and paraphrase. The real work comes as students try to find a way to get a word in edgewise.

In the junior and senior seminars, students are writing their first long, independent research papers. I think of these courses as writing courses primarily, where the key lessons are consistent with the argument of "Inventing." Students need to learn to do what they need to do—to produce close readings of texts. And they need a context, in this case the disciplinary context; they, too, need to learn to appropriately represent the work of others through summary and paraphrase, but nothing happens until they feel the pressure to speak on behalf of different, even competing interest groups: theorists of narrative, Faulkner scholars, the common reader, readers in school, their generation—and to do so with a sense that there is something at stake in all of this for the writer, personally as well as professionally. My job, as I see it, is to organize the writing assignments so that they are not doing everything at once, and then to ensure that these various figures in the text are all taken seriously.

English majors need to be able to speak on behalf of scholarship in the field (this is my belief but it is also an expectation written into our curriculum). And, as they do this, they need to also find a way of speaking on their own, or on behalf of what matters to them. And this latter is always a matter of revision, of attending to what the language is doing (as well as what it is saying), and, in the end, the rewards come with small signature moments inside a relatively conventional form. When I discuss sample papers in class, after reading a paper out loud, slowly and carefully, to get rhythm and intonation, the first question I ask is always: "What was your favorite moment?" I've learned over time that the most pressing critical discussions of student writing begin with appreciation. *So opp. I see the opposite, what they hate, more*

JS: What have been some of your own experiences in reading appreciatively? What has this process involved for you?

DB: I had the privilege and the pleasure of being asked to look in on Nancy Sommers's longitudinal study at Harvard, and so I had a chance to read across the full range of work of a few individual students, every paper they wrote over the four years of undergraduate education. I found it thrilling and ended up reading them as a form of epistolary novel. (Think Richardson's *Clarissa*, since these are stories of possession and resistance.) And one of the things I noticed was that there was a key moment when students began to speak on behalf of a scholarly collective: narrative theorists, scholars of religion, labor economists. I have no way of correlating my favorite student writers with their grades or class rankings or career placements, but the heroes for me were those whose senior theses pushed the field forward—sometimes conventionally but not always so. Students at Harvard (like students at Pittsburgh and other campuses) have published their senior theses, sometimes with faculty sponsors as coauthors, sometimes not. Students also, however, reshape (or reinvent or deform) the genres and methods that have become their tools.

I have one particular student in mind. She came to Harvard as a fundamentalist Christian. (Imagine the difficulties of maintaining this identity in such a secular setting.) She majored in religious studies. Harvard, being Harvard, made it possible for her to spend part of her junior year in Northern Ireland, working on a reconciliation project. Her papers as a junior were exemplary exercises in academic writing (she writes skillfully and eloquently from within the point of view of "scholars of religion"); her senior thesis has a conventional expertise until, at one moment, it uses the authority of the Bible to make its point. There was nothing else to do. I found it a remarkable moment. I don't know how this was read by her professor—if he (or she) in effect crossed it out or put an exclamation point in the margin. At this stage in her intellectual life, it strikes me as a signature moment and crucial to her development as an intellectual. She worked and worked until she reached bedrock, because the questions mattered to her, and her spade was turned.

I am on leave this year, as I said before, and I have been reading "ordinary language philosophy," primarily Austin, Wittgenstein and Cavell (whose writing I admire enormously). The questions they ask seem to me to be crucial to composition: how and when is ordinary language an instrument of serious thought? Cavell makes much of the passage I cited [earlier] in Wittgenstein's *Philosophical Investigations*: "'How am I able to obey a rule?'—if this is not a question about causes, then it is about the justification for my following the rule in the way I do. If I have exhausted the justifications I have reached bedrock, and my spade is turned. Then I am inclined to say: 'This is simply what I do.'" And, he adds: "Remember that we sometimes demand definitions for the sake not of their content, but of their form. [That is, it is a move in a specific language game.] Our requirement is an architectural one; the definition a kind of ornamental coping that supports nothing."

Cavell refers to this as "Wittgenstein's scene of instruction," and, in *Conditions Handsome and Unhandsome*, he says: "[. . .] the inheritance of a culture—the process of cultivation (or what is the point of spading?)—comes not to a natural end, or rather to its own end, but to one ended, by poor resources, or by power; [. . .] when explanations in particular circumstances run out, teaching becomes heightened while control over what it is that is taught, say shown, is lessened."

JS: How do you account for the staying power of "Inventing the University"—its legs? 25 years later, and it is still taught and cited, used as a significant point of reference. And how do you understand its relationship to what you have done since?

DB: I don't know that I *can* account for it staying power. Like anyone who writes, I am thrilled to have readers. I'm grateful to those who continue to read the essay and to include it as a point of reference in their work. I know that "Inventing" is still used in classes, which means that I now have readers across several generations. And I know that this audience includes undergraduates, because I get emails fairly regularly from students working on a paper and looking for help or a phrase to use in quotation. The question they ask is usually something like, "Did you really mean what you said?!" And that is a hard question to answer.

I first realized that the essay had become useful to the field, that it provided a reference to something that mattered, when you and Patty Harkin published *Contending with Words: Composition and Rhetoric in a Postmodern Age* (1991), where it was mentioned several times. *Contending* was a collection of excellent and provocative essays on composition and literary theory; it became a landmark book as it defined (and helped to produce) a new direction for research in composition by declaring composition's instructional moment (its materials and practices) as an arena for cultural study, and compositionists, those working in the field, as theorists. This list of authors in *Contending* provides a list of those who have gone on to have significant and influential careers: Bialostosky, Bizzell, Clifford, Covino, Crowley, Harkin, Herzberg, Jarratt, Schilb, Sosnoski, Vitanza, and Worsham. Their essays read the work of composition in relation to the work of major theorists, those whose work was circulating widely in cultural and literary studies: Bakhtin, Foucault, Marx, Althusser, Gramsci, Cixous, Irigaray, Kristeva, Lyotard, Deleuze and Guattari.

Between 1985 and 1991 (when *Contending* appeared), my own work followed a track set down by "The Study of Error" and "Inventing the University." I wanted to find a way to describe student writing for what it did (as opposed to what it didn't do) and as evidence of intellectual work (rather than its absence). I wanted to extend this analysis beyond the sentence (or sentence-level error). I took institutional judgments about error (what the academy took to be failures to think, read, or write appropriately) as evidence of the fault line between individual performance and institutional expectation. That, I decided, was where the action was. I wanted to be able to describe what was going on in these textual moments, and I wanted to do so from within both points of view, on behalf of students (and their work) and in order for the institution to reconsider its practices—its curriculum and its ways of staging, receiving, and valuing student writing.

In his book, *Introducing English*, Jim Slevin says that this *is* the work of composition—to attend to these difficult moments of contact—and, he said, if we do our job well, institutions will change. Jim and I had begun to share notes during this period (the late '80s). Even then I thought this claim a little grand, but I was committed to the idea that we could better manage the encounter between students and the academy, and I felt that the challenge to those of us working in composition was to teach others how to read and to value student writing as intellectual work.

The writing I did during this period is represented by the book *Facts, Artifacts, Counterfacts: Theory and Method for a Reading and Writing Course* and, more fully, by a series of essays published in various settings but collected in *Writing on the Margins: Essays on Composition and Teaching*. I also continued to participate in funded projects at

LRDC and, in these, continued to work with substantial collections of student writing, both from first-year courses and from writing intensive courses in the disciplines.

I also began to work on the textbook *Ways of Reading* with my old pal and colleague Tony Petrosky, and with Chuck Christensen and Joan Feinberg of (then) Bedford Books. The textbook began with courses Tony and I (and our colleagues at Pitt) had designed for the first-year writing program, including courses in Basic Writing. The task we set ourselves initially was to choose a reading list and to write assignments that would use reading and rereading, writing and revising to give students access to the work that was valued in the academy, essays by (for example) Michel Foucault and Edward Said, Gloria Anzaldúa and John Wideman, Adrienne Rich and Stephen Greenblatt. We wanted students to be able to participate in intellectual projects these leading figures had begun; we wanted students to be able to write with them, to do more than summary and paraphrase; we wanted students to be able to construct a reading on the page and, in doing so, to make room on the page for themselves, room to talk back, to make additions, to get a word in edgewise. We set out to write assignments that would enable students to bring their thoughts, words, examples and experiences into play with the thoughts, words, examples and experiences of leading intellectuals, writers of power and authority. I thought of the textbook then as I think of it now, as part of the work I do and not as something I do (or did) on the side.

Textbooks are a different genre and present different challenges to the writer. I should add, though, that the essays I wrote during this period have a very different look and feel from the essays in *Contending with Words*. The primary materials are student papers; the block quotations are drawn from student texts. In *Contending*, the primary materials are the theoretical texts and the writers are working to present the thinking of Marx, Foucault or Althusser (for example) and to understand its bearing on composition and the teaching of writing. The work is important and there are some quite dazzling pieces of writing—I remember Don Bialostosky's essay on Bakhtin as a Bakhtinian exercise and Victor Vitanza's animated prose enacting the difficulty of postmodern writing. I thought Pat Bizzell was exactly right about the absence of Marx in our thinking and writing. (I also remember Sharon Crowley identifying the writer of "Inventing the University" as the "bad guy" in the stories people wanted to tell about teaching and learning, a role he went on to play again in any number of books and articles.)

Contending with Words is an important book and the field retains its commitment to theory. In fact, it is not unusual to find that the "theorist" in an English department is also the specialist in rhetoric and composition. At the same time, it remains rare for a book or essay in our field to take a piece of student writing as its object of study or case in point. If "Inventing" has been influential, its influence has not extended to subject or method.

Jean Carr and I recently published Thomas Rickert's book, *Acts of Enjoyment: Rhetoric, Zizek and the Return of the Subject*, in our series with the University of Pittsburgh Press ("Composition, Literacy, and Culture"). I admire this book; I've taught it in a graduate seminar; it is exemplary for its attention to the scene of instruction in composition as an arena for cultural studies and for its theoretical speculation. It was the 2008 winner of the *JAC* Gary Olson Award. I believe I am correct in saying that Rickert was Victor Vitanza's student. His work is certainly in a line with the work begun in *Contending*. In the final chapter (as is often the case of "theory" books in our field), Rickert turns to the classroom to think about the implications of what he has been saying. There is one student writer featured in this chapter (and in the book), and he is *my* student, Quentin Pierce, who wrote the "Fuck You" paper I discuss in "The Tidy House." *I* provided the example of student writing. It comes from a classroom at Rutgers in 1973 or 1974. I find this to be so very odd. Rickert teaches writing and yet his courses and his students are nowhere to be found in this book. I think I understand why. And I am pleased to have provided a useful example. But I find this odd and telling.

I wrote the chapter on "Composition" in the most recent MLA volume, *Introduction to Scholarship in Modern Languages and Literatures*. (Susan Jarratt wrote a separate chapter on "Rhetoric.") The volume is meant for those who are making a decision about graduate school and a career. At the end of my chapter, and thinking about the future of scholarship in composition, and thinking about the manuscripts I review for the U of Pittsburgh Press, I say this:

The important questions are persistent, and for me the most important have to do with student writing—its value and promise. These questions are questions of value and should, I think, be a constant source of debate and controversy. What is a good student paper? What makes it good? What is it good for? What genres of writing are appropriate for the college classroom? Are there emerging or possible genres that we have not yet given appropriate attention? Can we establish a corpus of student writing for common reference? What are best practices for courses with varied goals and in varied settings? These are questions worth an adult professional's time and energy.

Can a young scholar build a career around such work? Yes, but not easily and not without risk. It is certainly the case that Assistant Professors at major research universities are less likely now to have a primary engagement with a freshman composition program than was once the case, to be the person charged to manage, organize and value the writing of hundreds or thousands of students. More and more programs are being turned over to non-tenure stream faculty, often quite brilliant teachers but without the resources, the time or the charge to think of the work as a scholarly enterprise. My sense is that departments are providing neither the motive nor the occasion for the "research" faculty to think about composition and teaching. The motivation is there, however, to think about history, about theory, about literacy, about linguistics or genre or document design or technology. I know that I will continue to receive outstanding manuscripts that follow the tracks I've identified in the essay above, and I will be eager to receive them. The manuscript I'm most eager to receive is one that

I can't easily predict or describe; this is every editor's dream. At the moment, it is always surprising to receive a manuscript with student writing at its center.

But you were asking me about readers and about the surprising shelf life of "Inventing." I've written other things that continue to be taught and cited, but nothing with the reach and persistence of this essay. As I said earlier, I don't know that I *can* account for this. But I am certainly grateful.

CHAPTER FOUR

[handwritten annotations: "The mistakes of students reveal their thinking." and "Copy style to Create new Content"]

Contest of Words

> What we can learn from looking at the institutions we can
> learn also from looking at the prose; just as we can see in the
> prose, as in the history of the time, certain new relationships
> struggling to be formed.

— Raymond Williams, "Notes on English Prose: 1780–1950"

LOOKING AT THE PROSE

In the fall term of 2016, I taught my last section of Seminar in Composition, our required first-year writing course, a course I had taught every year, sometimes twice a year, since I joined the English department at the University of Pittsburgh in 1975. I opened the course with a 2012 *Harper's Magazine* essay by Ben Lerner titled "Contest of Words: High School Debate and the Demise of Public Speech."

Ben Lerner had been my colleague at Pitt for three short years. As Chair of the English department, I hired him to his first tenure track position. Ben has since become a McArthur fellow, a Distinguished Professor at Brooklyn College, and a leading figure in contemporary American letters, recognized for his work as a poet, novelist, and critic.

It turns out Ben was also once the US National High School Champion in Extemporaneous Speaking. "Contest of Words" begins with Lerner as a high school debater in Topeka, Kansas, where he is sorting through three forms of formal debate: Extemporaneous

Speaking, Policy Debate, and a new form named after Lincoln and Douglas (and sponsored by Phillips Petroleum).

The latter, which he calls L-D, turned away from facts, data, and fine points of argument, where a team would win if it could present more arguments than the opponents could refute, to focus on "value," where the competition was between two speakers, and the winner was the speaker who presented the most compelling performance. Content, knowledge, policy: these were replaced by character, performance, ethos. The essay is pre–Donald Trump, so Ben's presidential example was the debate between Jimmy Carter and Ronald Reagan—where Reagan dismissed Carter as a dull, policy wonk by saying, "There you go again."

But Lerner writes also about rapping and free-styling, about drunken basement parties, and about his first year at Brown, where he began to identify with poets and poetry. The essay is about rhapsody, about finding oneself inside sentences, about being transported, about the "experience of prosody," about moments of speaking, when, he says, "grammar became pure possibility." (The essay ends with Occupy Wall Street and the human microphone, speakers passing a phrase from one end of a crowd to the other, but I don't have time here to connect all those dots.)

My students were taken by the opening sections of the essay. They could identify with character and scene—a smart (and smart-assed) kid in high school and at the university. And they could quickly recognize the language, at least in part. There is the ordinary language of a high school party ("getting fucked up," "getting my ass kicked") and there are a number of specialized or uncommon terms: somatic, glossolalic, syncope, rhapsode.

There was useful work to do with this essay, in other words, in order for students to move back and forth between these registers, to make these new words meaningful and to give the old ones a new context of use. And that was the work of the opening weeks of the course. You can't figure out what he means by *rhapsode* just by googling, I would say—or (as if this should even be imaginable) by pulling a dictionary off the shelf. You have to get inside the essay and its sentences. Try them on. See how they work. See if you can do something like that, too.

As I organized and directed the discussion in the classroom, and as I wrote comments toward revisions of first and second drafts, this was what I was trying to say. And it is why I find Lerner's essay to be so teachable. It does something that I want my students to try to do. This contest of words is like what I imagine knowledge to be.

Here is how Lerner describes Extemporaneous Speaking:

> I became in these transportative moments an acned rhapsode, and if the song that was coursing through me was about the supposedly catastrophic risks of a single-payer health-care system or the affirmative speaker's failure to prove solvency, I was nevertheless more in the realm of poetry than of prose, my speech stretched by speed and intensity until I felt its referential meaning dissolve into pure form, until I was singing the oldest song, singing the very possibility of language. In a public school closed to the public, in a suit that felt like a costume, while pretending to argue about policy, I, in all my adolescing awkwardness, would be seized, however briefly, by an experience of prosody.

And here is Lerner's account of free-styling. Note how these sentences, as those above, enact his argument. They are sentences where a reader can feel, however fleetingly, "grammar as pure possibility."

> And yet during those house parties, as some eighty ounces of Olde English malt liquor coursed through my body, I might again be seized by an experience of prosody that transcended

the stolen and perverted materials out of which it was made. "Freestyle" is a misnomer for a radically formal activity in which the pressure of rhyming in real time forces a speaker to prioritize the material attributes of language, its sounds and stresses, while still performing narrative tasks. Freestyling isn't about fitting preexisting content into rhyming and rhythmic forms but rather about discovering content, what's sayable, in the act of composition. I would sometimes manage to rise, I beg you to believe me, above the stupid violence of our battles and enter a zone in which sentences unfolded at a speed I could not consciously control. At that point it didn't matter what words I was plugging into the machinery of syntax, it didn't matter if I was rhyming about bitches or blow or the Canadian health-care system; it didn't matter that I looked like an idiot; what mattered was that language, the fundamental medium of sociality, was being displayed in its abstract capacity, and that my friends and I would catch a glimpse, however fleeting, of grammar as pure possibility.

These sentences give a reader the "experience of prosody." They do what they argue. They "prioritize the material attributes of language, its sounds and stresses, while still performing narrative tasks." A reader is swept up by the shape and rhythm of the sentences (until meaning dissolves into form), one sentence pushing forward in its enthusiasm, the next stopping and starting as it tries to bring the energy, briefly, back under intellectual control. This was the point I was trying to make in my teaching.

Lerner writes an extraordinary "ordinary language" essay, where the difficultly of the thinking is enacted in striking sentences that rely on everyday words and common experience in order to take a step beyond, to advance thought and expression. I finish a sentence or a paragraph (as I finish his novels or poems) aware again of the possibilities of written language. I often find myself writing "Wow" in the margins.

I've spent a career trying to teach just that—how everyday words can be turned this way and that in order to say something that matters. I tell my students that I am looking for (and will note) "Wow" moments in their papers, sections that I'll take time to read to my wife or to send off to friends. Class time is always organized around a close reading of sample student papers. (I don't, for example, lecture on Lerner. I direct discussions of Lerner as he is represented and understood in this week's student essays.)

The writing problems that matter will be seen generally across the students' work. I choose papers for discussion that present the most provocative readings in the most eloquent sentences. (And if I have none of the above, I know I'm in trouble.) I read these papers out loud slowly, and as expressively as I can, and I ask students to mark what they take to be the best moments. And I ask, what might come next? If the essay is to have another week's work, as it will, what might that work be?

This was the opening writing assignment.

I would like you to begin a project in the style of Ben Lerner's "Contest of Words." I'd like you to write about a language lesson, a relatively recent event or exchange (or a series of events or exchanges) that led you (or that can lead you) to questions about language and its use, about the ways it serves (or fails to serve) individuals and communities. (For reasons that I'll present in class, I want to warn you *away* from an essay on the language of the current presidential contest. It will be very hard to find a fresh angle, to find something new to say—hard for you and hard for your readers.)

Begin with a story. In fact, you can take the structure of Lerner's essay as a model. The story you tell should be important to you and rich enough in possibility to take 2-3 weeks of your writing time. It should be something you are willing to share with others.

Your audience? You can imagine that you are writing for a magazine or for friends and family or for a future autobiography. What a reader wants is a view of you and your world, not in the pen-pal sense of what you look like or what you prefer in music, but with the goal of understanding something more general, something about people like you, something about what it is that shapes and defines a person or a life or an identity in this place and at this point in time, something about what it means to live in and through language.

You are preparing a first draft. You don't have to begin at the beginning and you don't have to finish. We will be working together to find a sense of shape and direction. And you will return to this document more than once in the next few weeks.

I am trying to avoid the word "essay" in describing this project, since that word carries certain generic restrictions. And I'm trying to be fairly vague in describing what I want. My advice is for you to begin *not* with a generalization but with some specific scene or scenes. Begin with a story (or stories) rather than with an argument. Write from inside the scene. If people are speaking, you can, if you choose, let them speak as characters speak in fiction. You can, obviously, write in the first person.

Students write every week in this course. With each assignment, the second and third weeks are for revision, where I expect substantial additions and reformulations. Two-to-three-page papers (single spaced) become 6-8 page papers.

One student wrote an essay about social networks, digital composition, language change, and language variety. His examples, the sections in quotation, were all drawn from either street talk and dorm slang or from online written exchanges: tweets, instant messages, memes, blogs, Facebook postings, emojis.

The essay was interesting and provocative, but the prose that surrounded the quotations was, by an old form of measurement, and in its own terms, unfinished and ungrammatical. To my ear and to my eye, the prose was the prose of someone who had pretty good command, who was pretty well situated, but who couldn't (or wouldn't) be bothered to pay attention to detail.

The essay was a first draft. It concluded:

> Even I have found that shortening words has its benefits and have brought myself to missing punctuation and disregarding most grammar rules. As long as they understand what the general message you are trying to convey to them, it is a successful text. Yet this is not the only time that our language has been tarnished. In everyday speech, people are also loosing key elements to the English language and just blow it off and say that it is unneeded because they are speaking in a conversational method. . . . It takes time to move in this direction but over time can lead to people changing the English language to either accept the new ways or to find a way to get people to use English how it was intended to be used.

A *successful text. Everyday speech. Tarnished language.* A method that is efficient and *conversational.* These key terms can organize an interesting and useful discussion of language use. *English how it was intended to be used.* This is a great phrase, and I pointed to it when I wrote comments to direct the first revision. How might a writer sort out the differences between English as it is used and English as it is intended to be used? Whose intentions is he talking about? How might they be located?

I also asked the student to use this first draft as text, as exhibit A, as one example he was examining, studying, and preparing to bring to the table. As he revised a particular passage, what changes would he make to better serve the needs of a reader? What sentences or phrases would he point to as signs of his generation, its conventions and contributions to English, of those "new ways to use English" that he values and would defend? I wanted to provide the occasion for him to think both through and about what he was writing.

When I began teaching in the early 1970s, most of my students wrote in longhand on yellow legal pads. I can remember struggling to learn to read their handwriting. And I remember heated discussions among colleagues about the ethics of requiring typed final drafts, since more than a few students would have to hire typists to do the job, an additional step that some could ill afford and that, for all, would further distance them from the responsibilities of producing what we would have called a "clean, final draft."

In those courses, the sentences that demanded my attention were the sentences of working-class and minority students from inner city Pittsburgh, Newark, or Philadelphia, many of them first-generation college students. They struggled, and the struggle with the sentence enacted a national struggle for access.

Here, in 2017, things were different. Pitt had become a "reach" school rather than a fallback, and all students had become comfortable at a keyboard. The student who wrote the first draft of the "Lerner essay" had command of the new technologies of writing and all they provide in service of revision and presentation. He was fluent, confident, and entitled. A struggle with words was something I would have to teach, which is why revision has such pedagogical power.

Revision, as I say to my students, is where I can see them at work on their writing, struggling with sentences and beyond, trying to take a next step in thought and expression. And it is why, as I say in my course description, I base their grades on the work I see from draft to draft. I don't put grades on single papers; I evaluate what I see happening on a single project from one week to the next.

As I remember my students in the 1970s, they were not equally fluent. They struggled to get words on a page, and the struggle, as Mina Shaughnessy noted in her magnificent, groundbreaking book, *Errors and Expectations*, included handwriting. Nor did they have as similar a sense of confidence or entitlement, at least in placing words on a page.

Here is another way to say this. This student and his colleagues are in a better position to get started on the real work of writing. He had begun to gather his examples and to organize them in relation to an argument about language use and language change. What he didn't yet have was a way to take his own work seriously. But, to say that is to say that this was the opening week of a fourteen-week course in composition.

My classes met two days a week, usually Tuesdays and Thursdays. I hand out writing assignments, like the one above, on Thursdays. The papers are due the next Tuesday. (I don't want to read papers over the weekend.) I turn the papers back on Thursday, with comments toward revision.

To help to prepare students to reread and to revise their first essays, and to assist the classroom discussion of "Contest of Words," I created a set of exercises in "grammar as pure possibility." I asked students to write within the shapes and rhythms of some of Lerner's most performative sentences, like this one: "In a public school closed to the public, in a suit that felt like a costume, while pretending to argue about policy, I, in all my adolescing awkwardness, would be seized, however briefly, by an experience of prosody." Lerner would provide the form; they would provide the content. Here is a representative response: "In a library filled with IPhones, in a chair that felt like bricks, while pretending to do homework, I, through all the distraction, found a surge, intensely, of focus." In class, I asked the student what it was like to write a sentence like this. She said, "Oh, man, it was like building a cathedral, and 'I,' I was the figure at the top."

I learned long ago the importance of focusing attention on key sentences in the work I have assigned for students to read, sentences we can use to think about a writer's style and about the lessons it can provide. These sentences are often the least colloquial, the longest and most difficult to parse, and they are, then, sentences students have learned to ignore.

My courses always assume that students will reread before they write, going back to work on a text. They need to find passages that work and that will work for them. My goal is to teach that kind of attention, which is a form of close reading, although not the precious close reading of Brooks and Warren. It is more like "reading in slow motion," a phrase drawn from Reuben Brower's essay in *In Defense of Reading*, a book he edited with Richard Poirier. (The essays in that collection describe a first-year English course Brower and his colleagues had developed at Harvard in the 1960s.)

Below are some additional examples of student responses. This first one provides a lesson, for example, in the colon and semicolon, and in the pleasures and possibilities of the right-branching sentence. And, in fact, I learned to expect such sentences across the essays I would receive the following week: sentences that are right-branching, organized by dashes, a colon, and three semicolons. This is Lerner:

> Although high school debate is often considered the thinking person's—the nerd's—alternative to sports, my memories of it are primarily somatic: the starched collar of the dress shirt against my recently shaved neck, small cuts and razor bumps deepening the sensation; the constant gentle pressure of the tie; how my gait and posture adjusted under the direction of the suit; the way the slacks always felt high and tight because I normally let my baggy jeans sag to whatever level we white Midwestern adolescents had tacitly established as our norm.

Here is a representative response:

> Because high school football is often considered the barbarian's—the jock's—way to get away with violence, I remember it very physically: the sweaty padding of the heavy helmet against my constantly soaked scalp, the sun's heat magnifying the sensation; the constant soreness of my body, how I always collapsed after a long day of practice; the way my shoulder

pads slid across my chest because I felt the need to unbuckle them with the hope of accessing more air with each breath.

Here is another example, although the writer stumbles a bit after the colon (which is what I said to her when she prepared to revise):

> Although high school girls' lacrosse is often considered to be soft—easy—compared to boys lacrosse, from my experience, I would say quite the opposite: the small pocket of the stick makes catching, passing and cradling more difficult; the constant checking of the stick by opponents forces the ball out of your stick; the frequent reminder from the referees to not make contact with the other player made the differences between both men and women's lacrosse surprisingly far from each other.

I always took great pleasure from my students' delight in authoring long, complicated sentences, sentences drawn from the assigned readings. In weeks two and three of this course, they were "Lerner-like" sentences. Later, the sentence patterns would have other names: Appiah, Quammen, Laskas, Williams, Gawande. I'd make a point of chuckling over this when we discussed sample papers in class. Imitating was honoring; it was homage; it was learning. But, of course, it is also a case of "be careful what you wish for." After a couple weeks it became my job to rein them in. Not every sentence can or should be a tour de force.

I was teaching lessons in grammar and style. I also, however, wanted students to work toward a quick paraphrase of the key arguments in Lerner's essay, something they could use as starting blocks or points of reference if they cared, as I was determined they would, to bring Lerner's argument into an essay of their own.

This was the harder task. I have never taught summary as an endpoint, but I knew the importance of teaching toward this form of strategic comprehension. And I knew how difficult it was to try to summarize Lerner's argument. That difficulty was one of the things that drew me to that essay in the first place, that made it teachable.

As with the sentence exercises, I wanted to focus this writing problem (a summary statement) in Lerner's terms, and so I headed the exercise with a passage from his essay:

> My college application essay was about moving from debate, which conceived of linguistic exchange as a contest with winners and losers, to a more poetic understanding of the nuances of language in which writer and reader collaborated on the construction of meaning.
>
> Ben Lerner, "Contest of Words"

Below is a key moment in the essay, a place where you can feel (hear) Lerner trying to say something that is not easily said—that is, something not already prepared, packaged, and available. There is, in the prose, a "haltingness"; you can sense the "demand . . . for a new language." These moments ask (even require) a reader to collaborate on the construction of meaning. And this is a standard move in serious writing.

Let's imagine that you are writing about "Contest of Words" (using, say, the passage below in block quotation). If you did, you would need to follow Lerner's words with a kind of translation. The block quotation won't just speak for itself. You would need to write your sense of what Lerner is saying. To enter this space, you might write, for example: "in other words" or "here is what I think Lerner is saying" or "here is what I take from this."

For the passage below, I'd like you to provide your version of what Lerner is saying.

When I was in my Dillard's suit spewing arguments in a largely empty school, when I was a belligerent little wankster rhyming in a basement, when I was an ignorant undergrad abandoning the clichés of my macho Midwestern romanticism for the clichés of poetic vanguardism, I was, in all my preposterousness, responding to a very real crisis: the standardization of landscape and culture, a national separation of value and policy, an impoverished political discourse ("There you go again") that served to naturalize our particular cultural insanity. I was a privileged young subject—white, male, middle class—of an empire in which every available identity was a lie, but when I felt that language breaking down as I spoke it—as it spoke me—I felt, amid a general sense of doom, that other worlds were possible.

Here is one student's response:

Lerner addresses three moments of his life, which I interpret as turning points. As a high school debater, a teenager rapping in a basement, and an undergrad he highlights exchanging the "clichés" of his real, culturally accepted identity for that of a poetic character. He explains that exchange to be a response to a "crisis." I interpret this crisis as a response to the separation between value and policy. In other words, he's saying he was ignorantly making that exchange of his real self as a reaction to troubled political discussion and possibly a troubled culture/society. In addition, he mentions that accepted identity was a lie in our troubled society, but through language it was true, alive, and versatile.

The results, in general, were not promising. The students struggled to read beyond their quickest translations of what Lerner was saying. Or, to put it another way, they read it through the lens of deeply held desire, the commonplace of *finding one's true self*. Ben Lerner was a successful writer with an Ivy League education. Maybe he was a phony in high school, we all were, but he found himself in college.

I wrote to the class:

> Most of you, in your translations, focused on the first use of the word "cliché" and ignored the second. You had Lerner abandoning his clichéd years in high school for his true identity as a poet.

> Here is what I hope you will take away from the "construction of meaning" exercise: When the words are hard or used in odd ways, when the meaning seems hard to construct, you must focus in on the language and read even more closely. Let the context help you. You should *NOT* step back and translate the text into what is commonly said. The writing that is valued in the university is almost always writing that struggles to say something new, that struggles *NOT* to repeat the common phrase or the common wisdom.

I needed to move on, so I didn't ask students to revise these paragraphs. This was one of the moments where, as Wittgenstein says, you hit bedrock. The spade is turned. There was nothing I could think to do but to say, "No, that's not quite it." It was not a deft move, but a teacher has to know when to move on.

What we were moving on to was a chapter by Anthony Appiah, "Synthesis: For Racial Identities," that was part of his exchange with Amy Gutmann in their 1996 book, *Color Conscious: The Political Morality of Race*. For convenience's sake, in preparing the chapter for class, I referred to it as an "essay," and I shortened the title to "For Racial Identities."

Appiah's writing, like Lerner's, was difficult to read, and in all the best ways. Appiah was, as I would say to my students, reader-friendly. He knew and acknowledged the needs of readers who were not philosophers or political scientists. The argument was organized through key terms: scripts, identification and ascription, collective identities and individual freedom. The material Appiah brought to the table included classic texts from major writers, but also examples from his lived experience, from newspapers and popular culture.

And he knew where and when to clarify by using what a magazine writer (which he also is) would call a nut graph—something catchy and clearly stated that could nail down a difficult concept. Students always chose this passage as the best and most useful example of such a gesture: "If I had to choose between Uncle Tom and Black Power, I would, of course, choose the latter. But I would like not to have to choose. I would like other options."

The writing is difficult because of its learned range of reference, and it is conceptually challenging. It does not say the usual things. But, more than anything else, it is difficult because it requires attention to voice—to where and how Appiah locates himself in relation to the available terms and arguments, to ways of thinking and speaking that he (and his ideal readers) quickly recognize but that which, to undergraduates, just sounds "true." Here is what I wrote to my students to try to prepare them for this.

As you read "For Racial Identities," it will help to pay particular attention to voice—to the way the writer locates himself within available ways of speaking and thinking. Appiah writes as a philosopher. That is, he writes from within ideas, from within trains of thought. He is not necessarily endorsing these ways of thinking. They are not necessarily his thought processes, or ones he would endorse. He is trying them on, testing their consequences or limits, showing where they might lead.

You can't, in other words, quickly assume that an affirmative sentence expresses Appiah's own thoughts or beliefs. This is tricky. For example, listen to these sentences. Where might you locate Appiah?

> I have insisted that African-Americans do not have a single culture, in the sense of shared language, values, practices, and meanings. But many people who think of races as groups defined by shared cultures, conceive that sharing in a different way. They understand black people as sharing black culture by definition: jazz or hip-hop belongs to an African-American, whether she likes it or knows anything about it, because it is culturally marked as black. Jazz belongs to a black person who knows nothing about it more fully or naturally than it does to a white jazzman.

Appiah is not saying that he believes jazz belongs to a black person more fully or naturally than it does to a white person. He is saying that "many people" have a way of thinking about race and culture that will lead them to such statements or beliefs.

Learning to read along with a philosopher, with a writer who is thinking about ways of thinking, is challenging. As you read, keep an ear cocked for moments when Appiah gives voice to others, and be alert for those moments (and they are fewer) when he speaks for himself.

Appiah ends "Racial Identities" with a bravura sentence, a sentence with fling. I used it to frame a Lerner-like exercise in grammar as possibility.

Here is what I wrote:

Appiah: Grammar as pure possibility

As he prepares for his conclusion, Appiah offers a surprising list.

> In policing this imperialism of identity—an imperialism as visible in racial identities as anywhere else—it is crucial to remember always that we are not simply black or white or yellow or brown, gay or straight or bisexual, Jewish, Christian, Moslem, Buddhist, or Confucian but that we are also brothers and sisters; parents and children; liberals, conservatives and leftists; teachers and lawyers and auto-makers and gardeners; fans of the Padres and the Bruins; amateurs of grunge rock and lovers of Wagner; movie buffs; MTV-holics; mystery-readers; surfers and singers; poets and pet-lovers; students and teachers; friends and lovers.

A list like that is a generous gesture. It invites additions; it invites you to join in. It is also a leveling gesture—Jewish or Christian, gay or straight, poets and pet-lovers, fans of the Pirates and the Penguins (or the Red Sox and the Bruins). All of these identity markers have equal status.

1. Using the following prompt, make your own list.

In policing this imperialism of identity—an imperialism as visible in racial identities as anywhere else—it is crucial to remember always that we are not simply

but that we are also

2. Is there anything too singular, too close to your heart, too fundamental to be fractured, played, or treated with irony?

There were few surprises in the students' lists of available terms: socially awkward; disabled; athletes or nerds or artists; prospective engineers; journalists, doctors, economists, or businesspeople; light or tan or dark; gay or trans; doers or followers; peace seekers or God pleasers; Irish or Italian; atheist or agnostic; Shia or Sunni; suburban or ghetto; pro-life or pro-choice; numbers or résumés; ill or physically sound; upfront or ambiguous; rich or poor; privileged or underprivileged; those who look like thorn bushes; Roger Goodell haters; Southern, Jamaican, Caucasian; inexperienced and indecisive; social media addicts; *that which we don't necessarily choose.*

There were few surprises, but of course that is Appiah's argument. In the final paragraphs of the essay he says:

> So here are my positive proposals: live with fractured identities; engage in identity play; find solidarity, yes, but recognize contingency, and, above all, practice irony. In short I have only the proposals of a banal postmodernism. And there is a regular response to these ideas from those who speak for the identities that now demand recognition, identities toward which so many people have struggled in dealing with the obstacles created by sexism, racism, homophobia. "It's all very well for you. You academics live a privileged life; you have steady jobs; solid incomes; status from you place in maintaining cultural capital. Trifle with your own identities, if you like; but leave mine alone."
>
> To which I answer only: my job as an intellectual is to call it as I see it. I owe my fellow citizens respect, certainly, but not a feigned acquiescence. I have a duty to reflect on the probable consequences of what I say, and then, if I still think it worth saying, to accept responsibility for them. If I am wrong, I say,

you do not need to plead that I should tolerate error for the sake of human liberation; you need only correct me. But if I am right, so it seems to me, there is a work of the imagination that we need to begin.

In answer to my final question—Is there anything too singular, too close to your heart, too fundamental to be fractured, played, or treated with irony?—only five of twenty students said yes. And only three of the five gestured toward what that singular thing might be called: *sexuality, victims, survivors.*

WRITERS AND READERS AS "ACTIVE HUMAN BEINGS"

A newly active social sense of writing and reading, through the social and material historical realities of language, in a world in which it is closely and precisely known, in every act of writing and reading, that these practices connect with, are inseparable from, the whole set of social practices and relationships which define writers and readers as active human beings, as distinct from the idealized and projected "authors" and "trained readers" who are assumed to float, on a guarded privilege, above the rough, divisive and diverse world of which yet, by some alchemy, they possess the essential secret.

— Raymond Williams, "Cambridge English, Past and Present"

The work with Appiah carried us through midterm. I gave two separate writing assignments, each with revisions. One had students summarizing and paraphrasing Appiah's argument. It said that they should write an essay addressed to others of their generation—friends, people who mattered to them—presenting something Appiah said and why it might be considered important, or at least worth considering.

In the second, students were asked to write a narrative essay where they brought their own example to the table, to write about a moment from their own experience in a way that showed their engagement with what they had read, even if it didn't make direct reference to Anthony Appiah.

The assignment to summarize and paraphrase, as always, produced writing that was clumsy and often ungrammatical, particularly at the level of the sentence; some of it was writing beyond revision, all of it was frustrating for everyone involved: "Kwame Appiah is unafraid in his endeavor to delve into the realm of identities, labels, and the consequences of norm on the individual. In doing so, he has raised some questions as to the true output of his proposals. To do so, we much look at the role and effect of some of the varying modern forces within personal identity." The narrative assignment produced essays that were eloquent, moving, and often quite beautiful. And many provided sophisticated readings of Appiah. I had two students who won prizes for these essays—one in the Carnegie Mellon Martin Luther King writing competition and the other in our own Composition Program Writing Awards.

To give you a sense of what these essays *did*, how they worked, here is the opening section from the first of these. It was titled "Mixed Girl Problems." All of the students had learned (from Lerner and Appiah) to punctuate their essays with sections breaks. In the fourth paragraph, you'll see the use of colon and semicolon in the manner of Lerner.

"What do you say when people ask you what you are?"
"Uh . . . I say I'm Filipino."
"Haha, no, honey; *You say you're black.*"

There is a defaulted divide between black and white in society. My father told me that the first thing people will see, in terms of my ethnicity, is that I am black, not Filipino. The precedent of a white black divide has led people to identify me as only being black.

"What are you" is a question I have been asked almost a thousand times—people need a label. I love the question, however, because it has two answers: a simple one and a complex one.

I was enrolled and educated for fourteen years in the Union Free School District in New York. All throughout those years, my peers have always been of similar faces. Their faces were similar in the sense that they were variations of a particular shade, "colored," for lack of a modern term. All students in my district came from the same ten or so backgrounds that could easily be generalized into three: Black Americans; Black Caribbean Americans (Haitians, Jamaicans, and some Trinidadians); and Hispanics (El Salvadorians, Hondurans, Dominicans, and Mexicans).

The student population of my school was not "predominantly" populated by minorities; it was *entirely* populated by minorities. I can say, wholeheartedly, that we all had a fair contribution and ultimately a fair share of what I'd like to call a common culture. We shared our Uniondale slang, slogans, sense of style, and social gestures. However, there is always some form—human constructed—of a distinction that manages to individualize people deemed relatively the same. I was a mixed-black girl to some of my peers and a fake black girl to others.

"You're not really black though. I mean you're black, but you're *fake* black."

When a group of worshipers in Charleston was murdered in a mass shooting, I was black. When Mike Brown was shot, I was black. When Eric Garner was shot for selling cigarettes, I was black. When Freddie Gray died mysteriously from a head injury, given that the police took undocumented "stops," I was black. Yet years ago, a very good friend of mine placed me under the label of being "fake black." She did so in such a fleeting manner; it still resonates with me.

This leads me to discuss my emotional connection with the black community. It is a fair share of what Appiah refers to as *ascription* and *identification*. During the demonstrations of police brutality cases mentioned previously, I was expected by those within the black community, my peers, my teachers, my neighbors, and others, to realize an obligation as a person apart of that community. My unspoken, understood obligation was to stand with my "brothers and sisters" during the fight to diminish police brutality on black people—most urgently. It has been a great deal of pressure. It has left me confused. When I talk about my heritages, cultures, and backgrounds, I am just *mixed*, but when a tragedy occurs and it wakes the entire black community, if I do not stand up with the utmost quickness, passion, and anger, I am neglecting the obligations of my identity, an identity some people within the black community otherwise would not think I owe entirety to. Truthfully, it ultimately boils down to my ability to exercise my right to choose and I choose reality. The danger of the events that have been occurring are as real to me as it is to any other person who identifies as black. For the reality of the equal danger, is the reason why I choose to stand in such situations and demonstrations. The reality is that my experiences and the way I am viewed in society have influenced the way I identify myself. I am black too no matter what.

"You're not really black, though." My friend did not intend to offend me; she was subconsciously displaying her offense. However, she did downplay my choice to identify as black. She attempted to place me in a special category, a category in which I could not fully take on the label of being black. In her eyes, I was simply, genetically, and apparently, not entirely black and therefore not black enough. I did not have that availability to "claim the culture." Even a very good friend of mine, a friend I

still have to this moment, was inadvertently expressing her offense. That is, the offense she took to *someone like me*, a person
with half as much the "biological basis," taking entitlement in
my blackness. A cultural issue, not a racial one.

> "I'll never understand why these light skin, silky haired
> girls always think they the shit."

This writer is quick to locate Appiah's essay within a context she
can command—and about which she cares deeply. My instruction to
all the students asked them to write from within the scenes they chose,
and to honor and rely on the language that belonged to those scenes
(*these light skin, silky haired girls always think they the shit*).

You can also, however, hear this writer chewing on the question
of choice, trying to find a language she can use to think about the
difficult relationship between "ascription," "identification," and choice
(or individual agency). I wrote "Wow" in the margins by this pair of
sentences: "However, there is always some form—human constructed
—of a distinction that manages to individualize people deemed relatively the same. I was a mixed-black girl to some of my peers and a
fake black girl to others." It sharpened the distinction and located it
within the terms of the example she has brought to the table. It also
demonstrates the Appiah-like move from abstraction to epithet, from
theory to example. I knew from conversation and from earlier drafts
that she was frustrated by the ease with which Appiah could say: *it is
crucial to remember always that we are not simply black or white or yellow
or brown, gay or straight or bisexual, Jewish, Christian, Moslem, Buddhist,
or Confucian but that we are also.* . . . She said to me: "The thing about
Appiah is that he *is* Black African and openly gay. The *ascription* part
is not hard for him. But it is not that simple for everyone."

As she says in the opening, there are simple answers and there
are complex ones. She is in pursuit of complexity and it takes her
to her bedrock moment—the moment where the language, as is the
case with all serious writers, breaks down—or, in this case, resorts

to the usual commonplace: "Truthfully, it ultimately boils down to my ability to exercise my right to choose and I choose reality." As Wittgenstein said, "Remember that we sometimes demand definitions for the sake not of their content, but of their form. Our requirement is an architectural one; the definition a kind of ornamental coping. . . ."

If I were pushing for another revision, I would have circled the word "reality" and asked, "How else this might be phrased?" I would have said, "There is more work to do here." But a teacher has to know when enough is enough. There is always more that can be done with a piece of writing, but not always in good faith or in good humor. And it was time to move on.

I want to take a moment, however, to mark this student's progress in her work on this essay. Here is the opening of an earlier draft, one in which I had asked for summary and paraphrase of key passages in Appiah's essay:

The word identity has been used differently over time. Kwame Anthony Appiah, a philosopher and an ethicist, in a selection from his and Amy Gutmann's book *Color Consciousness*, brings fascinating prior experiences and calls to question concepts of identity. He argues throughout his essay that now more than ever before, the definition of identity has a sense of ferocity and importance.

Appiah is a pragmatist; in this selection he speaks from inside the logic of many ideas, actions, and concepts he does not necessarily agree with. However, he communicates his arguments upon identity, with the foundation of his own identification as a homosexual and African-American man, against "ascription"; the "label" in which people within a society inevitably use to categorize a person. He introduces and acknowledges both the social and psychological effects of a "racial label" (44). These labels are said to be consented inevitably, which is a paradox because what that says is that they are basically not consented at all—"I don't recall ever choosing to identify as a male, but being male has shaped many of my plans and actions" (45).

You can see, feel, and hear the writer struggling to put Appiah's words to her own good use, and to define a space where the two of them are speaking together, where she doesn't just disappear within the conventions of a "term paper."

And here is the final paragraph of her final draft. I like that the piece ends with a play on words, the reanimation of a tired phrase (*not mutually exclusive*):

> The people within the cultures of which I share "parts" seem unable to decide whether they'd like to welcome me in as one of them; that is, they cannot decide where the line should be drawn. However, that line is somewhat imaginary. It is drawn in a different position for everyone or sometimes, not drawn at all. The line when drawn has a role in creating a division that determines a sufficient aspect, a considerable part that represents a whole culture (whether it be through appearance, practices, language, and etc.). But, I am multiracial and multicultural: Filipino and African-American. I am not half and half, but whole and whole; my identity is not mutually exclusive.

In an interview with Richard Fleming (reprinted in *Philosophical Passages*), Stanley Cavell says: "I recognize words as mine when I see that I have to forgo them to use them. Pawn them and redeem them to own them." He has been talking about his reading of Derrida and Derrida's reading of J. L. Austin, about the notion that not only do we abandon our words to others, but we are, ourselves, abandoned to them, in them. I use these two sentences over and over again as an epigraph for writing assignments. With this student paper, with the paper that follows in this chapter, and with the earlier paper on the war in Afghanistan, I begin to understand again their importance and their implications for criticism and for teaching. "I recognize words as mine when I see that I have to forgo them to use them. Pawn them and redeem them to own them."

I also received an essay titled "To Anthony Appiah: A Rejoinder." It was not one of the prize winners, but I thought it was (as I still think it is) a remarkable piece of work. These students (and their colleagues) and these essays (along with many but not, of course, all the others I received) came to me as a timely gift in this, my final composition class.

In "A Rejoinder," a student wrote about the pressure to have sex, which he does, first with a girl and later with a boy. But, he wrote, he couldn't find himself in any of those moments. He just wasn't there. And as he (and others) tried to find terms of explanation, all the available sentences had him choosing between "straight" or "gay." And those words didn't work for him. In the end, everyone, friends and family included, decided that he was "confused." Here is part of the opening section:

As a child, it is normal for boys not to have feelings for girls. They're not developed yet, not knowing what it means to *like* someone in the big people connotation. However, once I hit puberty, that transition was much foggier than it was supposed to be. When I was about 15, I met someone who became my first real girlfriend. However, though I enjoyed her personality greatly, I never felt butterflies in my stomach when I saw her, never missed her terribly, and certainly never felt like writing her a poem to express my love.

It seems that, in those early pubescent days, I was in the relationship because that's what I felt like I had to do. I liked this girl as a friend, so clearly I was supposed to date her. And, since we were dating, I played by the handbook and we had

sex. I was doing everything right and yet, at 15, I couldn't com-
prehend why I felt like there was a misprint in my emotions, as
if something went wrong and the syntax no longer added up,
as if there were someone or something missing.

You can hear Lerner here in the reference to syntax, and in the
ways the writer brackets the failure of the usual ways of talking about
sex and love. From later in the essay:

I ended up meeting someone through a friend of mine, and
though I enjoyed his company, I was apprehensive to the whole
idea of being in a relationship. Every time that we would meet
up, it felt unnatural; I wanted to be his friend, not his lover. I
could never let myself make the relationship official, and again
I felt empty. Only once did he try to kiss me, and though I
let it happen, it was, yet again, the exact opposite of what it
was supposed to be. There were no fireworks, no oncomes of
extreme passion where I felt the need to confess my undying
love—just two lips touching two lips. I promptly ended things
with the guy, though he didn't take it too well. "What do you
mean you're not gay?"

Before, this would have comforted me, knowing that I
wasn't gay. However, now it had left me in a strange state of
mind that I had never before encountered—a state of mind
where I no longer had an identity to grab onto, gay or straight.
It seemed that everyone had blurred being metrosexual with
homosexual, and I was on the short end of that confusion.

However, I find it important to note that I wasn't confused.
During this time of my life, many people were quick to write
off my experiences as confusion, as a phase. That wasn't the
case; it wasn't that I was confused, but that I was lost. Confusion implies that I had these feelings and I was unsure how to
deal with them, possibly unwilling to confront my inner self,

but being lost, on the other hand, meant that I had no feelings for men or women and I genuinely wasn't sure what this meant for me or my future.

At this point in a long and compellingly detailed narrative, the genre of the classroom essay offers him the chance to conclude, to be done with it all, to say, "OK, I WAS confused," but the writer rejects the offer, as he will go on to reject other offers to conclude. He just keeps writing. And what follows are not the predictable set pieces of *They Say/I Say* but what I might call a "contest of words."

What I admire here is the writer's recognition that the work of the essay is not simply the work of narrative, of careful and detailed recall, nor is it simply the work of statement, example, and conclusion. It is also a struggle with terms, particularly the commonplace notion that late adolescence (and sexual experimentation) can be successfully accounted for as "confusion." Like the "mixed girl" essay, this essay pushed back on Appiah's notion that choice was bound by available "scripts." It deeply understood Appiah's argument, was inspired by it, but found, in the end, that it just didn't quite fit.

Here are the final paragraphs. Through the sentences in bold, I am tracing what I take to be the ways the writer rejects a set of foregone conclusions and struggles with the available language, struggles against what he is prepared to say. It begins, as it should, with "however":

> **However, I find it important to note that I wasn't confused.** During this time of my life, many people were quick to write off my experiences as confusion, as a phase. That wasn't the case; it wasn't that I was confused, but that I was lost. **Confusion implies that I had these feelings and I was unsure how to deal with them, possibly unwilling to confront my inner self, but being lost, on the other hand, meant that I had no feelings for men or women and I genuinely wasn't sure what this meant for me or my future.**

At this point, the only thing that really confused me was why I had to be described as confused, as closeted, or as a feminine man, with no room for anything in between. What confused me is why, because I had no sexual desire, I was considered less masculine. It seemed that, with every holiday dinner conversation, I was constantly bombarded with the question, "so do you have a girlfriend?" And every time I brought a female within close proximity of my family, they assumed it was a love interest of some sort.

Now, at the ripe age of 19, I feel the pressure more than ever before. I see my friends falling into committed relationships, planning their futures with their significant others. I see the movies, the media, the music, telling me that as a male college freshman I should be in sexual overdrive—trying to score any hookup I can muster. I see the LGBT and other "socially-progressive" peoples trying to tell me who I am, label my feelings, and tell me that I'm not alone, that there are other people like me.

I'm not buying it. I'm not trying to fall into these categories, to describe my sexuality and my feelings as this or that. I view sexuality as fluid, capable of coming momentarily in and out, capable of changing, capable of being inactive or active, capable of being curious and of being consistent. It does not need to be named; it does not need described.

So, what's the end result of all of this? Well, as for now, I would say I'm very content with my life. I have managed to dedicate my time to my friends and family while others dedicate their time to their significant others. Though I am still unable to see myself with a man or woman, I don't turn my back on the thought. Maybe one day I will feel the way others feel, but I am convinced it will be because of a change in my desires, rather than some sort of destined lover making a storybook entrance. I have learned that I complete myself, and it is not up to another entity to clarify or validate that.

My only worry comes with time. As I face more and more

real-world situations, I feel the weight of the world pushing down on me more and more. I hope to hold my ground, to stand on my position of fluid sexuality and self-satisfaction, but I would be a liar if I said I had no doubts. It is still true that I share the same first and last name as my father and grandfather; it is still true that most people marry and dedicate time to their partners, not friends; and it is still true that life can be financially and socially beneficial if spent with another. **I worry that, with time, my will to stand strong on the matter will erode, and I will succumb to one of the all-too-familiar lives available to me.** I can only hope that, should I find myself in love, it is a product of my feelings and not of what I am supposed to feel.

This essay was written by the same student who wrote the clumsy, ungrammatical sentences I used to represent the difficulty, even impossibility, of a summary: "Kwame Appiah is unafraid in his endeavor to delve into the realm of identities, labels, and the consequences of norm on the individual. In doing so, he has raised some questions as to the true output of his proposals. To do so, we much look at the role and effect of some of the varying modern forces within personal identity." The narrative essay provided a compelling rejoinder, a nineteen-year-old's rewriting of Appiah's story of free choice. The narrative essay had an argument. The argumentative essay, on other hand, struggled to find a way to begin.

It is hard to reconcile these two performances, two weeks apart, all from the same writer—one appearing as a failure to be articulate and the other as a success. I've spent much of my career thinking about this disjunction—these two writers in one body—and what this disjunction says about learning to write.

Raymond Williams calls this disjunction the "underlying unevenness of literacy and of learning," and, as I have recalled earlier, in "Notes on

English Prose: 1780–1950," he illustrated these moments by turning, for example, to the differences between the narrative language and the reported speech, the diverse voices in, say, the novels of Charles Dickens, Elizabeth Gaskell, and George Eliot. Here is what he says about Thomas Hardy: "But Hardy as writer was mainly concerned with the interaction between . . . the educated and the customary: not just as the characteristics of social groups, but as ways of seeing and feeling, within a single mind. And then neither established language would serve to express this tension and disturbance. Neither, in fact, was sufficiently articulate."

The educated and the customary—and neither is sufficiently articulate. In a wonderful book, *The Radical Soldier's Tale*, the cultural historian Carolyn Steedman transcribes and then reads an "unreadable" text, a late Victorian, working-class memoir by John Pearman, first a soldier in the Sikh Wars and then a policeman in Aylesbury, England.

I have taught Steedman's work often, including chapters from *The Tidy House: Little Girls Writing* (1982) and *Landscape for a Good Woman* (1986). Both became key texts in my undergraduate composition courses in the 1990s. The first book draws upon her work as an elementary school teacher; the second is a memoir of a working-class childhood in postwar London. Steedman was born in 1947 (and so we are the same age), and she is very much a product of Cambridge English. While she received her BA in English and American Studies from the University of Sussex in 1968, she completed her MLitt at Cambridge in 1974 and her Cambridge PhD in 1989. In a somewhat nervous aside, she once commented that she owed an "immense debt" to Raymond Williams, to his accounts of culture, schooling, and individual expression—that, in fact, her own work was, perhaps, only a long, elaborate set of footnotes to his. (The book you are reading, of course, documents my own debts to—and preoccupations with—Williams.)

John Pearman's memoir was written between October 1881 and the winter of 1882, two hundred pages of handwritten "memos," all in a prose that enacts a struggle with written English. The struggle is partly with orthography, punctuation, and the grammar of the sentence (Pearman repeatedly fails, for example, to close a parenthesis), but also with the conventions of prose memoir. It begins as a standard soldier's tale of comrades and battles, but then shifts dramatically to an argument against the church, imperialism, and those in power, appropriating the conventions and the evangelical rhetoric of the Chartist movement and of weekly newspapers like the *Freethinker* or the *National Reformer*.

Why would Pearman have written so much over such an extended period of time? He wrote it because, Steedman says, he wanted to learn to write, which meant learning to locate his story in relation to a larger, literate public. He wanted to be someone, someone on a page. Steedman concludes that while the effort is magnificent, he largely fails. The fractures in the narrative, and the errors on the page, are signs of his struggle to "capture the inchoate, the intense living and thinking that the words were meant to represent."

By the second half of the memoir, she says: "The political arguments he manipulated stopped short of allowing him to deal with what he knows of himself as a social and emotional being, and the shifts between argument and experience, are usually . . . abrupt." There is, however, one moment where he achieves a perfect balance:

> Look at the difference of the Start in life   our Queen had a noble start   compare that with the Gutter Children of the earth and look at their start   they surly have nothing to thank God for. Now by a Close Calculation of the birth rate it would take about 65 generations from the time of the Christian era to the present time to produce our Queen. . . . Now it would take the same number of generations . . . to produce me and when I look back for only the past two generations of my Family what an amount of temptations we have to endure to avoid   and to look at   if [of] what are parsons Calls sin to git a chance to live   while our Queen and the Lords & Dukes fare of the best, the poor Children of this—Carrupt earth   can get for them and then they cry moor moor....

[Note: I added the spacing to make the shape of these sentences more visible.]

Steedman says, "He is in perfect control of the argument here. The place where he enters his own calculation—'me'—is perfectly timed. It is at this point that he enters both this particular narrative, and the difficult history he is dealing with. He makes his theoretical mark upon the world, analysis and feeling working towards a delineation of himself within historical time."

He "enters his own calculation"; I love that phrase. A similar struggle, this time the struggle to enter the discursive world of the university, to enter its writing, to be present, is the topic of Mina Shaughnessy's magnificent book *Errors and Expectations*, a book that Steedman knew. Shaughnessy teaches us how to read and to understand a sentence like this one:

In my opinion I believe that you there is no field that cannot be effected some sort of advancement that one maybe need a college degree to make it. If a person feels that by getting a college degree would make him a better person although the jobs to fit his education might not be in demand of course it makes sense.

There is a simple declarative sentence at the core of this, one that clearly and correctly speaks a life's desire: **I believe that you need a college degree to make it.** But the writer knows that the occasion demands more, including elaboration, and the struggles of the sentence are the struggles of the writer to locate herself in that other, newly imagined grammatical context. Here is how I would chart the progress of that sentence:

In my opinion,

In my opinion, I believe that you

In my opinion, I believe there is no field that cannot be effected

In my opinion, I believe that some sort of advancement

**In my opinion I believe that you there is no field that cannot
be effected some sort of advancement that one maybe need a
college degree to make it.**

The timing is right. This is the moment when the student must enter
a newly elaborated narrative of education, to enter her own calculation,
to be part of a sentence she is learning to write. Here is Williams in my
epigraph: "What we can learn from looking at the institutions we can
learn also from looking at the prose; just as we can see in the prose, as
in the history of the time, certain new relationships struggling to be
formed." The point of the first-year writing course, as I understand
it, is to make that struggle possible, useful, and just.

ENVOI

I have been writing about my last section of First-Year Composition
(Fall 2016). Let me step back in conclusion to think about the arc of
my almost fifty years with this course, forty-six of them working with
and inside the composition program at the University of Pittsburgh.

Shaughnessy's genius, like Steedman's, is in her persistence with
resistant, unconventional texts, but also in the example of her readings.
She speaks of these students in terms of their logic and imagination
and courage and competence; she speaks of what they *do* rather than
what they fail to do, and she did this at a time when the university
knew only to speak of how these students fell short of expectation:
They can't even write a sentence.

Errors and Expectations was, as I said, a groundbreaking book.
In many ways, my career began with this book and her work and
her example. I went to Pitt to reorganize the Writing Center and

to develop a course in what was then called Basic Writing. My only other points of reference were the work of my colleague Bill Coles; my graduate professor, Richard Poirier; and through them the curricular experiment of Cambridge English that begins with I. A. Richards, engages F. R. Leavis and William Empson, and ends with Raymond Williams.

With Shaughnessy, my colleagues and I developed a way of thinking about error and about sentences, and we developed a pedagogy of proofreading and revision. And like Shaughnessy, we thought long and hard about what students should be reading and why, what subjects we could most usefully set before them, about how we might introduce them, prepare them as readers and writers, for the written work of a university education. (That work is reported in our book, *Facts, Artifacts and Counterfacts.*)

When it was time to think beyond the sentence, Shaughnessy struggled to think beyond or outside the key terms of the 1960 composition course, which relied on these units: *word, sentence, paragraph, essay.* Characteristically, the move beyond the sentence, the move to define the discursive units, the "basic thought patterns" in academic writing, resulted in little more than a renaming of standard, 1960 assignment prompts:

This is what happened—narration
This is the look (sound, feel, smell) of something—description
This is what ought to be done—argument
This is like (or unlike) this—comparison and contrast
This (may have, probably, certainly) caused this—process analysis
This is what someone said—quotation and paraphrase.

The Shaughnessy that I both remember and consistently imagine knows she has hit a wall at the end of her book. What *can* be done beyond the sentence? There is a sense of desperation throughout her book's last two chapters, titled "Beyond the Sentence" and "Expectations." *Errors and Expectations* was published in 1977. In 1978, at age fifty-four, Shaughnessy died of cancer.

At the end of the second to last chapter of her book ("Beyond the Sentence"), Shaughnessy turns very briefly to the notion of "academic genres." As an intervention in the first-year writing course, the reference to "academic genres" was a mixed blessing. It opened the door to what we now think of as Writing in the Disciplines. But the problems were several and they can easily be represented by recalling the textbook representations of academic genres: "Writing in the Social Sciences," "Writing in the Natural Sciences," or "Writing in the Humanities."

There is no single "genre" for writing in the social sciences or the natural sciences or, as we know, in the humanities. What was promoted was a kind of new formalism, and like the old formalisms, it was a trap. The distinction mispresented the work of the disciplines (and the work of writing) and offered little by way of method for teaching students to read and write their way into the academy. It offered a false sense of an endpoint, one where, as Williams reminds us, idealized "authors" and "readers" "are assumed to float, on a guarded privilege, above the rough, divisive and diverse world of which yet, by some alchemy, they possess the essential secret."

What is lost is what makes *Errors and Expectations* such compelling reading—the presence of students as *active* readers and writers, struggling to inhabit sentences in ways that matter to them and that can be valued by the institution as acts of knowledge-making.

At Pitt, and at a moment of some importance to the profession, our local response to the questions raised by Shaughnessy's injunction to teach "academic genres" was to (1) offer selections of serious writing by prominent intellectuals (Anthony Appiah and Ben Lerner or Gloria Anzaldua and Adrienne Rich), texts already circulating on campus, and (2) use these models as prompts for essays where students *did* something in kind, an homage of sorts, an effort to "test" or "extend" what Appiah, for example, was doing when he thought about questions of identity.

I have been drawing on these courses and writing about them in just about everything I've published throughout my career, including the textbook *Ways of Reading* and its instructor's manual.

I've presented the example of my student last fall, failing and succeeding in a two-week span with the same piece of writing. I've said his dilemma is like that of Thomas Hardy, John Pearman, and students of the open admissions classroom at City College, New York, in the 1970s. I've used all of them to locate writing as a struggle with words, words on a page. Writing those sentences was, I believe, a significant intervention—by the student and on behalf of the institution.

I think they show a student writer learning from a struggle with and within written language. Richard Poirier, my first link to Cambridge English, said: "Writing [when it is most alive] exemplifies the kind of effort that can and needs to be made by anyone who proposes to make more than submissive sense of the world as it now is." In that sense, I think the student writing I presented above has come alive. The writers work from inside sentences (Leavis's concern), they resist stock responses (I. A. Richards's), and they worry about words and how they mean what they mean (as in the work of Empson, Wittgenstein and, at Oxford rather than Cambridge, J. L. Austin).

Active reading. Active writing. *Active* was a key word for Raymond Williams, as it was for his teacher, I. A. Richards. It is the word they would fall back on to try to define what it was that mattered to them as teachers of English. And this they struggled to define with ease or precision.

There are lessons in reading and writing and thinking that cannot be learned or delivered elsewhere or in a medium other than writing on a page. Written language in use and a critical reflection on such uses. This is why revision, including close line editing, the tinkering with and the recasting of sentences, is such a powerful and essential exercise in a writing course. In the era increasingly empty of sentences, or their elaboration, it is easy to give up and to say that words no longer matter. I think it is our job to show how and why they do.

CHAPTER FIVE

Back to Basics

I sensed that I simply couldn't judge the students for anything they thought, at least in the beginning. Their backgrounds were too far removed from what I had known before coming to Fuling, and, like all young Chinese, they were surrounded by the aura of a troubled past. It was easy to forget this—it was easy . . . to smile at their childlike shyness, and it was easy to dismiss them as simple young people from the simplicity of the countryside. But of course nothing was farther from the truth—the Sichuan countryside is not simple, and my students had known things that I never imagined. Even if appearances were deceiving, the truth always came through in the ways they wrote about their homes and families.

— Peter Hessler, *River Town: Two Years on the Yangtze* (2001)

BASIC WRITING

I retired from teaching in August 2018. In the spring term of 2017, I taught Basic Writing, now titled Workshop in Composition, a first-year writing course I taught at Pitt in the spring term of 1976.

In 1976, my Basic Writing students were almost all working class, most were Black. They came from Pittsburgh, Harrisburg, Philadelphia, and small towns in between. In the spring term of 2017, my students were all Chinese. Many, but not all, came from privileged families. Their lives as students of English were demanding. I admired them greatly for their courage and resolve. All had sacrificed to be where they were in the United States, and they struggled with the course, which presented challenges beyond differences in language and culture. Still, this group struck me as possessing a deep sense of entitlement, with the confidence that ensued. They came from families with power and influence. Most were smartly dressed. The room looked like an ad for J.Crew, but for the exception of two persons: the rumpled professor and the young man sitting next to him who wore a T-shirt, rolled at the sleeves, and who had a hammer and sickle tattooed on his bicep. (The others, perhaps jokingly, said he was a mole, planted at Pitt to report back to the Chinese Communist Party.)

Why did I choose an *ESL* section of Workshop in Composition for my final semester? Perhaps the most compelling motive for teaching the ESL section was that I wanted to repay a series of favors. Once I stepped down as Department Chair in 2009, my wife and I became deeply involved with Pitt's Study Abroad program. This included two extended (five-week) stays with students in Beijing (at Capital Normal University). We were warmly received. We loved our time in Beijing. When I returned to Pittsburgh, I began to regularly sponsor visiting scholars from China.

We had also been traveling and teaching all over the world (Argentina, Brazil, India, South Africa, Ecuador, Cuba, Spain, the UK), where I had watched my students (and myself) struggle with our limited command of the language and, in spite of our best efforts, a limited sense of local culture and history.

One of these programs (called "PittMap") had a focused curriculum that relied on fieldwork. In Argentina, South Africa, and China, the faculty team included an epidemiologist from the medical school and an economist. During a full semester, at three sites, we were investigating local and national programs in public health, with a focus on HIV/AIDS. In South Africa, for example, we met with clinicians, government boards of health, the children and teachers at an orphanage (for children whose parents had died from AIDS), and the pharmaceutical company that was first to produce low-cost retrovirals (thanks to an intervention by Bill Clinton), among other sites.

Students made their own contacts with South Africans; this was the expectation of the writing course. The students were to be reporters. They had to find stories out in the field. Some found access to the townships, the shanty towns outside the city; some worked with a group producing Spaza Rap, a hybrid rap, English and Xhosa; some volunteered in an AIDS clinic; some worked out with sports teams from the University of Cape Town; one made close contact with the Jewish community and dined each week with a different family. (She wrote on the actions and inactions of the community during Apartheid.) Another stood in a long line at the Cape Town Medical School for AIDS testing, and this when AIDS testing first became a public initiative and, under the administration of Jacob Zuma, extremely controversial. He wrote a ground-level account of AIDS and its place on the Cape Town campus. After graduation, one of the students went on to work as a Peace Corps volunteer in Senegal. Several went on to programs in public health with an international focus.

At every site there were challenging and unforgettable moments of contact and encounter, but also, of course, challenging and unforgettable moments of misrecognition and misunderstanding. All became crucial to the work we did together, as students wrote weekly about where they were and what they were doing.

In my eight years with study abroad, the challenges were invigorating; the work felt pertinent and urgent and important. It seemed an extension of my early days teaching Basic Writing. And, in teaching the ESL section on our campus, I was eager for a chance at a semester-long reflection on language learning in a global context, within an already proven curriculum, and in the company of students who were good at this, who were experienced and successful at working in translingual/transcultural settings. The teaching assignment gave me the opportunity to work closely with a course designed by Marylou Gramm, my colleague at Pitt, an inspired and inspiring teacher whose commitment to translingual composition I admired. I knew I would learn something.

(Some who read an early draft of this essay wondered if there were another story to tell—of a shift in priorities on our campus. Had we diverted funds that once went to American students in order to attract and serve international students who could easily pay full out-of-state tuition and who did not rely on local scholarships or financial aid? So far as I can tell, the answer is no. It is certainly not the case that the University of Pittsburgh, or its English department, had abandoned its traditional commitments to Basic Writing. We continue to provide a range of support for US students who seek these courses or who are required to take them. I will note, however, that the institution remains far more accepting of language differences in the written English of "foreign" students than it is in the writing of US nationals. Of course, that is to be expected. And of course it is not.)

The essay that follows is not organized as an argument. And I want to make it clear from the outset that while I was teaching a course marked as ESL, it is the only ESL course I have ever taught. I claim no expertise in that field. I am speaking from inside the experience of one course to those who might be interested in the long trajectory of my career as a teacher.

This essay, then, collects a set of interesting examples and puts them in conversation, one with the others. I like this as a model for the essay as a genre. "Ordinary language philosophy teaches us how to think from within. It teaches us to think through examples." That's Toril Moi from *Revolution of the Ordinary: Literary Studies after Wittgenstein, Austin and Cavell.*

I was both pleased and surprised by the stories and examples that pressed themselves on me as I began writing this essay, some coming from a documentary instinct (to report on my final course, to think back on my career), but others popping up unexpectedly from the reading I had been doing over the past ten years in support of a graduate seminar on ordinary language, a course that had become focused on Cambridge English, the early attempt to create a university-level English curriculum that has served as the foundation for the modern English department in the English-speaking world. The key figures were I. A. Richards, William Empson, F. R. Leavis, and Raymond Williams. Wittgenstein was lurking in the wings. Of the group, Empson and Richards had spent a substantial period of time in China, teaching Basic English. The key term that will bring these examples together at the end of this essay is "translingual composition." Or so I believe. Translingual composition is represented at the outset by the example of Chinese students writing in English in a required first-year course at the University of Pittsburgh.

The course I taught in 2017 was structured exactly like the course I taught in the late 1970s. There were weekly writing assignments, drafts, and revisions, usually two of the latter, where the work of revision was initially the work of supplement and addition, later a questioning of key terms, so that two-to-three-page essays (single spaced, double spaced between paragraphs) became six-to-eight-page essays. These essays were prompted by assigned readings, but more on that later.

There were also weekly language exercises. I would present typical sentences from their papers, "common errors" we once called them, model sentences with a grammar common to this group of writers, one that varied from what, following Suresh Canagarajah, I called "Metropolitan English." I'm not sure this label is any less problematic than the old one, Standard Written English, but since most of my students aspired to use their English in metropolitan settings, it seemed strategically useful to name it so.

As a profession, and with colleagues in our institutions (willing and recalcitrant), we have learned over time to finesse and refine the ways we name exercises in proofreading and grammar, to find terms other than "error" and "correction." If I had called these weekly exercises "Corrections," my students would have known exactly what I was talking about, and so there was an advantage in renaming and reframing examples of language differences, and in thinking and talking about the source, context, and usefulness of these paired sentences without resorting to a simple binary—correct and incorrect. This is one of the important arguments of those who have been working to establish the notion of a translingual composition. Min-Zhan Lu provides a classic example of this exercise in "Professing Multiculturalism: The Politics of Style in the Contact Zone."

Although there were changes in the terms I used, and they are not unimportant, and most certainly changes in the grammatical patterns I was highlighting, I was teaching proofreading and sentence-level revision just as I had in a Basic Writing course forty-two years before. Why proofreading? Here is how we phrased it in 1975. Students don't make all the errors the English language allows. They make a predictable set of errors. They have their own "style of error," as Shaughnessy used to say. A personally tailored list allows for focused proofreading. And proofreading itself is a difficult skill to learn. Adult readers don't read each word on a page. They anticipate and fill in the blanks. A writer must *learn* the odd form of reading that is proofreading, paying attention to all the words, sentence by sentence.

Below is a language exercise from the fifth week in that fifteen-week term. Creating a handout like this is common practice wherever ESL is taught. There is nothing original or exceptional in what I am offering.

Language Exercise: Proofreading Guide

Here are student sentences (your sentences) that vary from what we might call "Metropolitan English," the English that circulates and serves as cultural capital in the world's great cities. When you proofread, I want you to set aside time to hunt for sentences like the ones I've indicated below. When you find one, I would like you to revise—and to revise with a Metropolitan reader in mind.

And, and this is important, I would like you to be prepared to talk about the changes you make—why you made them, what was won or lost in the bargain.

1. Sentence boundaries—Marking the beginning and end of sentences.

I consider myself a very <u>patriotic person, I am</u> so patriotic that I even love the countries like Pakistan and Russia which are good friends with China.

China's education environment is more competitive than the <u>U.S.A, students</u> have to get a high grade before they enter into a better school in next level.

2. Simple mistakes and typos—these tend to be hard to spot but easy to correct.

Even in this small town where <u>I was barn</u>, learning a foreign language has become an important thing for current students.

A few weeks before the first day of school, I started <u>loosing</u> sleep.

3. Shifts in verb tense—if the speaker, scene, or the action are set in the past, keep the verbs in past tense.

My parents weren't rich enough to move into a better district for a living, so they <u>have</u> to choose a second-hand apartment as a transitioning shelter.

My father was born in a rural place in Chongqing province. His family was poor, and he <u>has</u> two sisters and one brother.

4. Other errors with verb tense

The article said Chinese students <u>has been teach</u> these patriotic content, but these patriotic materials also help students to build their views for students' life.

5. Plural nouns—plural nouns normally take a final S.

Our English festival always started by watching English <u>mov-ie</u> and reading English books.

"Why is a raven like a writing desk?" Alice asked. The show Alice's Adventures in Wonderland was performing and drama is one of the traditional <u>program</u> in our English festival.

6. Definite article—"The"

Now, considering what Chinese government has done to Chi-nese kids as a bystander, I have my own point of view. _____ Chinese government utilizes different means to infuse red ideology into children and tries as much as possible to fetter their minds in order to create unity.

Though the show did shape my views towards _____ Long March and the Communist Party, it became meaningless when I was repeatedly forced to watch it.

7. Relative pronouns—blurred patterns

In the recent couple years, there are increasing number of students in <u>China</u> <u>do</u> not know about the past history at all. **(There are an increasing number of students in <u>China</u> <u>who</u> do not know about history at all.)**

As I did in 1975, I used class time for students, alone and in pairs, to reread (or proofread) their weekly essays and to revise sentences. I would circulate and help. Later, we would talk about individual instances and examples, particularly when a revision seemed partic-ularly inspired or particularly unsatisfying. I would ask students to add examples to their personal lists and to let me know if they saw examples I should add to mine or that might suggest a new numbered entry on my handout.

WRITING IN THE CONTACT ZONE

As has been the case throughout my teaching career, the writing assignments in this course were all prompted by readings, readings chosen because, although difficult (first-year college students are not the assumed audience), the writing is exemplary, and the essays touch upon subjects that, I believed, could engage both me and my students at our best. In this course, I wanted to provide my students with ways of thinking about where they were geographically and intellectually, and I wanted them to have interesting references they could bring into discussions beyond my classroom.

I opened the course with Min-Zhan Lu's much-traveled 1987 *College English* essay, "From Silence to Words: Writing as Struggle." Lu writes about her youth and young adult life in Shanghai, about learning English, about schooling under Mao Tse-tung, and about her family's persecution during the Cultural Revolution. It is a complicated and moving essay (an unusual combination, in my experience). I have taught it often, and it has always been a challenge.

I also drew from two books I admired, both by former Peace Corps workers in China: Peter Hessler, *River Town: Two Years on the Yangtze*, and Evan Osnos, *Age of Ambition: Chasing Fortune, Truth, and Faith in the New China*. I have had the pleasure of meeting and talking with both. My students and I spent an evening talking with Osnos in Beijing, and I helped to host Peter Hessler when he came to my campus for a reading at the invitation of my colleague, Michael Meyer, also formerly in China with the Peace Corps, and whose books I regularly teach in my course on travel writing.

I am not going to give an extended account of my use of these two books. I taught the opening chapter of *River Town* (including its brilliant account of teaching English composition in China). Here is an excerpt from the opening assignment:

Peter Hessler, "Downstream," from *River Town*

In "Downstream," Hessler provides his view of the Chinese students, teachers, and administrators at the college in Fuling, Sichuan Province, in 1996. Imagine that you are writing to his American readers, including students here at the University of Pittsburgh.

Where, in your opinion, is Hessler most accurate? Where is he at his best? Where does he show that he has a deep understanding of China and Chinese people? Be precise and provide details.

Have things changed since he published his book in 2001? What would an American reader need to know to be up to date? Be precise and provide details.

And where, in your opinion, does he miss something important or misinterpret what he sees and hears? What preconceptions does he bring with him about China or about the Chinese? Where, in his writing, do you sense or see this preconception? And how might that preconception be said to distort his vision or get in the way of understanding? Again—be precise and provide details.

Notes:

I'd like you to quote briefly from Hessler's writing and think about the precise words in the quote. That is, your reader will need to "hear" Hessler. This means that you will need to provide at least two good examples of the way he thinks and writes.

Note the page number (in parentheses) at the end of each sentence that contains a quotation or paraphrase. You don't need to list Works Cited.

Don't quote or summarize too much; otherwise Hessler, not you, will be writing this essay. Give plenty of time to your commentary.

I'm looking for at least two pages, single spaced, with a space between paragraphs.

Proofread when you are finished.

Osnos came last in the course. The chapter we chose, "A Chorus of Soloists," was about individual ambition and youth culture in relation to Chinese revolutionary history and ideology. As with the other readings, the assignment sequence took the essay through a first draft and two revisions. In the middle was an exercise in summary and paraphrase. Here is the opening Osnos assignment:

Evan Osnos, "A Chorus of Soloists"

In the chapter from *Age of Ambition*, "A Chorus of Soloists," Evan Osnos tells the story of Han Han and his phenomenal presence in Chinese popular culture as a novelist, a blogger, and a media superstar. He was, Osnos says, "a seductive spokesman for a new brand of youthful defiance" (169). (Did you read *Triple Door*? Do you know people who did?) Han Han, according to Osnos, did not "reorder the political life of Chinese youth, or force the hand of policymakers, but he was a powerful spokesman for the joys of skepticism" (175).

And Osnos also tells the story of Michael, the student from Li Yang's Crazy English who perfected his English by listening to American advertisements. Michael, he says, "framed the study of English as a matter of moral entitlement." He told his students, "You are the master of your destiny. You deserve to be happy. You deserve to be different in this world" (180).

I would like you to write an essay of about four pages. You'll have two weeks to finish it and one week to revise.

> **Week one** (two pages, single spaced): I would like to hear your account of some area of youth culture that has captured the attention of your generation. What is it? What are its attractions? What needs and desires does it serve? How might it have spoken to you? How and when might you have chosen to be "different in this world?" (These questions are meant to get you thinking. Please do not use this list of questions to organize your essay.)

> Whatever you choose as your subject, you will need to describe it in close detail. And you will need to pay close attention to its reception—to your interest, but also to what you have heard others say. It would be helpful to have more than one person speaking in your essay.

> You can imagine a thoughtful, interested American reader. Your reader, however, knows nothing about Chinese popular culture.

Several students wrote about video games (of course), several about TV shows (*The Voice*; *Happy Camp*; *FeiChengWuRao*, a matchmaking show; *Where Are We Going, Dad*, a weekly family travel adventure). One wrote about *Wei Bo* (like Twitter), and one about the Monkey King, a folk figure who has reemerged in digital form.

To vary the pace and rhythm of the course, I also provided some shorter exercises in reading and writing. I would clip articles about China from the *New York Times*, and I introduced students to a new genre, the letter to the editor. I reprinted a short column by Didi Kirsten Tatlow (*New York Times*, September 2, 2016), "For China's Children, a Resoundingly Patriotic Return to School?," for example. Here is how it opens:

Sparkling red stars and bloody tales of military sacrifice accompanied 200 million Chinese children into the new school year this week, with the Education Ministry requiring them to watch a television show extolling the spirit of the Communist Red Army as it escaped its enemies on the Long March.

"Be unrelenting!" was the message of the 90-minute event, "Flag of Our Ancestors," broadcast on CCTV, the state broadcaster.

In a sign of how wide-ranging the government's propaganda efforts are, the Education Ministry asked schools to instruct parents to ensure their children watched the show, at 8 p.m. on Thursday, the first day of classes. Some asked parents to send photographs as proof that their children had complied.

And it concludes:

Since 1949, Chinese schools have sustained a diet heavy in patriotism and Communist Party propaganda. But the annual back-to-school show, which began in 2008, has moved more sharply in that direction with the ideological tightening under President Xi Jinping, as he has cracked down on corruption and freethinkers alike and deployed the language and symbolism of a purist form of Communism to unify the country.

I received many spirited responses in defense of propaganda. Some sounded like prepared responses; some sounded more halting. Here is one that sounds practiced; it very skillfully brings US history into play:

> I am not an expert of politics or history, but if there is one thing I know, it's that patriotism is not a bad thing. Countries are carriers of people's culture. In a world which has 193 nations, the idea of patriotism is the last bunker to protect country, people and culture. Look at the people who didn't have their own countries: the Jews were slaughtered before they built their own country; native Americans lost their home because they did not fight back when outsiders stepped on their lands. That's why China is "brainwashing" its children with patriotism, because we've been bullied for too long. We were first invaded by Western developed countries around 1900s and forced to "rent" out our territory; then the Russians and Japanese came and took over half of China. After the establishment of the Peoples Republic of China, we were still despised by other more developed countries, even India and Vietnam can step on us. . . .
>
> And now, we are finally powerful enough to protect ourselves against invasions; we can finally say we are proud to be Chinese; our government can tell the children: "Hey kids, remember, the deeds done by our ancestors did not go to waste, we didn't let them down."

But I also received several letters to the editor, equally spirited, that while they appreciated the government's initiative said, in effect, "Give us a break, Ms. Tatlow. Do you think Chinese students have no sense of irony, no sense of spectacle—that, as young people, we can't both be in school and out of school all at the same time?!" Here are three brief excerpts.

1. Like students in the United States or students in any other countries, students in China have their own opinions towards the government they have, towards the educational system in which they 'suffered' a lot, and even towards tiny 'society' like their schools.

2. When I entered the middle school and was asked to write about the show again, I got bored. I knew exactly what was going to be in the show, but I had to write an essay to tell how moved I was and how meaningful the show was. Later in high school, the tradition went on. I could write an essay about the show without watching it. All I had to do was to tell the greatness the Community Party had achieved.

3. It does seem that the government has achieved great success—almost everyone is following the instructions and requirements. However, is it true success? For me, I reckon, what the government is doing is a ritual. That is a superficial meaning of success. Deepen inside the surface, are students really affected or really touched by what they are doing? In my heart, those over glorified programs or events will not affect me anymore. While a few very innocent students, who I was one of them once, indeed accept and embed the red ideology in their minds without further thinking, I believe nowadays Chinese students will not be moved by the show, the speech or the movie; rather, they regard these as onerous tasks, just as homework, to undertake.

The trope of irony is slippery, difficult to manage in the play of language as it crosses boundary lines—the teacher's desk, national borders, local languages, divisions of power and authority. This is

Empson's argument in *Some Versions of Pastoral*, where he argues that irony (which often cannot be "pegged out in verbal explanations") "can, often magnificently, show us what there is to be looked at, prove there is a crossroads where we so far have seen only a single, well-trodden track."

Later in the semester I took students to visit the Carnegie Museum of Natural History, just across the street from the Cathedral of Learning. (I love this building, the Cathedral; it is, itself, a test of irony and its management.) The Carnegie is a nineteenth-century museum and features rooms full of dead animals, stuffed and posed in dioramas. Each tells a story. A mother grizzly bear protects her cubs while catching and eating salmon. They are threatened from above by eagles, and from in front by a male grizzly, skillfully placed beyond the glass, out in the hall next to the spectator.

One student wrote about a display of a mother leopard and her cubs. It was touching, she said, until she thought about who shot them and how they arrived at this spot in Pittsburgh, Pennsylvania. She wrote,

> The scene was superficially a harmony one, but deeply a ferocious one. I even thought I was guilty to stand there and watch them happily without thinking about their pains. Maybe this was the Americans at that time. They believed they could conquer the nature; they could get anything as long as they and the other Americans wanted it. I knew Americans had a tradition of moralism. With the feeling of exceptionalism and righteousness, they believed they were moral example for the rest world. But it seemed to me that it was so contradictory.

This is skillful writing, and part of its achievement is represented in the way she (correctly) imagines what it is I hope to hear. What do I write at the bottom margin? Good job? Or, "Why do you put those last two sentences in past tense? *Americans had a tradition of moralism?*

. . . they believed they were a moral example for the rest of the world. There is a grammar lesson with an edge. Is she putting me on? Am I putting her on? I had an easier time knowing where and how to push with my US students.

This is the odd conundrum of teaching, one that haunts a book like Bill Coles's *The Plural I.* When is student writing a step forward in thinking and in living the world, and when is it not? When is it just submission? Themewriting. Stock response. Here is I. A. Richards on stock responses (from *Practical Criticism*).

A stock response, like a stock line in shoes or hats, may be a convenience. Being ready-made, it is available with less trouble than if it had to be specially made out of raw or partially prepared materials. And unless an awkward misfit is going to occur, we may agree that stock responses are much better than no responses at all. Indeed, an extensive repertory of stock responses is a necessity. Few minds could prosper if they had to work out an original, "made to measure" response to meet every situation that arose—their supplies of mental energy would be too soon exhausted and the wear and tear on their nervous systems would be too great. Clearly there is an enormous field of conventional activity over which acquired, stereotyped, habitual responses properly rule, and the only question that needs to be examined as to *these* responses is whether they are the best that practical exigencies—the range of probable situations that may arise, the necessity of quick availability and so forth—will allow. But equally clearly there are in most lives fields of activity in which stock responses, if they intervene, are disadvantageous and even dangerous, because they may get in the way of, and prevent, a response more appropriate to the situation.

The danger or disadvantage of the stock response. To be sure, these play out differently in the People's Republic of China than in the

United States, and hence I had no good instincts for where and how to push in the ESL course, but the concern to move beyond stock responses has been the guiding principle of my teaching for forty-five years.

WRITING AS STRUGGLE (1)

I opened the course with Min-Zhan Lu's essay "From Silence to Words: Writing as Struggle," first published in *College English* (1987). From the late 1970s through the 1990s, I taught our Teaching Seminar, a required course for new Teaching Assistants/Teaching Fellows. The course was not an Introduction to Composition as a field; it was a semester-long reflection on the course everyone was teaching (and we taught from a shared syllabus), with a few readings from key sources (Richards, Burke, Shaughnessy) meant to provide context for discussion, much of which was devoted to student essays, writing assignments, and possible new readings for the following semester.

Because I wanted the course to be centered on actual practice (rather than the usual fantasies of who writers are and what writers do), for the opening writing assignment I asked students to write about an important writing lesson, in school or out of school, a time when they learned something meaningful, when they took a significant step forward as writers, and to do so from the inside, as memoir.

Lu's essay for the seminar was an early draft of "From Silence to Words." There were, in fact, two essays from that course that were published and that went on to wide circulation, including publication in composition textbooks. The other was "From Outside, In" by Barbara Mellix, a writer in our MFA program. Her essay was first published in the *Georgia Review*, also in 1987. Mellix, an African American, wrote about the language of home and the language of school, about taking Basic Writing as an undergraduate and now being in a position to teach it.

I want to take time to summarize "From Silence to Words" in detail. The essay is a classic, I know, and widely read, but classics tend to lose their edge. This one benefits from rereading. Here is how it opens:

> My mother withdrew into silence two months before she died. A few nights before she fell silent, she told me she regretted the way she had raised me and my sisters. I knew she was referring to the way we had been brought up in the midst of two conflicting worlds—the world of home, dominated by the ideology of the Western humanistic tradition, and the world of a society dominated by Mao Tse-tung's Marxism. My mother had devoted her life to our education, an education she knew had made us suffer political persecution during the Cultural Revolution. I wanted to find a way to convince her that, in spite of the persecution, I had benefited from the education she had worked so hard to give me. But I was silent. My understanding of my education was so dominated by memories of confusion and frustration that I was unable to reflect on what I could have gained from it.

"From Silence to Words" is the occasion for that reflection. You can trace her further thinking through many of her publications, including "Conflict and Struggle: The Enemies or Preconditions of Basic Writing?" (1992), "Professing Multiculturalism: The Politics of Style in the Contact Zone" (1994), "Redefining the Literate Self: The Politics of Critical Affirmation" (1999), "Living-English Work" (2006), and her memoir, *Shanghai Quartet: The Crossings of Four Women of China* (2001). The latter, I believe, is not as widely known as it should be.

"From Silence to Words" turns first to the several languages of her early upbringing, each connecting her to a different world of experience, thought, and feeling. She grew up speaking a Shanghai dialect, something later shared only with her servants. In school, she learned to read, write, and speak in Standard Chinese, "the official written language of New China." And at home, she spoke English with her parents, her sisters, and their tutor, a Scot. This she thought of as private, a family language. She says, "While I was happy to have a special family language, until second grade I didn't feel that my family language was any different than some of the classmates' family dialects."

As she grew older, and as China "was making a transition from a semi-feudal, semi-capitalist, and semi-colonial country into a socialist country," the family's English identified them as imperialists, enemies of the people. Her father was a physician. His practice served a wealthy, English-speaking community in Shanghai. He (and the family) would become a target during the Cultural Revolution, 1966–1976, when she was in high school and beyond. She learned to use English only when she was at home.

And in school, she learned to master Standard Chinese and, through it, to identify as a proper working-class subject. She says,

> As school began to define me as a political subject, my parents tried to build up my resistance to the "communist poisoning" by exposing me to the "great books"—novels by Charles Dickens, Nathaniel Hawthorne, Emily Bronte, Jane Austen, and writers from around the turn of the century. My parents implied that these writers represented how I, their child, should read and write. My parents replaced the word "Bourgeois" with the word "cultured." They reminded me that I was in school only to learn math and science.

She says,

> I learned a formula for Working-class writing in the composition classes. We were given sample essays and told to imitate them. The theme was always about how the collective taught the individual a lesson. I would write papers about

labor-learning experiences or school-cleaning days, depending on the occasion of the collective activity closest to the assignment. To make each paper look different, I dressed it up with details about the date, the weather, the environment, or the appearance of the Master-worker who had taught me "the lesson."

She tells a chilling story of her first day in junior high school:

We were handed forms to fill out with our parents' class, job, and income. Being one of the few people not employed by the government, my father had never been officially classified. Since he was a medical doctor, he told me to put him down as an Intellectual. My homeroom teacher called me into the office a couple of days afterwards and told me that my father couldn't be an Intellectual if his income far exceeded that of a Capitalist. He also told me that since my father worked for Foreign Imperialists, my father should be classified as an Imperialist Lackey. The teacher looked nonplussed when I told him that my father couldn't be an Imperialist Lackey because he was a medical doctor. But I could tell from the way he took notes on my form that my father's job had put me in an unfavorable position in his eyes.

The defining moment comes when she is assigned a report on *The Revolutionary Family*, a novel that represented an appropriate working-class consciousness.

In one scene the [mother] deliberated over whether or not she should encourage her youngest son to join the Revolution. Her memory of her husband's death made her afraid to encourage her son. Yet she also remembered her earlier married life and the first time her husband tried to explain the meaning of the Revolution to her. These memories made her feel she should encourage her son to continue the cause his father had begun.

She was, she says, "moved" by this scene. And "moved" was a word her mother and sisters used to talk about what they valued in the English novels they were reading, novels like *Jane Eyre* or *David Copperfield*. The genre of the book report, she knew, required her to emphasize the mother's revolutionary spirit. She chose this scene to illustrate the point.

The next morning, however, she knew that she could not turn in this book report. "I had dwelled on [the mother's] internal conflict, which could be seen as a moment of weak sentimentality," a virtue in one context but a sign of weakness in the other. She rewrote the report, "taking care to illustrate the grandeur of her Revolutionary Spirit by expanding on a quotation in which she decided that if the life of her son could change the lives of millions of sons, she should not begrudge his life for the cause of the Revolution."

Writing this book report, she says, "increased my fear that I was losing the command over both the 'language of home' and the 'language of school' that I had worked so hard to gain." One way of thinking and writing "interfered" with the other. To a writer for whom words matter, and in a context where identity is taken seriously, "code-switching" is not an easy fix. And the rest of the essay considers the difficulties Lu had managing the competing languages of family and school, defined in terms of liberal humanism and revolutionary commitment. There is a short final section that proposes a writing class that will allow, even promote, competing voices within a single text.

Although I feel that I know Min-Zhan Lu well, I know very little about the period in her life between the middle school girl, writing a book report on *The Revolutionary Family*, and the woman in her midthirties, a wife and a mother who arrived alone at the University of Pittsburgh in 1982 to study for a PhD in English, writing first on Theodore Dreiser and later on Mina Shaughnessy and Basic Writing.

The United States didn't establish full diplomatic relations with the People's Republic until 1979, just three years before her arrival. Lu arrived long before there were well-established protocols for student and faculty exchange, and long before the steady flow of students from China into graduate programs at US universities. Lu's trip was an extraordinary step across time and place, one requiring great courage, inventiveness, resilience, and resolve.

In *Shanghai Quartet*, she says: "Most immigrants know how to package their life according to the standard expectations for a straight story." I understand Lu's writing (and teaching) as an effort to avoid the traps of the standard narrative, pastoral or heroic. There is no straight story in this writer's formation, but there is a clear line of effort and imagination in her work as a teacher on behalf of writers who share a sense of always being out of position, who hear the "dissonance among the various discourses of one's daily life." This is the program she outlines in "Professing Multiculturalism: The Politics of Style in the Contact Zone":

> . . . I am most interested in doing three things: (1) enabling students to hear discursive voices which conflict with and struggle against the voices of academic authority; (2) urging them to negotiate a position in response to these colliding voices; and (3) asking them to consider their choice of position in the context of the sociopolitical power relationships within and among diverse discourses and in the context of their personal life, history, culture and society.

I deeply admire the commitments in thought and action throughout this exemplary career. I admire Lu's determination to "stay on line with the voices that matter—that is, voices which can bring us the intelligence, humor, imagination, courage, tolerance, love, respect, and will to meet the challenge of hanging together as we work to end oppression in the twenty-first century."

Although I do not have the time and space to treat him at length, I cannot help but recall another great teacher/traveler, I. A. Richards, also determined, I believe, to stay on line with the voices that matter.

Richards taught English in China during several extended stays between 1927 and 1979. He was in China for a total of fifty-two months between 1927 and 1938; he was in China for six months in 1950 and three months in 1979. After publishing their first book, *The Meaning of Meaning*, I. A. Richards and Charles Ogden began to work on a program of instruction that they called Basic English—that is, the English language reduced to 850 words and a simplified grammar.

Richards held a professorship at Cambridge and had recently finished a visiting position at Harvard. He had emerged as a leading figure in English studies, and he would quickly be identified (wrongly, many believe) as a founding figure in a group that, in the United States, came to be called the "New Critics." Yet his next career move was to put it all aside to move to China, where he would work with middle school teachers, preparing them to teach a new, experimental entry-level curriculum designed to make the learning of English more manageable.

I can't be alone in finding this decision to be remarkable. And Richards did this at a time of war (the Japanese had invaded China), and at a time when widespread poverty meant that the conditions of living and of travel were difficult and primitive. At one point, he and his students had to move from Tsing Hua National University in Peking to the "University in Exile," Liana, in the mountains of Hunan Province, to avoid the bombs and pitched battles on the streets of the city.

Basic English is often condemned as an imperialist project. It lost its momentum with the Second World War and with the Communist Revolution in China. Richards's primary motive had always been to improve basic instruction, although it is true that Richards (and Ogden) believed that a simplified English might become a global means of communication, as it has. The First World War had been a defining experience for Richards. In developing and promoting Basic English, as in the teaching of English to English speakers, Richards's stated motive at this early stage of his career was to improve communication, avoid misunderstandings, and prevent the conditions of war.

It was also the case, however, that Richards was fascinated with the difficult meeting of the two cultures and the two languages. Travel suited him. His time in China provided material that would enable further thinking about reading, writing, and the difficulty, even the impossibility, of interpretation and translation. Below is a story that Richards liked to tell. It is one of my favorites. I'm taking this account from John Paul Russo's excellent biography of Richards. Although there was not so much at stake for Richards, it speaks to Lu's story of the two book reports, one for home and one for school:

[Richards] taught *Tess of the D'Urbervilles* to a class of about 40 Chinese. At the end of the novel, the black flag is unfurled, signaling that Tess has been hanged for child murder. When Richards read the climatic lines, "The President of the Immortals had ended his sport with Tess," the class burst into spontaneous applause for the only time in the course. In a state of amazement, Richards passed out protocols, and back came the universal response: Tess had shown disrespect to her father at the beginning of the novel. The students had been waiting for the just punishment that a great artist like Hardy would surely mete out.

This is the Richards of *Practical Criticism*, a book built around the initially unpredictable readings of poems by students and colleagues at Cambridge in the 1920s, gathered through written responses ("protocols"). There, as here, his response to difference, to ways of reading and thinking that are initially distant from his own, is to make those differences a matter of consideration, of discussion, part of the course and part of his research. It was not to correct them or to make them disappear. As I said earlier, Richards is often considered a founding figure in the American New Criticism. His practice, however, was far from theirs. The American New Critics had little interest in how students read. Whatever student responses might emerge, they would be quickly replaced by the brilliant example of a professor elaborating a reading of a poem before a group of silent admirers.

In the 1930s, while teaching in China, Richards wrote *Mencius on the Mind: Experiments in Multiple Definition*, as a way of thinking about how a mind might hold two systems of thought without, he said, "reciprocal disturbance." His last visit, just before his death, was in 1979, and it included a lecture in Shanghai on "sequenced language learning." I take delight in thinking of Richards and Lu crossing paths somewhere on a sidewalk in the French Concession. Between sequenced language learning and reciprocal disturbance, they would have had something to talk about.

WRITING AS STRUGGLE (2)

Below is a shortened version of the assignment I gave to my students. It was their opening writing assignment. There was much buzz and consternation among the students over my suggestion that they need not necessarily start at the beginning or end with the end.

Writing Assignment #1: Due 9/12

For your first assignment, I'd like you to begin your work on a brief literacy narrative. For this first draft, I would expect 2-4 pages. Here are some suggestions to help you to begin:

You can use "From Silence to Words" as a model. I would like you to write about an important recent lesson as you have been learning to read and write in English, to do the kind of advanced work that is expected of you here as a student at the University of Pittsburgh. You do not, however, need to write about something you learned in class or directly from a teacher.

You are preparing a first draft. You don't have to begin at the beginning and you don't have to finish. You will return to work on this document in the following week. We will be working together to find a sense of shape and direction. You can draw upon anything you included in your in-class essay.

My advice is for you to begin *not* with a generalization but with some specific scene or scenes. Begin with a story (or stories) rather than with an argument. If people are speaking, you can, if you choose, let them speak as characters speak in fiction. You can, obviously, write in the first person.

The first set of papers were a real disappointment. All told the same story—about hard work, rigid teachers, late nights doing homework, and the tyranny of the Gaokao, the national SAT-like exam used to direct students to their slot in higher education. I later learned that this is essentially the approved narrative of high school education in China—survival in the face of parental pressure, young lives drained of fun, students who learn to follow the rules. Here is a sample from a first draft: "Fortunately, I learned how to make my paper be ample and how to make my argument be strongly supported the same time with struggling to meet the minimize requirement of my assignment."

And I said, "No. Please. I want you to reread Lu's essay and, when you write, I want you to think *in the manner of* Min-Zhan Lu. Yes, of course she was formed at a different moment in the history of your country, but what was it like for you? I used this exercise in class:

Lu Exercise 1: "Future Proletarians"

In "From Silence to Words: Writing as Struggle," Lu recalls this scene from her schooling:

> One of the slogans posted in the school building read, "Turn our students into future Proletarians with socialist consciousness and education!" For several weeks we studied this slogan in our political philosophy course, a subject I had never had in elementary school. I still remember the definition of "socialist consciousness" that we were repeatedly tested on through the years: "Socialist consciousness is a person's political soul. It is the consciousness of the Proletarians represented by Marxist Mao Tse-tung thought. . . . It is the task of every Chinese student to grow up into a Proletarian with a socialist consciousness so that he can serve the people and the motherland." (440)

Let's assume that all schools in all countries (including the United States) are designed to turn students into future *somethings*—if not working-class heroes, then characters who can occupy some ideal or acceptable social role. What was it like for you?

Please prepare brief answers to these questions—one or two sentences. I won't collect these, but I *will* ask you to read aloud in class.

1. What ideal role was presented to you and your friends once you moved beyond elementary school? How was your experience different from you parents' experience?

2. Did you find it easy to assume that role? Does it make sense to think of education as a "struggle"? If so, why?

3. Was English necessary for that role?

4. Was learning English a struggle? Was it in any way a *Min Lu–like* struggle—that is, a struggle over identity? A struggle to reconcile a Chinese point of view and an American or Western point of view?

5. Min Lu says that she spoke (and thought) one way at home and another way at school or in public. Would you say this was true for you? If so, can you provide an example?

These were pressing questions for me. My children had each spent two full years in a small-town Spanish school—first elementary school, and then high school. No one spoke English. And, as I have said, I had spent six semesters with Pitt students studying abroad. I was trying to imagine the extraordinarily complicated set of forces that had shaped these young Chinese lives—turned them to English and then to a four-year undergraduate program in the city of Pittsburgh. They didn't make these decisions on their own. Private fantasy was at play for sure. (What will I do? Who will I be? Where will I go?) But there was a complicated array of other interests at play here—state and local ministries or boards of education (or whatever they might have been called), family, and certainly some areas of youth or popular culture, among others.

Hessler said of his students, "I brushed against people just long enough to gain the slightest sense of the dizzying past that had made them what they were today." I wanted the students to understand that I was not just setting an exercise. I wanted to learn something about China and about their generation of young Chinese men and women. They were my primary sources.

The essays, in the end, were mostly predictable, partly, I think, because of an unwillingness to leave anything behind that could get a person into trouble, or slow him or her or them down on their chosen path. I had the sense that writing in English was always and only a move on the chessboard, a way of writing whatever they needed to write in order to move on to something more important. It was hard to spark a sense of joy or passion or confusion. But this is old news to anyone who teaches composition. Still, the conditions of restraint must be different for Chinese students (and in ways I will never understand).

It was also the case that, with the very substantial amount of time I needed to devote to sentences, my students could not give much to revision. Or perhaps this is what I want to say: they were very good at and interested in additions, in searching around for more and more interesting examples; they weren't as willing or able to pick away at the key terms governing the search.

These essays were long. I've chosen from those that seemed the most ambitious and surprising. I've cut them to show the range of examples (and the willingness to linger with examples), but not the general shape of the essay. I've not made any other changes.

This was the first to break the pattern of thesis and conclusion. It sent a buzz around the room when I read it out loud, slowly, trying to honor its tone and rhythm:

> I consider myself a very patriotic person, and I am so patriotic that I even love the countries like Pakistan and Russia which are good friends with China. There were three "Russians" in my high school's class. I called them "Russians" only because they spoke Russian, but actually one of them was Ukrainian and the other two were Greeks with Ukrainian/Russian lineage. I liked to think of them as Russians because I like Russians, and I liked them, so I tended to combine them with the characters I liked, which I am sure was a very natural thing for humans to do.
>
> Despite their feelings, I kept calling them "Russians," "comrades" or "the Red Children." They've expressed some negativities toward these names, but I ignored them, since as far as I could see, they were just like all other nicknames, like Timmy, Matty, Sasha and Vladya. Eventually, they asked me

formally to stop calling them like that, and I stopped, but that came later.

When Russia sent its troops to Crimea, it became a big topic in our social study class. Of course I was on the Russians side because I love Russians. In my opinion, Crimea belonged to Russia, and actually, even Ukraine should belong to Russia. Since Russia was the biggest power in the Soviet Union, all the small countries around Russia should belong to it. From my now perspective, that idea was very foolish, probably even Vladimir Putin himself would not think like that. But I was young and naive. I told my thoughts to my "Russian" friends: "Putin is not invading, he is just taking back the land his fathers used to own." Unexpectedly, the Ukraine girl went nuts after she heard this. She started yelling to me that Crimea is not part of Russia. Ukraine is an independent country and so on. Then I realised what a giant mistake I've just made. I might even break our friendship by saying that. Luckily, after I apologized to them, they still treated me as friend. . . .

Until recent, I just noticed how wrong it is to think someone as what I would like them to be. After I moved into college, I met some new people and made some new friends. One of a new friend I made has a Taiwanese roommate. When he told me about his roommate's nationality, I tried to correct him by saying : "Hey, Taiwan is part of China, you know that?" and he said: "Yeah, I know, but he want to be known as Taiwanee." I suddenly understand why my friends were not happy when I called them "Russians." Though they speak Russian, that does not mean they are Russians. I should not put tags on them. I need to treat people in the way of how they want to be treated. I think of myself, I don't want to be called as "the god dam commie" (although I am a steadfast communist). Just like Confucius said: "Don't make others do things you don't want to do."

Still, the idea of racial identity confuses constantly. I asked my Hispanic friend: "When you think about your self, do you think of your self as an American first, and then Hispanic? Or is it the other way around?" He looked at me and said: "It depends." "What about right now?" "Hispanic." Then I asked his roommate who was laying on the bed: "What about you? American comes first or White?" "Definitely American." He said. I am very confused about their different answers. One seems care more about his ethnic identity than his nationality, and the other one seems think the opposite way. For me, I always think myself as a Chinese and then a communist. . . .

So yesterday was Sam's birthday. Everybody on my floor was saying happy birthday to him in GroupMe. (In case you don't know, that's a group chat app.) Then, a Chinese guy texted him happy birthday in Chinese characters and all the sudden, people started saying happy birthday in their own languages. At first, there was Russian, and then Arabian, Spanish, German, Japanese, Korean, and a native Nigerian language called Bohop or something. . . . There were in total of 10 different languages!

I didn't know there were so many different language speakers on my floor, and I was shocked. What's funny was that the Nigerian guy didn't actually say happy birthday, instead he said something about Sam's mother. We knew that because Luke, another pretty funny guy on our floor who texted happy birthday in Spanish, translated all the languages into English.

I don't think the essay would be improved by some final discussion of diversity. I told the writer that I would love to see him write another section, of equal length, this one turning to the different languages, peer groups, and political affiliations within the group of Chinese students on our campus. But we were at the end of the cycle of draft and revision, and it was time to move on.

What all the students admired in this piece, as did I, was its energy and sense of fun. There was a recognizable person in here rather than a stock figure. My composition classes almost always are defined by an early moment where a writer appears as a compelling character with a "real" voice. That was how this essay was read by the class, but there were not many who followed suit in their revisions.

This next student paper was remarkable, to me at least, for its length and range, and for its straightforward (neither melodramatic nor overly self-conscious) account of what seemed to me to be the crushing cost of making the passage to Pittsburgh. It is also a wonderful reading of Lu's essay. At one point, the writer defines herself as "unobscured and adventurous"—what a lovely phrase!

"Unobscured" became a term of use for me in that class. In this essay, the writer was writing about her parents, and it is the stories of their lives that allow her to become "unobscured." This coining is proceeded by another interesting pair of terms. Their age and her travels to the United States ("geographical craziness") all led, she said, to "concurrence and controversy." In these pairings (and in the precision of the terms) she is searching for a third term, a somewhere in the middle that can't be found, as it shouldn't. But the searching for terms and the unusual coinings, like "unobscured," are signs of a writer at work trying to make her language do something new, something important, something other than stock response (what the language is prepared to do, or used to doing).

There are moments in the essay where she enacts (and not just narrates) her version of the "conflict and struggle" of Min-Zhan Lu's learning to write in Shanghai. I think it is brilliant. And I said so. And to frame the discussion, I asked: "Where else in this essay, on the page, do you see this writer as 'unobscured'"?

My father was from a small town in Henan, the middle east of China; my mother was from a little village in Inner Mongolia, the most northern part of China; I was born in Henan, then I lived in Georgia for three years before moving to Pennsylvania. On top of the geographic craziness, the age difference among the three of us were quite drastic as well. My father is fifteen years older than my mother, and they had me when she was thirty. This variation of our experiences lead to both concurrence and controversy. We could have profound discussions on the topics from literacy, medicine, to policy during afternoon tea. My father and mother would always have something fascinating to say, and I brought the youth's and western thoughts to the table. Their experiences helped me to be unobscured and adventurous.

My middle school was a boarding school, the top one in Henan Province. Because it was a province school, it was in the capital of Henan, which was a two-hour drive from where we lived. It was my first time living away from home and away from my mother and father. A few weeks before the first day of school, I started losing sleep. I did not understand why I would have trouble falling asleep since I considered myself being one of the best sleepers in all of the people that I know. My mother told me that my sleep problems were caused by a thing called "excitement." "Ha! Now it makes sense!" I was excited to potentially start a new life at this new place with all those new people. But I was nervous at the same time, especially about living at a dorm with six other girls.

Move in Day was literally a race to get to the room and claim our territories, so that we could get the "good" spot. The room was approximately ten square meters. It was set up with four sets of gun metal lockers standing against the wall near the red metal door; two sets of bunk beds with wooden boards as the "mattress" on each side of the room; a small glass door to our washing area where we had three sinks, one toilet, and one shower. I was a little bit let down by the fact that as many as seven people were shoved into this little tiny space. I could not help to complain, "this place is terrible, how can I live here for three years?" Then I saw both of my parents laughed, and my mother said, "honey, back in the days when I was getting my associate degree, it was so much worse than this." My mother had not told me a lot about her college life, and my reaction to her comment was, "you lived in a dorm too? I thought . . .

well, I don't actually think about life way back then. So what was it like, mom?" She and my father both chuckled, and then sat down on the naked wooden board, and started telling the story from her youth years—

"Your grandfather was in the army, so he and your grandmother moved to Inner Mongolia under the order of the commander to help exploit desolate areas there in October 1954. Then your aunts were born, I was born, and your uncle was born last. We grew up in that little village. Oh, the one you visited last time when you went back." "You mean the one that we drove up the mountain for two hours to get to and we did not see any human being or any types of transportations on the way up there?" I interrupted with great inconceivable, "I mean, they weren't even houses, they were [made of grass] bricks! How does that work? It gets super cold in the winters there."

My mom nodded undeniably and continued with her story. "Your grandfather used to make these trousers with cottons for us. Those trousers were so thick that they could stand on there own! Your grandparents had one room, and the rest of us had the other. I didn't like sleeping in the same bed with four other people. But what could I do? Nothing. So I told myself everyday that I had to get out of that poor little village. When I was about ten, my sisters and I started working as mushroom pickers in the mountains to get some extra money for stuff that we wanted really badly. For me, I wanted a pair of white sneakers, and they cost 0.5 yuan. I finally worked my hours and got the money to buy these wonderful shoes.

But guess what your grandmother did? She beat me the second I walked into the house. She blamed me for spending money on useless things and accused me of being too much of a vanity. All she wanted us to become were good students at school, and obeying children at home. That was when I swore to myself that I would become the best mom if I ever have a child.

I worked extra hard at school, because I wanted to get out. And I succeeded! I achieved my goal by getting the top scores and came to Henan for high school and then college after that. Speaking of residential life, we used to have a bed that was as wide as the room, which probably was about eleven meters long, and twelve girls slept in the same bed. Although there were disagreements about snoring and showering here and there, I enjoyed it. We would turn off our lights and all be in bed before the RA comes to check on us, and then chat about everything, classes, friends, fashion, boys, all kinds of stuff, until really late. I think it was a unique experience, and taught me how to be around people. Don't complain, and never give in without a fight."

. . . .

The entire family on my father's side was Hui Chinese, thus they were all Muslims. I did not believe in the Islamic faith. My grandparents were pure Muslims. My grandfather had a big white beard just like Muhammad. My grandmother married my grandfather when she was fourteen and had been a virtuous wife as the Islamic culture set her to be since. Both of them grew up in a small village where everyone were Muslims; everyone had the same last name; everyone was related to everyone. However, there were never any sparkles or clicks between my "family faith" and I.

My father used to tell me bedtime stories from the Quran. I enjoyed them, but they were simply entertainments to me. Celebrations to traditional holidays on the Islamic calendar were just exciting parties that had amazing food. I did not like the Islamic faith, and I was glad that my father allowed me to not like it. I disliked it because of the forceful element to it. It is difficult for me to accept my identity to be a Muslim strictly because my father is one. In my opinion, the freedom of thoughts and believes should be a necessity to human beings. I should be able to choose what I believe in and no one can put me a group based on my family history. Maybe I valued freedom more many Chinese due to the American novels I read and movies that I watched. I never liked it, let along believing this faith of my family's.

My father had always wished that I could believe in something. He wanted me to learn more about other cultures and faiths, so that I would one day have a spiritual sustenance. My father did not agree sending me here to the US. when I first proposed it. He thought that Americans discriminated Asians, and it was not as safe as China due to the problems with gun controls. The drugs and alcohol at American high schools and college he saw from TV shows or movies made it even more challenging to convince him to let me study in the US. Finally, he gave in, but under one strange condition, that was for me to go to a Christian school. I took this offer with great pressure because I was eager to learn anything new.

. . . .

I arrived in the US in August, 2014. My host family was Christian. We went to church every Sundays. Most of my classmates were Christians. I had a bible class everyday. We celebrated Christian holidays instead of Islamic ones. Everything was different. The first bible class was full of confusion. Everybody but me in the classroom got the biblical references the Mr. Wilson, my bible teacher, made. I did not know what "Roman 6:15" meant; I did not know when or where Jesus was born; I did not know who Abraham was. On top of all the previous knowledge that I lacked, my vocabulary seemed to vanish when I read the bible.

There is no rush here toward a Conclusion, and the detail comes from within the scene. The turn to her parents and grandparents was, perhaps, inspired by the example of Hessler's students, who also located themselves in a family history. But you always believe (or the students and I were quick to believe) that she was writing about people and places and ideas that mattered to her. Part of this is in the loving attention to detail, which *unobscured* the scene, the place, and the time:

[The boarding school room] was set up with four sets of gun metal lockers standing against the wall near the red metal door; two sets of bunk beds with wooden boards as the "mattress" on each side of the room; a small glass door to our washing area where we had three sinks, one toilet, and one shower.

But the writer's achievement is also in her willingness to bring forward the terms of an unconventional life. The Hui Chinese are one of the fifty-five ethnic minority groups in China. While they are not actively persecuted, as in the case, for example, of the Uyghurs, they remain marginalized. This is what I meant when I said that she wrote about something that mattered because it mattered. Her subject was not determined by a standard narrative. She struggles that it be unobscured. And when she succeeds, you want to say, "Wow."

I tried very hard to move students away from the sorts of conclusions that sum everything up, speak in a loud voice, and leave the world a happy place, part of the drill of Chinese (like American) writing instruction. I have had pretty good success with this in other courses. Here I couldn't make much of a dent. The biggest change came with the ways students gathered and considered examples—slowly, thoughtfully, and at length, as something other than props, support, or proof. And Lu's essay was exemplary in this regard.

Here is part of the conclusion of my student's essay, above:

Luckily, I have two sets of family on each side of the planet. My American parents would explain to me phenomena in the US, and they were always excited to listen to me expressing my Chinese point of view. My father was surprisingly supportive when I presented him with my interest in Christianity. We talked about the similarities and differences from the Bible and the Quran regularly. His perception on America became weaker after getting to know this country. My appreciation toward my diversified and accepting family grew stronger as I acquired more knowledge from other languages and cultures. The opinions and experiences my parents shared with me were precious. They helped resolve the struggle that I had with discourses of Chinese and English.

SOME VERSIONS OF PASTORAL

In the opening chapter to *River Town*, Peter Hessler tells a story about his friend and colleague, Adam, the other Peace Corps volunteer in Fuling. In a moment when he needed to usefully fill classroom time, Adam turned to his students and, in a phrase familiar to us all, said: "Write about anything you want."

> At the end of the hour, Adam collected their papers. They had written about anything they wanted, and what he had was forty-five shopping lists. I want a new TV, a new dress, a new radio. I want more grammar books. I want my own room. I want a beeper and a cell phone and a car. I want a good job. Some of the students had lists a full page long, every entry numbered and prioritized.

In the 1970s, when I started teaching, stories like this would often begin or end a conference paper at CCCC. They provided the punch line or the pivot, a demonstration of the gulf between the haves and the have-nots, evidence of the impossible task of teaching composition in the era of open admissions. *We inhabit different countries, different planets*—that was the subtext. *I could be a good teacher if they would just send me good students, students whose writing I can read.*

Hessler, however, uses the story to set up the passage I placed as my epigraph.

I sensed that I simply couldn't judge the students for anything they thought, at least in the beginning. Their backgrounds were too far removed from what I had known before coming to Fuling, and, like all young Chinese, they were surrounded by the aura of a troubled past. It was easy to forget this—it was easy . . . to smile at their childlike shyness, and it was easy to dismiss them as simple young people from the simplicity of the countryside. But of course nothing was farther from the truth—the Sichuan countryside is not simple, and my students had known things that I never imagined. Even if appearances were deceiving, the truth always came through in the ways they wrote about their homes and families.

It was easy to dismiss them as simple people from a simple countryside. Both the invitation to dismissal and the speech act to provide cover were the subject of William Empson's *Some Versions of Pastoral* (1935), where he considers the "trick of language," the form of "magical thinking" that allows us to construct simple binaries, like complex and simple.

Empson, following Richards, taught Basic English in China in the late 1930s, and then again from 1947 to 1953. (He taught in Japan in the early 1930s. He posthumously published a book on *The Face of the Buddha*.) Empson had difficulty finding a permanent position at an English university, and he was restless. His first full-time appointment was at the University of Essex in 1955.

Empson had spent his early career seeking out the thorniest, most difficult passages in all of English literature in order to do the work he wanted to do. His first book, written while he was an undergraduate at Cambridge (and studying with Richards), was *Seven Types of Ambiguity*. The title was an Empsonian joke, demonstrating the craziness of any precise account of imprecision, of words, sentences, and passages that had multiple meanings. And, as I said, each chapter is built around readings of some of the most difficult passages in all of English literature: Chaucer, Shakespeare, Donne, Pope, Hopkins, Eliot. How should (or might) readers (or writers) locate themselves in moments where meanings are multiple, where the language is slippery, when passage or utterance defies paraphrase, defies all attempts at understanding? He is interested in moments where readers and listeners (writers and speakers) stumble, when they stumble and when that stumbling cannot (should not) be attributed to a failure of education, class, will, or attention.

And so, of course, Empson would take the opportunity to live and teach in China. His interest in travel was, like Richards's, part of his interest in the limits of language, the problems of knowledge, translation, interpretation, "the structure of complex words," to use the title of the book that followed *Some Versions of Pastoral*. Empson's argument, following Richards, was that meaning was always contextual and contexts were changeable and unpredictable. With language, verbal or written exchanges were always fraught and contingent; someone was always out of step; misunderstandings were inevitable. Knowing this was the proper preparation for a life in the world.

The opening example in *Some Versions of Pastoral* is Thomas Gray's poem, "Elegy in a Country Churchyard." In it, the poet reflects on rural labor and rural laborers—one of them buried here in a country churchyard, forgotten and unheralded, perhaps a "mute inglorious Milton," an example of opportunity wasted.

> Full many a gem of purest ray serene
> The dark, unfathomed caves of ocean bear;
> Full many a flower is born to blush unseen
> And waste its sweetness on the desert air.

Empson is always quick to pull the curtain on the wizard. He says, "What this means, as the context makes clear, is that eighteenth-century England had no scholarship system. . . . This is stated as pathetic, but the reader is put into a mood in which one would not try to alter it."

The trope of the pastoral, what Empson calls a "trick" of language, erases difference in order to serve the needs and desires of power. But the power he is concerned with is not rooted in class or capital. It rests with the tropes deployed by a writer or reader. That is, Empson considers the trope in the context of working-class as well as highbrow literature. He argues that these speech acts conveniently represent the difficult, unequal relations between, say, rich and poor—or, in later chapters, the wise and foolish, adults and children, life and death, spirit and body, conscious and unconscious, gardens and heath, the "best" and the worst. And, we might add, teacher and student. Pastoral (as a trick) allows these unequal relations to be fixed in image and phrase and, so, to appear "beautiful," "natural," inevitable, part of nature or god's plan. It is a way of ignoring difference as though such ignoring were a generous thing to do when, in fact, the gesture (or the trick of language, as Empson has it) is a way of pushing others aside, erasing them, placing them in the standard narrative of high and low, ignorance and experience, and so on.

The Hessler of my example does not fall for the trick. He doesn't settle on "simple," nor on its complement, "complex," which would be equally dismissive and patronizing (the "inscrutable oriental"). He wants to know things he has never imagined, and so he turns to the singleness of the cases before him—presenting one student paper after another and, later, one instance after another—all from his teaching and his life in Fuling.

And, in doing so, he enacts what I understand to be both the methods and the ethic of "translingual composition," which I take to be a new way of conceiving the motives and methods of what we used to call Basic Writing. I'm drawing, now, from Bruce Horner's definition of translingual in the chapter "Language" in his most recent book, *Rewriting Composition: Terms of Exchange*, but I'm referring broadly to the publications of a larger group of colleagues. Translingual composition locates writing temporally as well as spatially—always in process, always in motion, always a negotiation. Translingual composition is an orientation rather than a specific set of practices. Translingual composition produces and requires a "set of dispositions"—tolerance for variation, humility and a willingness to negotiate meaning, letting ambiguities pass, a recognition that language is changing, not static.

Perhaps the founding document for translingual composition is the *College English* essay "Language Difference in Writing: Toward a Translingual Approach" (2011), written by Bruce Horner, Min-Zhan Lu, Jacqueline Jones Royster, and John Trimbur. Here are some of its resolutions:

> The translingual approach we call for extends the CCCC resolution [on "Students Rights to their Own Language"] to differences within and across all languages. And it adds recognition that the formation and definition of languages and language varieties are fluid.

> The translingual approach encourages reading with patience, respect for perceived differences within and across languages, and an attitude of deliberate inquiry.

> The translingual approach asks of writing not whether its language is standard, but what the writers are doing with the language and why. For in fact, notions of the "standard English speaker" and "Standard Written English" are bankrupt concepts.

As the term "Basic Writing" once opened up new possibilities for thinking about English in use, and about composition as a school subject, so, I believe, *translingual composition* has that power now. It reanimates all forms of writing as a negotiation across languages. It speaks equally to Basic Writing, to all forms of first-year composition, to Writing in the Disciplines, to introductory courses in journalism and nonfiction, and, as I note, to study abroad.

In this essay I've wanted to account for a Basic Writing course I taught in my final semester, and I wanted to think back to where I began as a teacher and a writer. And in thinking about where I began, I couldn't help but make connections to Cambridge English, here represented by I. A. Richards and William Empson.

Why Empson and the trick of the pastoral? Because, as I continue to read this odd and difficult book, *Some Versions of Pastoral*, I always find myself thinking about the problems central to what we are talking about when call up a term like "basic writing." From a certain humane perspective, it is tempting to assume that language differences don't matter. That they can be overlooked or overcome. This is one of the tricks of pastoral. To celebrate a common humanity, differences must be erased. The shepherd and the lord of the manor can/should speak, think, and feel as one. One must be consumed by the other.

What Empson shows is how very difficult it is to think otherwise, to productively, for example, inhabit and engage diverse ways of thinking, speaking, and feeling. And to do so without resorting to hierarchy, where one utterance, one sentence, for example, must be replaced by another for the text, or the utterance, to be acceptable.

Composition courses are ground zero in these struggles. What I have learned late in my career is to see the importance of bringing our energies to the fundamental problems of writing in a global context, and there is no better testing ground than undergraduate courses that combine travel and travel writing, where the opening assignment, for example, may be to write about South Africa, to write about South Africa without being South African. And even if you could inhabit such a position, Empson asks, which South African might you then be? Or which and what kind of North American do you become? Or might you become? Empson doesn't solve the problems of Basic Writing (or travel writing), but he is brilliant at showing all their forms and manifestations. And he does so with great delight.

Perhaps the simplest and most elegant statement on language diversity comes from Raymond Williams. What Williams knew was the product of his close study of the history of writing in English. But he also lived and worked and found himself and placed himself in the midst of diverse linguistic practices and expectations. Williams was a professor at Cambridge; he was also Welsh, working class, the son of a railway signalman. He was a distinguished academic; he also devoted fifteen years to teaching adult education courses through the Workers' Educational Association. He was closely and deeply aware of language difference—of different "structures of feeling" as well as the different habits of thinking and writing. A culture, he said, "is always both traditional and creative." A culture is composed of "both the most ordinary common meanings and the finest individual meanings." And the problem of having to choose between an "educated" or a "customary" style, he would say, is that neither is sufficiently articulate.

CHAPTER SIX

The Historians of Cape Town

On Teaching Travel Writing

with Rene Lloyd

Note: This chapter reverses my usual practice. In the early chapters I embedded student writing in an essay of my own. Here, my comments are embedded in the full text of an essay titled "Historians of Cape Town," written by one of my undergraduate students, Rene Lloyd.

"Not only is Cape Town beautiful, with the ocean and the mountains and the greenery, not only is it beautiful, it is strategically significant!" the cab driver declared as his car—a Cadillac with blue and white striped fleece lining on the seats—sped toward town from Mowbray. He took one or two breaks to breathe during his history lesson, which both began and ended with "beautiful! and strategically significant!" He recited every year that South Africa changed political hands. He pointed out all the major buildings. He talked fast. His accent was thick. Very clearly, though, at the end of the ride, he said, "be safe."

We are driving from Long Street up to Spring Hill on a day when the wind in Cape Town is sweeping people inside. Elly is saying that all the leaders in Africa are filling their countries with death. Or did he say debt? Originally from Zimbabwe, Elly came to South Africa because back in his country, "you have to be a criminal to survive." You have to steal to get by, he said. "I was coward enough to get out. So I drive all day, every day." He drops us off with his phone number at the foot of Lion's Head Mountain and tells us to call him before it gets dark. Later, as the city lights up and hikers descend from a mountain-top evening, Elly is quick to pick up our phone call and quick to pick us up.

He can't be going more than fifteen miles per hour descending from the trailhead into the city bowl. He said once he tried to climb to the top but had to turn back—he was too out of breath! His attempt to climb Table Mountain was the same story. The nine young people squished in the back of his seven person cab laugh with him and ask if he could go a little slower: "we're finding it hard to breathe!" a boy from Belgium yells. Elly laughs contagiously. His meter is broken but he tells us exactly how much it will cost to get to Orange Street then to Strand then to Mowbray. "I would rather just drive the girls, you know, but it's okay, you boys can stay now."

Elly tells us he has three sons. "The eldest, he's almost your age, he's fifteen!" Once they get a little older, the five girls left in the car can all marry his sons. We exchange smiles in the backseat as Elly commences his defense of polygamy in the name of his sons. He hears protests from the sweaty mountain women behind him and he responds that in fact it is fair. There are more women than men on the planet.

The windows in the back of Elly's jeep—an unlabeled cab—are held shut with small bungee chords. The fabric lining the seats is faded; it must have been from the 1980s, once colorful and reminiscent of the bounty of African flora. He gives us his phone number and says to always call him, and he'll remember the girls from Mowbray. "Be safe," he says.

In 2011, and then again in 2013, I was faculty coordinator in a newly developed University of Pittsburgh Study Abroad program, PittMap. The program occupied our spring semester (fifteen weeks), and it was built around a focused curriculum, including core courses taught by Pitt faculty, a required language/culture course taught by faculty at our host university, and local electives, also taught by host faculty.

In 2011, with a colleague from the School of Medicine and another from Economics, our topic was public health, with a focus on HIV/AIDS. We spent five weeks each in Buenos Aires, Cape Town, and Beijing, meeting with doctors, researchers, and public health officials; visiting clinics, hospitals, research centers, and pharmaceutical companies. We wanted students to see the world; we wanted them to visit cities American students seldom visit; and we wanted to provide a comparative perspective on public health.

In 2013, with a colleague from Political Science, we were five weeks each in Florianopolis (Brazil), Hyderabad (India), and, again, Beijing. Our topic was "the politics of inequality." We were studying the efforts to serve the poor and the disadvantaged within the political and civil sectors of these three emerging economies. For fieldwork, we visited schools and clinics, NGOs and government offices, women's groups and other centers of local activism (within the Dalit community, for example, in India).

My wife and I (and our Pitt colleagues) lived with the students in student housing. I had a graduate assistant who served as a student counselor, problem-solver, and resident assistant. It was my job to make sure all the parts were working, that spirits were high, and to step in if there was a crisis (problems with local courses, visa problems, or, as was the case in Hyderabad, a terrorist threat). For my teaching assignment, I taught a course in travel writing. The writing course, as I conceived of it, would serve two purposes. It would provide a motive to be out on the streets, paying close attention to people and places, and it would create a quiet, reflective space each week in the middle of a demanding and chaotic travel schedule.

To be a good travel writer is to be a good traveler, or so I said in my course description. You need to know how to look and listen, how to let a scene speak for itself, how find the stories that are there waiting to be heard, how to get yourself and your preconceptions out of the way. You need a notebook and you need to use it when you have a quiet moment alone. When you are out in the field, you need to make contact and to talk with people *not* in our group; you need courage; you need to pay attention. And, as Elly said, "Be safe."

I found that I could not, as was my usual practice, work from published, professional models. Most of the travel writing in the Best Of book series, minus some of the very best (by writers like Peter Hessler), tended to be self-centered and dismissive. The focus was on the "writer's journey" rather than the place of encounter. Think *Eat, Pray, Love.* I wanted a genre that would honor detail over generalization and that would take students outside of themselves and their preconceptions. I quickly developed a library of exemplary student writing that I used as assigned readings.

This chapter presents one of them, "Historians of Cape Town," written by Rene Lloyd, then an Environmental Studies major. After graduation, she served as a Peace Corps volunteer in Senegal. At the time of this writing, she is a graduate student in the School of Public and Environmental Affairs at Indiana University. "The Historians of Cape Town" provided a defining moment in the 2011 PittMap travel writing course. I've used this essay as a model in almost every writing course that I have taught since then.

Note: The section that follows includes a reference to Ernest Cole. Cole was a self-taught, Black South African photographer whose work won international attention in the 1960s. In 1967, he published a collection, *House of Bondage: A South African Black Man Exposes in His Own Pictures and Words the Bitter Life of His Homeland Today* (New York: Random House). We attended a retrospective of his work at the National Gallery in Cape Town.

A bird's eye view shows a train station at rush hour. In the foreground a few white men with briefcases amble in wait. An invisible line separates them from masses of black people, no room to stretch between them. The line is invisible. It separates first and third class.

The photo by Ernest Cole tells the story of apartheid with a simple image of people waiting for a train. It hangs in the National Gallery, amongst other images depicting the lives of black people around the 1960s. Other photos show people running over train tracks toward unmarked trains, hoping they choose the one that's going home. Faces, one on top of another, stare into Cole's lens.

There is still first and third class on the trains in Cape Town. There is no second class. The trains still don't have signs telling where they are going, and they don't follow the schedule. In fact, in early February 2011, the city discontinued fourteen of its trains citing vandalism and extreme weather as reasons. Commuters wait on concrete, shadeless slabs for hours to get to work.

After at least a half an hour on the cement, we hop into a train going the direction we want, all of us complacently uncertain, a familiar feeling after a few months away from the United States. Guidebooks and tour guides tell people to make sure they ride first class for safety and comfort. When the train rolls up, though, there's no way to tell which door will lead to first and which lead to third.

Arms are straight up, armpit odors and hairs bearing, as people cram into the train car. This is third class. A middle-aged man is telling jokes to the women and children sitting on the bench in front of him. He's hanging on to the top bar with both hands—taking up at least three spots where people could stand. He is speaking in Xhosa, laughing the whole time.

The windows are opaque grime and half open; the mountains with crowns of clouds roll by and the smell of the ocean breaks in through the doors and through the sweat every time the train stops. Fish and salt and wind beating beaches, trash bursting through the windows with each gust of wind, following twirling trails of sand.

"Chocolate bars, candy," comes from a monotone voice snaking its way through the densely packed car. A toddler, just learning to walk, wanders through the sea of shins to a man squatting next to me, who smiles lovingly and picks up the child. Another man standing holds the child's outstretched hand. Everyone in the car is watching the baby and smiling. The train stops and the man walks over to a woman sitting, hands her the child, and he exits the train. He didn't know that child.

People smile at the man as he leaves the train, and at each other, too. Xhosa clicks mix with English words. A boy—not quite adolescent, yet—runs through the train to a spot that's clear. He starts singing with his guitar he made from a stick, a plastic gallon jug, and nylon strings. After two songs, he holds out his instrument and lets two women donate a few rand; he yells something when the train stops and runs to the next car.

A man in a red baseball cap that says "Jesus is Lord" tells us he's dropping at the Muizenberg beach, so we should drop when he drops. Hopefully, "to drop" means "to get off." "Drop when I drop" was a lot better than, "wait for three stops after this one, and then get off at the second one after that." Following a dropper might be easier than counting. We couldn't see the signs of the stations through the windows so we were feeling somewhat helpless; eventually we saw the nod of the red cap through the new onslaught of passengers and scurried off after it—we dropped. The man with the red cap walked away holding hands with a woman before we could thank him.

"Why are you going to Gugulethu?" asks the woman who has been glancing at us while the conductor tries to fill up the taxi at the station. She hasn't heard of the hip hop concert we're going to, and that's where the conversation ends. She speaks with the man next to her calmly. At most the taxi should hold twelve people but won't leave until there are fifteen. The whipping wind that starts once we get on the NY-1 highway alleviates the heat of the day. The driver swings the unmarked van around bends and jolts to stops at traffic lights. Bare leg to bare leg, sweaty arm to sweaty arm, we are crammed in the back, hunched over.

We drive past Barcelona, a township named after the city in Spain. Hundreds of huts made from corrugated metal and cardboard seem to be pushing each other over but maybe they are holding each other up. A billboard whizzes by: *The N2, pathway from slums to success.* The wind prohibits conversation, but my friend leans over and reminds me that the internet says there are two murders every day in Gugulethu.

Hodael had said to get off at the police station. We were stopped at a gas station, the front driver's seat was smoking, and the driver and conductor looked at it nonplussed as the rest of the passengers looked out the windows. I tell Hodael we are at a gas station. "I'll come there now," he says and hangs up before I can describe where it is. Off guard, afraid of catching fire, we push hurriedly out of the taxi.

Milling about the gas station, my friends look at me questioningly. It's what seems to be the center of town. There is the smell of grilling meat. Friends are walking slowly along the street or sitting in the shade outside their houses or shacks. The sun shines on us and it seems like everyone is staring from the shade. Spaza, Hair Salon, Barber, Tailor, Meat. Then I see Hodael waving from across the street—sunglasses on and the same green shirt he was wearing the first time I met him.

We stand waiting for a half chicken to be grilled and sauced and make conversation with Hodael. He's the coordinator of the event today. "There's going to be contemporary dancers, an open-mic hip hop session, and a screening of a film shot here in Cape Town." He walks us slowly along the road. Old Cadillacs full of people stutter by on the street—"these are the cabs here," he says, "they are five rand no matter where you go in Gugulethu but they can't go on the highway because they'll get arrested," or they'll break down. "The drivers never really learned how to drive."

From inside shops people watch us walk by. Kids wave and Hodael smiles, "you guys are popular." I met Hodael at a performance art festival in Station Square. He coordinates and records events for hip hop and jazz bands, mostly from Gugulethu and other townships. He and his friend Thulani had invited me here: "bring everybody, we're going to rock your time in Cape Town."

Walking past brightly painted huts scattered between brightly painted houses, toward the sound of a thumping bass beat, Hodael points to a school. "Because of all the art projects going on here in the past few years with the school, this place has gotten way safer." He holds out his cell phone: "it used to be that if you walked around with this thing on this street you would get it stolen, no doubt. Now, people walk around like this all the time."

"It's crazy how people think of Africa, man. They come down here expecting that we'll be swinging from the trees, hunting animals with spears." He pretends to throw a spear and makes the outline of a loincloth on himself, laughing. "I'd love to go to other places and get to know other people's cultures, but it's too expensive." He talks about a program in Berlin that is soliciting art from South Africa. He lets out a sigh, "Man, if I could just get something together. . . ."

Inside the shack that has been hollowed into a music venue, groups of friends are gathered around tables with bottles of soda and hard liquor, making drinks for each other. We get beer and find a place near the back of the crowd. The man next to me has a playboy bunny tattoo on his neck. He is really feeling the rapper on stage, dancing and responding to each line delivered. I lean over to ask what language the guy is rhyming in. It's Xhosa. Right. "Where are you from?" The states, I say.

"Where are you staying?" Mowbray.

"Oh, yeah, yeah, all the students from the U.S. stay there; I should have known. I dated a girl there once for six months but then she left and broke my heart." He keeps looking me up and down, especially wide-eyed when I tell him we took taxis to get to the show. The tattooed man asks how I like Cape Town. I smile and say it's really interesting and point to where I'm standing to signify that I prefer where I am at the moment. He nods, still dancing to the music. He's from the Northern Cape but has spent twenty years in Cape Town and doesn't want to leave. "I love it, man! Every Sunday they do this," waving his arms to embrace the whole place.

"Cape Town, *in town* feels like anyplace else. You don't get the real vibe of Africa until you come to the townships. This is Africa," says the tattooed man. *TIA*. Charles and G, our student mentors from University of Cape Town, told us the first day we were here that *TIA* is their motto. It's a term of dismissal as well as contentment. *This is Africa*. People get mugged, *this is Africa*. Trains take a long time, *this is Africa*. There's no personal space on public transportation, *this is Africa*. It's an answer to frustration and indignation. It is a reminder of the past. It says nothing about the future. The playboy bunny–necked man's version of *TIA* is different. It's an answer to the question, *what is Africa?* This place, these people, this sound, this is Africa.

Thulani, who I'd also met at the concert in Station Square, grabs my hands and leads me out into an open sandy area. We are standing between the hip hop shack and the film screening shack. The way Thulani is holding my hands makes me wonder if he's about to propose. He apologizes profusely for losing his phone and not being able to call me. He's wearing a safari hat and large sunglasses. When he smiles infectiously I think he must really mean what he says, that it's really important that we came.

Under orders from the emcee, everyone scuttles out to the street where two dancers perform. The man and woman are simultaneously feathers and rocks. They lift each other and jump off and onto each other. They fall on the dusty pavement and jump higher than most basketball players. They are hostile and rough with each other, then suddenly soft and dependent. Their bodies, moving to an unimpressive English song, make it beautiful.

Back inside after the dance a rapper comes on. He yells something about Cape Town and the crowd yells back. The man with the tattoo from earlier tells me they're saying, "Burn it!"

The emcee comes back on stage. "It doesn't matter if you're white or black, old or young, man or woman; it doesn't matter if you have a fucking purple scar. There's only one god, one love."

A few weeks later, this emcee, named Smokey, would spend all night in our backyard helping explain the gang system in South African jails and teaching Sarah to step dance. He would criticize our pies and hike to Rhode's Temple with us proclaiming, "All the statues in the world should be destroyed!!" And we would have a handstand contest.

On this Sunday he takes a break to talk about his uncle from Tanzania. "I tended him when he had AIDS for the last six months of his life. He taught me everything I knew about guns, but I never touched one. He was in war, so this song is for him. Crossing border lines, watching out for mines, I'm looking out for mine."

Thulani squeezes through the crowd listening to the hip hop— where Green Panda from University of Cape Town has taken the mic—to urge us on to the film screening. Hodael is behind the stage talking to performers, writing things down. He grabs his camera every once in awhile and disappears into the crowd. He is smiling almost every time I look at him, but busy and intent. His baseball cap is ripping at the edges and his sunglasses cover most of his face.

Sunday afternoon is creeping slowly toward sleep. Our guidelines tell us not to stay out after dark, and it could be a long ride back to Mowbray, so we climb in a taxi, tired, full of half chickens and Heinekens, girls on boys' laps, young people moving over for elders. Some people stare down at phones and nails and freckles, and most people look out the windows at the mountains. Windows are closed on the quiet ride back to town.

Mountains are always in the background here. In the townships they are far away, sometimes invisible through haze or fog; but in the paintings for sale on the side of the road, the paintings where houses are cut out of tin soda and beer cans, the mountains are always there.

Over and over in my head I keep thinking about Smoky saying, "I've got a six pack but no father figure."

In the PittMap writing course, students wrote two essays at each of the three sites, the final versions composed from the weekly drafts and revisions. I asked that at least one of the two essays touch on the theme of the trip, public health. In the end, the explanatory essays were shorter, although important, and the personal essays (or travel essays) much longer.

In earlier chapters, I've provided detailed materials from my courses. Here I will just provide a rough outline to account for *my* work in the course, beyond reading the papers each week and providing commentary and editorial prompts. I was introducing students to a genre, what I was calling "travel writing." This was partially an established genre (you can easily find examples of travel writing online and at the bookstore), and it was partly a genre that belongs to this course only, shaped by my expectations for how and why to write while traveling. (I was not preparing students for a career in journalism; I offered no expectations that they could publish their work.) As I said earlier, Rene's essay quickly became a model for the writing that I thought could best serve the goals of our program—to have a comparative view of three major cities and three state-sponsored public health initiatives, and to learn how to be citizens of the world.

These are the features of the course that I think had the most bearing on how students reread and began to revise essays at each site.

Fragments: Each week students wrote two brief sketches or fragments focused on a particular person, place, or moment in time, five hundred to one thousand words, and they revised a piece they had begun the week before. The sections would eventually need to be organized in the form of a John McPhee or *New Yorker*–styled essay—an essay made up of sections, numbered or marked by dingbats, not necessarily arranged chronologically, and where a reader had the challenge (and pleasure) of making the leap from one to the other. There would be a thematic focus but no stated transitions. (One of the readings in the course was

John McPhee's *New Yorker* essay "Structure," later collected in *Draft #4*. Like McPhee, students spent time with pages on the floor or posted on the wall, thinking about how they might be arranged.) "The Historians of Cape Town" was written over the five weeks we were in Cape Town and revised during the travel break as we headed off to Beijing. It has six sections.

I found the notion of the "fragment" to be particularly useful. It made it possible for students to sit down quickly to write in the midst of a very busy schedule of fieldwork and class sessions. The task was manageable. And it made it clear that the purpose of the writing was not to master or to command a subject but to record and explore a day's work in the field. And it assumed that the larger, reflective moment would come later, once they had a better sense of where they were and what they were doing.

Beginnings and Endings: The students were not English majors or writing majors. There was a lot that needed to be done early on to get them started and give them confidence. Working initially from fragments was one prompt. I wanted to quickly replace the term paper or the classroom essay, where a writer is stating a theme and pushing conclusions, and to move them toward good journalism, where a writer is receptive to a scene, attentive to detail, scrupulous about listening to others, and unwilling to force a conclusion or to editorialize. I wanted nothing like what they had learned to provide by way of Thesis, Introduction, or Conclusion.

In revising and assembling fragments (and in making cuts or filling in gaps), students needed some governing sense of form. I prepared an exercise made up of opening and closing paragraphs from essays I had admired—a chapter from Stephanie Elizondo Griest, "Beijing," from *Around the Bloc: My Life in Moscow, Beijing, Havana*; the opening chapter, "Through the Front Gate," from Michael Meyer's *The Last Days of Old Beijing: Life in the Vanishing Backstreets of a City Transformed*; and David Quammen's essay "Deadly Contact," published in *National Geographic*.

From these we developed a set of guidelines, "fast tracks" for beginnings and endings. For example: "Begin with a scene of action. Write from inside the scene and use the language that belongs to that scene. Get other people talking as quickly as possible. Don't step out of the scene to provide commentary or to editorialize. Assume a reader who wants to see and know something about Cape Town.

(Forgive me, I said, but the people at home who will read your essay will not be interested in your conclusions and generalizations, your ideas. They'll want to be with you on the ground and to see what you saw. And besides, you don't know enough about South Africa to be making generalizations. Stick with scene, dialogue, and detail.)

The closing should be quiet, not loud. It should offer a final image or scene, something to carry away, perhaps someone else saying something memorable. It is not the place for the writer to make pronouncements.

Here, again, is Rene's opening:

"Not only is Cape Town beautiful, with the ocean and the mountains and the greenery, not only is it beautiful, it is strategically significant!" the cab driver declared as his car—a Cadillac with blue and white striped fleece lining on the seats—sped toward town from Mowbray. He took one or two breaks to breathe during his history lesson, which both began and ended with "beautiful! and strategically significant!" He recited every year that South Africa changed political hands. He pointed out all the major buildings. He talked fast. His accent was thick. Very clearly, though, at the end of the ride, he said, "be safe."

I'll wait to comment on Rene's closing paragraphs. But I think they are brilliant.

Editing: When I read, I offered comments that pointed toward revision—what I thought might be added to the week's fragment (or section) and what I thought might be interesting for the next week. I found that I needed to say over and over again—you need to get someone else speaking in this essay, someone other than you. And, of course, that is the hardest task—to be in conversation with the people of Cape Town. Students had access to the people who hosted us during our fieldwork, and made good use of it. Some, like Rene, found their way into the communities around us.

I knew the students and what they had been doing, and so my editorial suggestions were informed and specific (like those offered by a "real" editor). And I knew that, in the end, most would follow their own hearts if they were hot on the trail or deeply engaged with what they had begun. This was the case with Rene, who was completely committed to thinking about this encounter in the townships, this brief meeting of Pittsburgh students with men and women who reside in Gugulethu.

Line editing: And then I found that the most surprising and useful editorial intervention I could provide would be to just make cuts, most of them at the level of the sentence, and all in order to get the writer out of the way and back into the scene, writing from inside and in the language that belonged to that moment (rather than a moment of reflection or pontification). As is often the case, a personal narrative quickly veered toward the heroic or the epiphanic—and then I overcame all odds, and then I saw. . . . I wanted to preserve the fragmentary integrity of their essays because I wanted to postpone for as long as possible the moment at which the writer stepped out of South Africa and was once again in the United States (and a US classroom).

For each student I would take an early, middle, and late paragraph and cut it to the bone. I wouldn't rewrite, or at least not much. I would just cut words until the prose was direct, quick, and uncluttered. The students took this to be an engaging lesson, not hard to learn and, with only a couple exceptions, were eager to try out this clipped style.

Again, I was not preparing professional travel writers. I was, I thought, teaching students how to be present *in* a scene (not hovering over it), which meant I was teaching them to be better travelers. This comes from a student writing about working with immigrants in Italy:

With cuts:

> I ran back to the map that stood in Piazza Garibaldi, trying once more to get my bearings. When I couldn't find the street name, I decided it would be best to head toward the water. If nothing else, L.E.S.S.'s office was in that direction. I hurried down a street I had previously tried, but abandoned. There, on my left, I saw the office building.

Here is the original:

> I ran back over to the map that stood in Piazza Garibaldi for a third time, trying once more to get a sense of direction. My anxious state of being was prohibiting me from processing the confusing rendition of the surrounding streets. Not being able to find the specific street name, I decided it would be best to head toward the water as I knew that, if nothing else, L.E.S.S.'s office was in that direction. I walked in a direction that I had previously attempted but had turned back halfway

as I thought it could not be the right way. After making it down the remainder of the street, I came to where it merged with the main street along the water. I looked to my left and saw the office building—relief surged through my body.

"Hip hop is the perfect thing for our culture," says Dat outside of *Seventies 80s* on Church Street. Suzanne and I are sipping apple juice with lime, complements of Thulani on behalf of his newly opened venue. Dat is considered by his friends and the internet to be one of the founding fathers of spaza—or township hip hop. He started loving music at age six in church choir with his friend Asande, who is sitting next to us on a bench. Hodael is standing up, his green shirt rolled up to reveal thin and chiseled arms, listening attentively to his friend.

"Look, look at our culture now. People don't like reading or writing. It's because generations ago our culture just stopped writing. They used to, but then they started telling stories and singing songs around the fire. And look how long we went without getting good education. Now, with hip hop, it's like hanging out with a friend. You put a CD in and you get a story. You hear about history and what's going on in the world now. I learned about what was happening in Harlem from hip hop, and I never left Cape Town. You hear real stories, not fantasies like in rock music."

Asande tells me that his music tonight is going to be mostly in Xhosa. "Mind my language. So much of what we hear here is influenced by American culture—what we watch, what we see, what we read. All the kids are attracted to that because it's cool. But I try to keep my music African. That's what I am!"

Asande's voice is incredible. He fills the small retro venue with true reverence. His black baseball hat is turned backwards and he's wearing a light yellow sweater vest over a white collared shirt. "This guy is really good." The audience members look entranced. Dat and Hodael translate some of the lyrics for Suzanne and I. "That means

I see you." Dat sings along to most of the songs, too. The rest of the audience joins in for "Miss Gugulethu," a beautiful and tortured story showing off Asande's tremendous vocal agility. Another song, "Malaika"—which means *angel* in Swahili—enchants us deeper.

Thulani brings out plates with coconut-covered marshmallows, Doritos, and trail mix. Asande takes a break after an hour of singing and winning hearts. He flops down beside Hodael and me to touch our hands before stepping outside for a cigarette. Hodael and I sit listening to the interval music from the 1970s and talk about family. Van Morrison's "Brown Eyed Girl" comes on and Hodael laughs in surprise that I know all the words.

He has a younger sister and brother. All he wants to do is find a place in life where he can take care of them and be happy. He admits his all-consuming motivation to expose upcoming artists to the world stems from stubbornness as well as this desire to take care of his family. "I usually forget to eat," he says, as he makes his way gently into a marshmallow.

Hodael looks around the dimly lit room. We both lean forward off of a small bench covered with a sheet. I drink my ten-rand glass of red wine. "We break the rules here. We don't care. Back then I would get arrested for sitting next to someone like you. Things like that have changed." A call comes in on his cell phone about a band, and then he continues, "Well, things have changed a lot for upper class people. But for poor people, things really haven't changed."

"Is this the freedom," sing Yonelisa and Lalinda. Lisa's voice is a mixture of the British singer Adele and an old time blues singer like Billie Holiday. He is primarily a vocalist for another band, but tonight he is playing only with Lalinda and his guitar. Lalinda is a poet. She sings and poeticizes over some of Lisa's songs like "Freedom." More people filter into *Seventies 80s* as he starts playing Bob Marley's "Redemption Songs." Everyone in the venue is belting along, hands waving with him while he tries to put his own spin on the classic. Thulani brings out more small plates of corn, carrot, and chard with tripe and barbeque sauce.

Lisa sings a song in Xhosa. Hodael leans over and says, "It means,

I told you so." It's a song for everybody who's ever had someone telling you what to be when you just want to be you. Dat tells me later that his whole family wanted him to be a sangoma, a traditional healer. So, he gets what Yonelisa was talking about. He resisted and now his sister is a sangoma, "thank God!"

The music goes on until 11:30 or so. *Seventies 80s* is making the most live music on Church Street. Hodael sits in the corner of the room observing, looking tired but content. Dat is chatting away on a couch and singing along. Thulani is behind the bar counter, dancing more than anyone else and smiling wide. Asande sits by himself playing harmonies on his guitar quietly to match Lisa's. Later he gets back on stage—under the only lit lamp—for a second round of songs. When it's over the woman next to me says, "You can tell a guy is good when the band leaves and the people are still sitting."

Outside, Hodael tells Asande that he's perfect.

I can't help but think to myself that these people are starting something very important. Despite all my attempts to be objective in my observations, the passion with which these young men and women are cultivating expression around them is groundbreaking in Cape Town's climate. Languages mix, but the base is Xhosa. Stories mix, but freedom is always there, love is always there. "We're trying to make this sustainable."

As we're leaving, hugging goodbye and making plans for next time, Thulani grabs our hands and thanks us for coming. "You made my night, oh my god, you're the best! You really made my night!" His friend who helps him run *Seventies 80s* says, "Come back and tell us honestly how you feel so we can make it better every time." He tells us that we can say we were there at the beginning.

"Say I was a painter." Clara and I have asked this guy's name at least three times but can't catch it over the music. He is more excited to talk than to give his name, anyway. He works with Hodael—and wears the same sunglasses—coordinating artists in Gugulethu. "If I came up to you and showed you a canvas and it was all white or all black or all red, I wouldn't be a good artist. You'd be like, *who is this guy?*

"But God is a designer! He puts a little white here, a little black here, a little red here, making things beautiful. It doesn't mean anything. Look, you shouldn't feel strange for being surrounded by black people. And we shouldn't feel strange when we're surrounded by white people, it doesn't mean anything! God is like us, he's a designer."

We are back walking down the streets of Gugs toward Mzoli's Meat Restaurant, the one tourist attraction in the township. "Oh, right here is where I got stabbed," Hodael says. "I was riding my bike and these guys came at me. I fought back because I told them they could have everything but my SIM card, but they wouldn't give it back to me. Then I saw they had knives and I started running. I fell and they stabbed me three times." That was 2006.

"Mugged every day," he grumbles after an old man walks up to him and takes his newly lit cigarette.

After being shuffled around in a shebeen and popping out with a few drinks each, we make our way through the Mzoli's crowd. I squat next to Hodael against a wall away from everybody else. He starts rolling a joint and tells me he misses me when we don't see each other. "What's your love life like?"

"Oh god," I laugh nervously, "interesting." He says nothing but I can feel him prodding through his huge sunglasses. "It was complicated for a long time but now I'm traveling. And I'm single. And I'm pretty happy right here." I move a chicken bone around with my shoe. Then, quickly, "what's yours like?"

26 years old. He hums. A few years ago, long distance. She was in Pretoria but I was crazy jealous. Facebook. Visits. Suspicion. *This sounds familiar.* No more messages, no answer to the calls. This was all years after a promiscuous adolescence. I'm looking for a real connection now. "Living for the fuck"—as Hodael put it—is no longer sufficient, but it's a reality for every fifteen year old who wants to be somebody in town.

"We're going to go to a jam session and then you guys should get going before it gets dark." Through alleyways that smell of urine, through newly planted parks and deserted malls we walk. Women walk in and out of their houses doing chores as the day's heat dissipates. An older lady leading a child down the road takes my hand and says women should always walk between the men. Another woman cries, "I love you," and kisses me hard on the neck. She kisses Clara, Suzanne, and Caitlyn, but not the baffled males.

The clouds are getting darker and the wind is picking up in Gugs. Outside an elementary school we stand watching DJs and rappers as the crowd swells. All day people have been doing this. We take a Cadillac cab to the taxi station in Nyanga with Hodael and Dat and the talkative friend—the painter—who jumps out of the cab halfway there. It takes ten minutes of negotiation to find a taxi going to Mowbray. We say goodbye to Hodael and Dat with promises of more music and possibly an apple pie. "Take care you guys," they say, patting the back plate of the taxi as it drives away.

Over signal hill the sky is pink and deepening blue. I sit in the back corner of the taxi with my arm out the window and sunglasses on to protect my eyes from the wind. We come to a stoplight on the NY-1 going back toward Table Mountain.

A dark green car pulls up beside us. "Come here," yells the man to me from the back seat of the car. Everyone in the taxi giggles uncertainly. "Look, you gotta see this. You four in the back, come here; whites in the back and black people all in front." The taxi passengers in front of us erupt into laughter and clicks of Xhosa. Only one looks back at our faces. The light turns green and the taxi accelerates. The green car turns right. *This is Africa.*

Here, again, are Rene's two final paragraphs. Formally, they bring the essay to a close by mirroring the opening scene—a ride in a cab—and by repeating the catch phrase, "This is Africa," that appeared earlier in different scenes and contexts. Everything is the same but something is different. I think that is what a reader is invited to say at the end.

Over signal hill the sky is pink and deepening blue. I sit in the back corner of the taxi with my arm out the window and sunglasses on to protect my eyes from the wind. We come to a stoplight on the NY-1 going back toward Table Mountain.

A dark green car pulls up beside us. "Come here," yells the man to me from the back seat of the car. Everyone in the taxi giggles uncertainly. "Look, you gotta see this. You four in the back, come here; whites in the back and black people all in front." The taxi passengers in front of us erupt into laughter and clicks of Xhosa. Only one looks back at our faces. The light turns green and the taxi accelerates. The green car turns right. This is Africa.

What impresses me most is the way this ending complicates any rereading or remembering of what came before. This time there are whites and blacks riding together as passengers in the cab, but still in segregation. The writer believes enough in her work to resist the temptation to write a *perfect* ending.

The final phrase, "This is Africa," appears to be spoken by the writer, but it is a re-speaking, a quotation, a saying again what has been in the air and what had been said by Hodael and the South Africans, and, as *they* spoke the words, "This is Africa" became an ironic recapturing of what was said as a complaint by white South Africans and white visitors.

Everyone is speaking at once, although in the cab the white riders are silent. In this mix of voices, the phrase "This is Africa" refers at once to both failures of expectation and triumphs of will. In a sense, everyone is speaking at this point—and what they are saying remains up for grabs. The writer, as a speaker, is in the scene and speaks with the others. It is a very skillful and effective piece of writing for all the ways in which it tries to report on the scene without taking it over and turning it into gold.

I chaired the second MLA literacy conference, "Responsibilities for Literacy" (September 1990), and I invited Mary Louise Pratt to be one of the keynote speakers. Her talk, "Arts of the Contact Zone," was then published in MLA's journal, *Profession* (1991). The essay, the metaphor of the "contact zone," and the notion of "transculturation" have all traveled widely in the field of composition/rhetoric, and not just through the channels of citation. If you google the title, you will find a raft of student papers on the "Arts of the Contact Zone" (some for sale), an entry in Bartleby Research, and several free PDFs taken from the text as it appeared in the textbook *Ways of Reading*.

A section of the lecture is included in the opening chapter ("Criticism in the Contact Zone") of her landmark 1992 book, *Imperial Eyes: Studies in Travel Writing and Transculturation*. I taught *Imperial Eyes* as the core text for a section of my first-year composition course in the early 1990s, long before the PittMap course. To my delight, Mary Pratt happened to be in Pittsburgh that fall giving a lecture. I invited her to join the class, which she very generously did. After about twenty minutes of discussion, one of the students asked the question on every student's mind: "Why is this book so hard?" Pratt said, "It is hard to read because it was hard to write. If, after writing it, I were to write it again, it would be easier for both of us. But that's not how we do things."

I used chapter 3 from *Imperial Eyes* as a reading when we were in Cape Town. The chapter is titled "Narrating the Anti-Conquest," and it centers on four accounts of travel in South Africa: Peter Kolb, *The Present State of the Cape of Good Hope* (Germany, 1719); Anders Sparrman, *Voyage to the Cape of Good Hope* (Sweden, 1775); William Paterson, *Narrative of Four Voyages in the Land of the Hottentots and the Kaffirs* (Britain, 1789); and John Barrow, *Travels into the Interior of Southern Africa* (Britain, 1801).

In short form, the argument of the chapter is that eighteenth- and nineteenth-century travel writing was one of the ways

Europe took possession of Africa (and, in other chapters, South America). The new narrative of travel goes something like this: after a difficult and heroic crossing, a European finds himself in a "new" world. "There is nothing here," he exclaims as he stands high on a promontory looking out over green hills and valleys, calling up the story of the Garden of Eden and Adam naming the plants and animals. But, of course, the land has been occupied for centuries. The plants and animals already had names and stories. There is a history there. And culture. But the eye (and the "I") of the writer commands the scene, empties it of meaning, rewrites it in European terms, and turns it all to gold, where land and animals and people become resources available for European use.

The narrative of "anti-conquest" is a version of Empson's pastoral. It turns violence into peace. This trick of language is present in both the scientific accounts of flora and fauna and in the sentimental narratives of manners and customs. It is the trick of language that provides cover to a writer and allows him (or her) to imagine (and to represent) an innocent encounter with the new world. Pratt says,

> Even though the travelers were witnessing the daily realities of the contact zone, even though the institutions of expansionism made their travels possible, the discourse of travel that natural history produces, and is produced by, turns on a great longing: for a way of taking possession without subjugation and violence.

Why do I turn to *Imperial Eyes* in my presentation of a student travel essay? Why am I collapsing distinctions between high and low, professional and amateur? Because student writers are caught in the same dilemma as faced by Kolb, Sparrman, Paterson, and Barrow. They are writing alongside, and along with, legions of writers who have written about places not their own. The problems of writing are the problems of writing, and it would be just wrong to say that the student who wrote this essay wasn't aware of the dilemma or that she was not yet ready to confront it on the page, in the writing of sentences. Where she succeeds, and I believe she does, it is an achievement. Where she struggles or fails, she struggles or fails at exactly those moments when the available language has its own agenda, an agenda with a long history. And for that, see Pratt, *Imperial Eyes*. One would struggle to find a published piece of travel writing that was beyond "criticism in the contact zone."

I once gave a presentation on PittMap to a faculty "diversity" seminar on my campus. More than one participant made the observation that American students will always be American students, carrying with them an imperial point of view, and that this is an insurmountable problem. How could you lead such a trip? I was asked.

The discussion reached the point where the only available conclusion was that US undergraduates, all of them, anywhere, should simply *not* be invited to leave the country. They will only embarrass us and themselves. Or, if we did sponsor such trips, we would need to first be sure that our students had a solid command of postcolonial theory and a deep knowledge of, in this case, the history of South Africa from the era of European conquest through Apartheid. That was the prerequisite.

Which means, of course, that no one could or would go. It means that learning and doing are different spheres of human activity. It is like the English professor who refuses to allow students to write about a poem until they've heard the official version, what the professorate might say. I've heard similar arguments about teaching Foucault in a first-year course, which I have done. You can't read Foucault, I would hear, without a thorough grounding in Heidegger, Marx, Lacan, Derrida, and so forth.

But of course you can. I can prove it. I have the papers, some brilliant and others not so, but all examples of serious work. The rejection of student writing (and student traveling) is an odd variant on the old argument about Standard and Nonstandard English, about what is acceptable and what is forbidden.

There is a lovely phrase early in chapter 3 of *Imperial Eyes*. Pratt says:

> Despite the upheavals of the period, by the late eighteenth century, the spread of settler society was making interior travel in southern Africa increasingly feasible for Europeans. The flowering of natural history made it increasingly desirable, and the emergence of new narrative paradigms made such travel increasingly writable and readable.

To make travel writable. That was my goal in the course. I thought it could bring rewards in both venues—on the street and on the page. Travel writing is something worth doing because it raises questions about transculturation, brings them forward, makes them a part of everyday life, and not because it can or should somehow solve the problems of a colonial legacy. It is something worth doing.

"The Historians of Cape Town" is exemplary for the ways it negotiates writing in a contact zone. Could it be revised? Of course—all writing can be revised. But we were moving on to Beijing. It was time to start over again. That is just how we do things.

CHAPTER SEVEN

From Arrigunaga to Yoknapatawpha

Ramiro Pinilla and William Faulkner, A Writing Lesson

LAS CIEGAS HORMIGAS

In 1961, Ramiro Pinilla published *Las ciegas hormigas* (The Blind Ants), winner of the 1960 Premio Nadal, one of Spain's oldest and most prestigious literary awards. The announcement was made in early January 1961, and it was for Pinilla, as one reviewer noted, like winning *el gordo*, the fat one, Spain's big-purse Christmas lottery.

As the novel opens, a British cargo ship has run aground in bad weather on the rocky shoals off Arrigunaga, a beach below the village of Algorta on the northern Basque coast of Spain. The villagers, who are facing a hard winter, steal coal from the ship. This is dangerous work. The seas are high and the winds and rain are torrential. The coal must be hauled up over the cliffs that separate the village from the beach. There are old scores to settle within families and between families—and all fear the presence of the Guardia Civil, Francisco Franco's police force.

The novel offers the struggle of one family, the family of Sabas Jáuregui, to represent the struggle of the Basque people after the Spanish Civil War. Algorta was a fishing and farming village to the north of Bilbao, where the Nervión river empties into the Bay of Biscay. Its people and its traditions were under severe challenge. The area was a center of resistance against the fascists and, under the dictator, faced severe repression. And the river was now lined with blast furnaces, the *altos hornos*, or tall ovens producing steel for postwar Europe. Industrialization brought workers from all corners of Spain; the river and the harbor became clogged with traffic and waste. The new history of the region threatened the old orders and patterns of life. The genius of the novel is its intense concentration, locating the forces of history in the struggles of a single family in a local community sharply defined and easily recognizable to Spanish readers. More than one reviewer referred to it as "epic."

And, in trying to describe this novel, more than one reviewer mentioned Faulkner. Pinilla was quick to encourage this reading. When asked about his favorite authors, he mentioned only US writers—Steinbeck, Faulkner, and Caldwell. Throughout his career, he would frequently acknowledge his particular debt to Faulkner and to *As I Lay Dying*. (He hadn't, he said, yet read Hemingway.) In an interview with *Revista Gran Vía*, one of many where he echoed Faulkner's Nobel Prize speech, he said: "I live among these people. I know how they think, what they do, how they live. And I believe in them. Their lives are harsh. . . . I will always believe in the dignity of the human spirit to overcome all that is dark and tragic."

The prize brought national recognition. Until that moment, Pinilla was largely unknown, and the press coverage made much of this fact. (The second prize in the competition went to Gonzalo Torrente Malvido, the son of one of Spain's leading literary figures in the 1960s, Gonzalo Torrente Ballester.) The Premio Planeta was awarded at a gala event, thirteen hundred people at the Hotel Ritz in Barcelona. Pinilla was not there. He was, they wrote, at home in Algorta, on the hills above Arrigunaga, the setting for his novel. In the morning after the prize was announced, they said, Pinilla was up early and back at his job with the gas company in Bilbao; in the afternoons, he would enter the offices of a small publisher, Fher, writing the text for illustrated books and for *cromos*, trading cards for children's albums. (Fher's product list in the 1960s ranged from *Superman* to *Mary Poppins* to *El Cid*.)

According to the reviewers, Pinilla was, like the characters in his novel, an ordinary man. He did not travel in literary circles. He was not an intellectual. He did not sport a beard (like the existentialists); his clothes were not "from Saint Germain de Paris." He was thirty-eight; he had three children; he served two years as a mechanic on the big ships coming in and out of the port of Bilbao, a job he hated (and left) because it kept him from his family. He commuted to two jobs in Bilbao and struggled to make ends meet; he worked in his garden; he kept chickens; he loved to fish and to walk the cliffs along the Bay of Biscay.

So, how to account for this serious, important, and compelling novel? Pinilla did, in fact, work for the gas company, and he did not see himself as an intellectual. He gave himself freely to the newspaper accounts of who he was and where he came from—a simple man who lived in a village to the north of Bilbao. In the late fifties, he began to build a house in Algorta, where he had summered as a child. He named this house "Walden" (having found a companion spirit in Thoreau), and the move from Bilbao to the cliffs above Arrigunaga was, for him, a kind of declaration of independence. By this time, however, Pinilla was already a published writer. He had been writing and publishing detective novels, all (or most) under pseudonyms. (It has been difficult to establish a complete bibliography of his early work.) And, although he was in many ways opposed to organized religion, he had written stories and biographies on commission for the Catholic Church. Pinilla wrote regularly and he wrote for publication; he was not a newcomer.

None of the earlier work, however, would have predicted a novel like *Las ciegas hormigas*. The critics rightly admired its complexity and intensity. They referred to its (or its author's) "profound moral sensibility," one rooted in sharply rendered experience and offering more than the standard argument or stock literary gesture. Pinilla's politics were always on the left. He was, in the 1960s, a member of Spain's Communist Party. In general, however, he felt that all political parties quickly become religions, barriers to individual thought and personal freedom. An "epic novel," by universalizing struggle, gave him a way to speak on behalf of both the essential and the specific. In the prologue to the 2010 edition of *Las ciegas hormigas*, Pinilla said that this novel was, in fact, his "first cry of freedom," a cry of freedom from within and against the historical context of fascism, Franco, and the dictatorship.

The most distinctive feature of this novel, however, is that it was written from multiple points of view, in the manner of, say, *The Sound and the Fury* or *As I Lay Dying*. Pinilla was looking for a way to disappear behind the story, to be, he said, "invisible," to let the story tell itself. He needed to move readers, to invite them into close engagement with the historical moment, here the period after the Civil War, but he could not (or would not) provide a single, controlling narrative presence. As Pinilla said over and over in interviews, what was important to him as a writer was to let the story come from its characters, to leave room for a reader's independent judgment. No single person, the author included, should command the scene.

After the surprising success of *Las ciegas hormigas*, for the next two decades, until 2004, Pinilla wrote regularly but published very little—or, what he did publish received little national attention. This history is complicated and difficult. As a leftist, but not a Basque nationalist, Pinilla was oddly positioned in relation to cultural politics. The mainstream press was conservative in its values; the more experimental press in the Basque country was promoting a literature in Euskera, the Basque language. And Pinilla's relationship with his publisher, Destino, was fraught and contentious. Destino had full control of the rights to the novel and seemed to have little interest in consultation or cooperation—or sales. With a friend, and as a statement, Pinilla developed his own small press in Algorta, Libropueblo, designed as an argument against standard editorial practices, against the high price of books, and against the commercialization of literary culture. Libropueblo's business plan was to promote local authors, to provide workshops and a space for writers to meet and talk—and to sell books at cost from a table in public plazas in the village. There was no plan for broader distribution. Pinilla also edited a magazine devoted to local arts and politics, *La Galea*. In 2000, the offices were firebombed and destroyed by ETA, the terrorist wing of the most radical of the Basque nationalist political parties.

Some of Pinilla's work, then, was self-published, with limited circulation, including two collections of stories set in Algorta. Others were published with small presses in Madrid and Barcelona. By the early 2000s, however, Pinilla had completed a manuscript of about three thousand typewritten pages, a huge novel with a cast of more than fifty characters that told the history of the Basque country through the multigenerational story of two extended families living above the beach at Arrigunaga. It took the saga that was begun with *Las ciegas hormigas* and expanded it to cover the period from 1889 to 1961, from the restoration of the monarchy, through the Spanish Republic and the Civil War, to the era of Franco and the development of Basque nationalism. Like *Las ciegas hormigas*, the new novel was epic in its narrative ambition, and it was told from multiple points of view.

Pinilla struggled to find a publisher for this project until he signed a contract with Tusquets, another Barcelona publishing house, and the editors at Tusquets turned the manuscript into three volumes, all published under the general title *Verdes valles, colinas rojas* (Green Valleys, Red Hills). The individual novels were: *La tierra convulsa* (2004, "The Earth Trembles"), *Los cuerpos desnudos* (2005, "The Naked Bodies"), and *Las cenizas del hierro* (2005, "The Ashes of Iron"). In total, they number more than 2,100 pages. *Verdes valles, colinas rojas* won multiple awards (Premio Nacional de la Critica, 2005; Premio Euskadi de Literatura en Castellano, 2005; Premio Nacional de Narrativa, 2006) and established Pinilla's reputation as one of the most important writers of his generation in Spain.

The title *Verdes valles, colinas rojas* refers to a central thematic division between the green valleys of the old rural order, located on one side, the Arrigunaga side of the Nervión river, and the red hills on the other side, on the left bank of the Nervión—red for the iron ore mined in the mountains, leaving rust in the soil and the streams, and red for the fires of the blast furnaces. The narrative is divided between representatives of two families, the Altubes and the Baskardos, who stand for the competing ways of life in this area: rural and urban, traditional and industrial, wood and steel. And running through this fundamental division are the intertwined, ideological threads that, for Pinilla, define the political history of the Basque country: the church and the monarchy, democracy and dictatorship, nationalism and other varieties of resistance, from the union movement to communism to terrorism.

UN HUECO (A SPACE OR A GAP)

I first came to Algorta with my family in 1982, when I was a Fulbright lecturer at the Universidad de Deusto, in Bilbao. We've come back regularly ever since, just about every six years (for a year) on a sabbatical cycle. I'm writing this essay from our flat, near Arrigunaga, where I walk or bike several times each week. I first met Pinilla in the spring of 2010. He was reading from *Las ciegas hormigas* and taking questions from the audience in a local bookstore, all part of a celebration in honor of the new edition by Tusquets. I spoke with him after and he signed the copy I have next to me on my desk.

While I came to *Las ciegas hormigas* as someone who knew (and loved) Algorta, I came without the usual credentials. I'm not a scholar of Spanish language and literature, nor am I a Faulkner specialist. Long ago I wrote a dissertation on Thomas Hardy, an author often used in comparison with Pinilla. Like Pinilla, Hardy set his novels in a specific, local area, one he called Wessex, in the south of England. But I have spent most of my career teaching writing to first-year college students, which means I have thought long and hard about how to most usefully engage students with written sources.

My concern is to prepare students to work with and from assigned readings, to do more than copy, summarize, paraphrase, or quote. The problem with an undergraduate education in the United States, I think, is imagining how a novice can do meaningful work in the presence of experts—how they can have something to say in the presence of other very powerful and persuasive speakers, how they might get a word in edgewise, how they might use the work of someone else (Edward Said, Adrienne Rich, John Berger) to enable and inspire work of their own, work that can legitimately be said to be original, innovative, memorable, theirs. Pinilla appealed to me initially as a writer who brought me familiar scenes and local history; I came to see his work as an important point of reference to both my teaching and my interest in writers and the work of writing.

In August 2014, my wife and I spent an afternoon with Pinilla in his study in Walden, his house in Algorta. He was open and gracious and generous with his time and attention. We were interviewing him with an article in mind, one that might include a translation of a section from *Las ciegas hormigas*. It seemed to us then, as it seems to us now, odd that his work has not been translated into English. We intended to follow up in the summer of 2015, but, sadly, he passed away soon after we left. (A chapter of the novel, in translation, is now available in Valerie Miles, *A Thousand Forests in One Acorn: An Anthology of Spanish-Language Fiction*.)

We spoke at length about Faulkner. Pinilla was, he said, attracted to the passion and the sense of the "primitive" in Faulkner, to his attention to the land and to place. He was drawn to the edginess and the darkness in Faulkner (*acidez y sombria*). Before his encounter with *As I Lay Dying*, he had been writing regularly, biographies and genre novels, one about every two years, all located in the area, but the writing was never what he had hoped for. He said that *As I Lay Dying* opened for him *un hueco*, a gap or entryway, a working space that allowed him to do something he had not done before. After finishing the novel, Pinilla said to himself, "I can do that." Faulkner, he said, became for him a neighbor, a teacher (*maestro*), a colleague and companion, *un semejante*.

Here is how he described this first encounter with Faulkner in a 2006 interview with Javier Celaya:

> In the 1950s, I discovered Faulkner and became familiar with
> the literature of North America, and this at a time when Spain

was not encouraging cultural exchange. Nevertheless, there was a new American library in Bilbao and I had the luck to get to know its books. Among its authors, the one who made the greatest impression on me was Faulkner, and I was fascinated, above all else, by the sense he gave as a writer of not having, himself, said anything. I came to dislike the feeling, as a reader, that an author was trying to put something in my head, and Faulkner, with his distant language, sometimes prolific and sometimes torturous, gave the impression that he didn't care if anyone understood what he had written, that he was writing only for himself. It bothers me when a novel just ends and everything is wrapped up—period, end of subject. To finish one novel and then begin another, a new one, just doesn't seem to me to be a serious undertaking. . . . I always dreamed of doing something in the manner of Faulkner because his style squared with my way of being in the world and with how I understood story telling.

FAULKNER, THE US STATE DEPARTMENT, AND LA CASA AMERICANA IN BILBAO

Pinilla first encountered Faulkner in La Casa Americana in Bilbao. Founded in the early 1950s (most likely in 1951), Bilbao's Casa Americana was one of seven such centers in Spain. The others were in Barcelona, Cádiz, Madrid, Valencia, Sevilla, and Zaragoza. And there were similar centers throughout the world, including South America. They were managed by the USIA (the United States Information Agency), a branch of the US State Department. They were part of a postwar/ Cold War project to promote American interests throughout the world by providing occasions for an exchange of ideas and cultural values.

The programs sponsored by Casa Americana were not simply focused on American art and culture, however; the organizers also brokered meetings between engineers, architects, physicians, corporate executives, and politicians. In 1960, the director of the Casa

Americana, Abraham Hopman, spoke with Joseph Barr, the mayor of Pittsburgh, Pennsylvania, about formalizing the relationship between these two great, smoky, industrial cities.

And there were obvious links between the US-sponsored initiatives to establish goodwill and mutual understanding and NATO's desire for military bases on the Iberian Peninsula. US national interests were at stake; these were what justified the investment of resources. Still, the libraries served local interests and local readers, like Pinilla, by providing an "American" space in a Spanish city, whatever that might have meant at the time, and by featuring materials that might otherwise not have cleared Franco era censorship.

The Casa Americana in Bilbao contained a library of books, magazines, and newspapers, and it sponsored a regular series of lectures, readings, screenings, performances, and colloquia. According to one report, it had as many as five thousand members, and the library served up to ten thousand readers each month. In 1952, its programs in Bilbao (and at the other Spanish centers) were augmented by US-sponsored "Institutes for North American Studies." The Casa Americana was closed in 1961, although its library and schedule of cultural events were continued through the offices of the US consulate in Bilbao until 1996.

It is tempting to say that Pinilla stumbled on Faulkner, but the encounter was not simply the product of chance. In the 1950s and 1960s, Faulkner was much promoted by the US State Department through its various programs. His books were front and center in libraries like Bilbao's Casa Americana. And he was often sent abroad on tour—to read, to attend conferences, to be interviewed by the press and on radio and television. Faulkner was, as Catherine Kodat said, "one of America's first Cold War cultural celebrities."

In the 1950s and 1960s, Faulkner visited Paris, Cairo, Lima, São Paulo, Tokyo, Manila, Rome, London, and Reykjavik. He proved to be particularly valuable to the State Department in Latin America. Faulkner's first Latin America trip was to Brazil, Peru, and (briefly) Venezuela in 1954; his second was in 1961, when he returned to Venezuela. Faulkner was often asked to discuss US race relations and the politics of the South during and after reconstruction. By both humanizing and historicizing the presence of African Americans and the rural poor in the United States, he provided a view of the country that countered the prevailing image of brute, colonial power. After his 1961 trip to Venezuela, according to Deborah Cohn, an embassy official wrote back to Washington:

> I don't think any other living North American could have affected the minds and hearts of Venezuelans as [Faulkner] did during his two weeks here. . . . The most hardened press elements, the politically unsympathetic, all fell before his charm and his unwavering integrity. Even if nothing else of cultural note happens to us, we will be able to feed upon the effects of his visit for a long time to come.

It should be said that Faulkner was not always a willing participant in cultural exchange. He had to be prodded and cajoled in order to agree to these trips. He resisted the position of official spokesman, and his drinking episodes on the road became part of the mythology that trailed him throughout his career. For US scholars, teachers, and reviewers, his role in relation to the State Department was critical fodder for both the right (who saw him as promoting un-American values) and the left, for whom he was the unwitting pawn of US imperialism. His form of literary modernism was promoted (by, it was said, "New York intellectuals") as valuable because it was abstract and difficult to parse, resistant to statement or summary, something that stood in stark contrast to Soviet-style realism and yet could be said, in its difficulty, to promote both freedom of thought and freedom of expression. (This account is not far from what Pinilla said he valued most in Faulkner's prose—its argument on behalf of freedom.)

How odd, one might say—a high modernist author serving American foreign policy during the Eisenhower administration. In an essay on American studies and its roots in the Cold War, Michael Bérubé looks at the Congress for Cultural Freedom, another international program linked to the CIA, and speaks to this odd conjunction:

> In a perverse yet entirely unremarkable sense, the years of the Cold War were the good old days for American artists and intellectuals—the days when . . . 'the CIA was the NEA. . . .' Imagine if you will, if you can, a time when the work of abstract expressionists and twelve-tone composers was considered vital to national security, a time when the establishment of the pax Americana required the funding and nourishment of a noncommunist left with high-modernist tastes in arts and letters. It is hard to tamp down a sense of nostalgia.

However he was being marketed by the State Department, and whether he did or did not fully serve its ends, Faulkner's work came to be deeply important to an impressive list of Latin American writers, including Jorge Luis Borges, Gabriel García Márquez, José Donoso, Carlos Fuentes, Guillermo Cabrera Infante, Juan Carlos Onetti, Juan Rulfo, and Mario Vargas Llosa. Faulkner's novels, some argue, enabled a break with more restrictive, European forms of realism and helped to shape the role of the novel in the Latin American "Boom." There are many dangers in trying to generalize the Spanish-speaking world in the 1960s. The struggles for political and cultural freedom were not the same in Spain and, say, Colombia. But it was clearly the right time for Pinilla and García Márquez to be reading Faulkner.

It was also the case that Pinilla had Spanish authors (some of them also attentive readers of Faulkner) whom he could have taken as models—Juan Benet, for example, in *Volverás a Región*, and Elena Quiroga in *Algo pasa en la calle*. We know that Pinilla was reading Ramón del Valle-Inclán's *El ruedo ibérico* in the early 1960s. He mentions this in more than one interview, but he mentions it in passing and makes very little of the connection.

El ruedo ibérico was another massive project. The first novel in the series, *La corte de los milagros*, was published in 1927. The original plan was for three trilogies, nine novels in all, covering the period in Spanish history from 1833 to 1898, between the reign of Isabel II and the end of the Spanish-American war. Valle-Inclán only completed the first three novels, but he remains a major figure in Spanish modernism and the novels' important experiments in narrative, particularly in relation to point of view, were innovative. Valle-Inclán wanted to recount history from the point of view of the people, construed broadly, rather than from the point of view of privileged individuals.

Pinilla, in other words, could have worked from (and referenced) Spanish writers, both modernists and his own contemporaries. But he didn't. He chose to reference American rather than Spanish or European literature as a source of inspiration. The American connection meant something to him; it deserves our attention as readers.

The point I have been making is that Faulkner's novels didn't just happen to be circulating in translation in Bilbao and Cartagena. They were there by design. And when Pinilla encountered Faulkner's *As I Lay Dying* in the Casa Americana in Bilbao, the timing was perfect. He was ready for such a book; in that sense, he was the State Department's target audience. In his life and in his writing, Pinilla was looking to define a freedom that he came to associate with "America," a freedom that was Emersonian, individual rather than derived, lived rather than argued, more a course of action than an affiliation with political parties. (Remember: Pinilla named his house Walden. The name remains today, mounted on the stone wall that encloses his garden.)

And for Pinilla in the 1960s, this notion of freedom adhered to (was located in or confirmed by) certain American cultural products, in books and movies—and in popular culture as well as high. One of Pinilla's first publications was a police novel, *Misterio de la pensión florrie* (1944), which was published under the pseudonym Romo P. Girca. It was inspired by *Seven Keys to Baldpate*, a pulp novel written by the US author Earl Derr Biggers (and first published in 1913). *Seven Keys* was made into a Broadway play by George M. Cohan and became the source for several Hollywood films (in 1917, 1929, 1935, and 1947). Biggers would become the author of the Charlie Chan mysteries.

(From a distant point of view, fifty years later, and from the point of view of a native of the United States [from my own point of view, that is], Pinilla's version of America is far too idealized and unexamined to be simply celebrated or taken at face value. But then I suspect that my friends and colleagues in Bilbao would say the same of me—that my appreciation for things Basque, including Pinilla, is idealized and, therefore, a form of misreading.)

Pinilla didn't read his way to Faulkner, at least not as the story of influence is usually told in literary histories. *Las ciegas hormigas* was not the product of broad or focused reading; it was not the result of a thorough study of the traditions of the genre, whether American or European. And when Pinilla encountered *Mientras agonizo* (*As I Lay Dying*) in the Casa Americana in Bilbao, that meeting was as much the legacy of Cold War cultural politics as an instance of literary inheritance. So where (or how) as readers might we understand the work of an author in such a setting?

In a *Paris Review* interview, García Márquez said that while critics like to speak of his debt to Faulkner, he saw the connection largely as a matter of coincidence: "I had simply found material that had to be dealt with in the same way that Faulkner had treated similar material." It was a coincidence, an encounter that opened up new possibilities for an author, a reorientation to place (whether Aracataca or Arrigunaga) and a new way of imagining the relation of place to narrative. I find García Márquez useful as I try to think about the Faulkner in Pinilla. In the *Paris Review* interview, I hear García Márquez describing his version, while reading Faulkner, of finding a *hueco*:

> Around 1950 or '51 another event happened that influenced my literary tendencies. My mother asked me to accompany her to Aracataca, where I was born, and to sell the house where I spent my first years. When I got there it was at first quite shocking because I was now twenty-two and hadn't been there since

the age of eight. Nothing had really changed, but I felt that I wasn't really looking at the village, but I was *experiencing* it as if I were reading it. It was as if everything I saw had already been written, and all I had to do was to sit down and copy what was already there and what I was just reading. For all practical purposes everything had evolved into literature: the houses, the people, and the memories. I'm not sure whether I had already read Faulkner or not, but I know now that only a technique like Faulkner's could have enabled me to write down what I was seeing. The atmosphere, the decadence, the heat in the village were roughly the same as what I had felt in Faulkner. It was a banana-plantation region inhabited by a lot of Americans from the fruit companies which gave it the same sort of atmosphere I had found in the writers of the Deep South. Critics have spoken of the literary influence of Faulkner, but I see it as a coincidence: I had simply found material that had to be dealt with in the same way that Faulkner had treated similar material.

García Márquez, like Pinilla, was one of Faulkner's most interesting and insightful early readers. (*Leaf Storm*, first published in 1955, like *Las ciegas hormigas*, is often linked to *As I Lay Dying*.) Both writers were drawn to Faulkner's approach to land and people, to place and point of view, to Faulkner's way of attending to and recognizing the extraordinary in the local, the epic in ordinary people and in their lives.

READING FAULKNER

It is interesting to think of Pinilla, in the late 1950s, early 1960s, reading Faulkner (in translation) as partner to those US readers who were learning to read Faulkner through the writing and teaching of Cleanth Brooks, one of Faulkner's most important early US critics and champions. From *William Faulkner: The Yoknapatawpha Country* (1963) to *William Faulkner: Toward Yoknapatawpha and Beyond* (1978), and *William Faulkner: First Encounters* (1983), Brooks was determined to teach readers how best to deal with the most confusing and compelling elements in Faulkner's novels.

Yoknapatawpha was the name Faulkner gave to the setting for most of his novels. Faulkner prepared a hand-drawn map of this fictional landscape (as Pinilla drew a map for Getxo, the area that included Algorta), and it closely corresponded to Lafayette Country, Mississippi, his home.

It would be wrong, according to Brooks, to see Yoknapatawpha simply as quaint background, as local color. A reader must attend to landscape and history, and Brooks provides both a history and sociology of Mississippi to counter what he sees as misreadings. But it would also be wrong to think of the novels as "sociology" alone, he argued. They are works of art with their own expressive logic, including exaggeration. The connections between story and history, "fact" and "aesthetic value," were central to Faulkner's fiction and yet could easily be missed or misunderstood by a reader. From the first of these books, *The Yoknapatawpha Country*, Brooks expressed his concern that readers will misconstrue the relation of truth of fact to aesthetic value—of "truth of relevance" to "truth of coherence."

The relationship between the two truths is rarely a simple one. It is not a simple one in Faulkner's novels. Faulkner critics are prone to confuse matters by saying that since the fiction is good, the "facts" must be correct, or that since the facts are incorrect, the fiction is bound to be poor. Faulkner's novels and stories, properly read, can doubtless tell us a great deal about the South, but Faulkner is primarily an artist. His reader will have to respect the mode of fiction and not transgress its limitations if he is to understand from it the facts about the South—that is, he must be able to sense what is typical and what is exceptional, what is normal and what is an aberration. He can scarcely make these discriminations unless he is prepared to see what Faulkner is doing with his "facts."

And, Brooks argued, it was equally misleading to focus on "symbols" and to lose a sense of connection to the particulars of the American South ("a responsible context with its own network of interrelations" and *not* a "grab bag out of which particular symbols can be drawn"). This would be "a grotesque parody of anything like an adequate, careful reading." (Much of the Spanish scholarship on Pinilla's novels, I should add, has been to similarly document and attest to the "real" history, sociology, and geography that underlie his fictions.)

Brooks's account of Faulkner's use of multiple narrators in *As I Lay Dying* sounds remarkably similar to Pinilla's own:

> If the plot of [*As I Lay Dying*] is very simple, the technique of presentation is not. Nothing is told by the author in his own person and on his own authority. Instead, the novel is broken into fifty-nine segments, each assigned to a character in the novel. We are not told to whom the character is addressing his comments. Sometimes, in fact, he simply seems to be talking to himself. Naturally, Faulkner is careful to have each person speak in character, but, since few of the people who figure in *As I Lay Dying* are very literate, Faulkner often endows them with a vocabulary that they do not in reality possess. This is a literary convention that the reader has to accept, and that acceptance, once made, pays handsome dividends. We are thus enabled to penetrate much more deeply into the complexities of their minds than we could otherwise, for we must remember that Faulkner has in this novel denied himself the privileges of an omniscient author.

And, he concludes, "Faulkner's technique of presentation bears directly on an important theme in this novel: the ultimate isolation of every human being from the rest of humanity."

The point of this comparison is not to suggest that Pinilla read Brooks. He most certainly did not; he didn't work that way. What

I hope to suggest is that Pinilla's novel can and should be read as a serious critical reading (and reworking) of *As I Lay Dying*, a reading and reworking whose product is a work of fiction.

ON TRANSLATION

Pinilla said that he would often begin a writing day by reading from *As I Lay Dying*, reading for the rhythm and the music of Faulkner's sentences. This would launch him toward sentences of his own.

I've often wondered just what that might mean—or what it was that Pinilla might have heard and then carried with him to his own prose. Pinilla was, after all, reading Faulkner in translation, and what falls out in a translation is exactly what a native speaker would hear as the rhythm and music in Faulkner's sentences—the odd and insistent syntax, the local idioms, the nonstandard English of the characters. This, in fact, is what those who study translation say about Faulkner, that his language is so specific to local varieties of American English and to the communicative properties of nonstandard English that a close translation is impossible. A translator can follow form (as Pinilla did by creating multiple narrators), but at the level of language, Faulkner is untranslatable.

The language of the monologues in the Caballero/del Hoyo (1956) translation of *As I Lay Dying* (most certainly the translation Pinilla borrowed from La Casa Americana) is largely conventional—there is, for example, no attempt to create the nonstandard syntax or lexicon of a less educated or fluent speaker. And you find the same to be true in *Las ciegas hormigas*. There are occasional words drawn from Euskera, the Basque language, like *txitxiposo*, *caserio*, or *zaborra*, but the Spanish is generally conventional, a "standard" or radio-ready Castilian Spanish.

The most distinctive Faulknerian turn in *Las ciegas hormigas* is at the level of syntax. Pinilla's early readers noted the unusual length of his sentences. According to one reviewer, Pinilla was a better novelist than writer. The novels, he said, were compelling but the language was prolix and the paragraphs unending (*inacabables*). Let me examine this claim by turning to one of the narrators, Ismael, who speaks/thinks in long, insistent, right-branching sentences. Some are several pages long. When they work, they provide a driving forward rhythm, seemingly or potentially unstoppable, and a sense that the world is too full and too compelling for full stops.

And from Faulkner, let me offer the example of Darl, one of the sons in *As I Lay Dying*. You should note the pattern in the syntax—phrases and clauses added one after another after the verb, indicating a kind of driven intensity, one meant to characterize a way of being in the world. (The syntax in the Caballero/del Hoyo translation follows quite closely.) In this passage, Darl is describing his brother, Jewel, as he tries to tame his horse:

> When Jewel can almost touch him, the horse stands on his hind legs and slashes down at Jewel. Then Jewel is enclosed by a glittering maze of hooves as by an illusion of wings; among them, beneath the upreared chest, he moves with the flashing limberness of a snake. For an instant before the jerk comes into his arms he sees his whole body earth-free, horizontal, whipping snake-limber, until he finds the horse's nostrils and touches earth again. Then they are rigid, motionless, terrific, the horse back-thrust on stiffened, quivering legs, with lowered head; Jewel with dug heels, shutting off the horse's wind with one hand with the other patting the horse's neck in short strokes myriad and caressing, cursing the horse with obscene ferocity.

And below is a passage from *Las ciegas hormigas*. In it, Ismael is describing the scene as the villagers head to the cliffs in the midst of the storm to collect the contraband coal. I think the similarities with the Faulkner passage will be obvious, including the punctuation.

To save space, I will provide only the opening and closing of a three-page sentence. This long sentence piles phrase or clause on top of phrase or clause, everything tumbling out at once to indicate both the richness and the inevitability of the scene—first a line of men and animals headed toward the cliff to gather coal, then an extended view of the full community that stands behind them, along with the details of their daily lives, from young to old. At the end of the final passage, after the last semicolon, there is a sudden shift from a sleepy summer Sunday afternoon back to the present time of the violent storm:

But I had just seen them, because we were now there on the top of the hill and seconds later we would become part of the strange caravan: carts like ours drawn by oxen, wagons pulled by donkeys or mules, even animals on their own dragging nothing: mules and donkeys, mostly, with baskets spilling over one and the other side of their flanks, ears pricked, suffering the downpour the same as their masters: people from Algorta, San Baskardo, Berango, Sopelana, Azkorri, accustomed from the time they could barely walk to go down to the beach for coal, not only at first to grasp the net and enter the water up to their waist, but also to help to stack on the highest part of the beach the coal their elders would snatch from the sea, then load it onto the donkey and take it to the caserio; people going from the factories to the fields, where they nevertheless could dedicate two or three hours a day, after their factory work at the drill or lathe or the coke oven or the milling machine, and in the summer even more, not counting the fact that they had to get their animals in the stables ready for the day before they could leave for work in the morning early enough that the blowing of the factory horn could be heard practically on top of them. . . .

. . . boys who would also be occupying themselves by shining their soccer boots, or inflating the ball, or putting both things along with their uniforms, pants and shirts in team colors into the large shared basket that would be carried the next day to the station, or the bus stop, the eleven players and the three or four substitutes, reveling in the task, while they talked of tactics or the girls they had invited to watch the game that afternoon; those from 25 to 45 years old, during those same moments, could be found lying, alone, in their big rustic double bed, the one they had inherited, whistling or reading the sports pages of the local paper, in order to choose the game for that same Sunday afternoon, while they could hear the wife finishing up in the kitchen, gathering the remains of their dinner, now that the little ones were asleep, knowing that that night she would not find her husband asleep when she went in to bed; most all of them silent, punishing the animals unnecessarily, as if they were at fault for finding themselves out of doors that night, bearing up under the wind and the water and having to remain on that seaside cliff until one or another would become so accustomed to it that the moment would arrive (and they would know it beforehand) in which it would no longer matter that the weather kept punishing them or not.

If you read the two novels together, you can find many echoes—some offered, I think, in the spirit of homage, as a gesture toward a teacher, and some drawn initially to provide a kind of scaffolding, to give shape to the early stages of a project whose end was still unimagined and unseen and whose methods were still untested. I'll list just a few as examples.

Both novels take place in the course of a few days, as a family struggles to overcome obstacles en route to a fixed end (the interference of neighbors and acquaintances in both; weather in both; taking a mule cart across a swollen river in one, driving an oxcart and hauling coal up steep cliffs in the other). In both cases, the struggle includes a dead body (a mother, a brother) that must be delivered and buried well past the expected time. Each family (the Bundrens, the Jáureguis) has five children, four boys and a girl. The brothers in each novel share defining characteristics: Fermín (*Hormigas*) and Darl (*Dying*) are both psychologically troubled; Cash, who is building his mother's coffin in *As I Lay Dying*, is preoccupied by his tools; Cosme, the son who is a hunter in *Ciegas hormigas*, his new shotgun. In *As I Lay Dying*, Jewel's father sells his prized horse to complete the journey; in *Las ciegas hormigas*, Cosme's mother gives away his shotgun to protect the family. The youngest child in each novel is defined by an odd preoccupation—Vardaman, in *As I Lay Dying*, for a dead fish, which makes him think of his mother; Nerea, in *Las ciegas hormigas*, for the kittens that must be drowned, kittens she attempts to suckle at her breast. There are older characters in each that speak the language of the church and the Bible, and, in each novel, that language is found to be empty, just words.

There are also important differences. The father's failures of character in *As I Lay Dying* are, for example, central to the plot and to the novel's argument about the American South and its history. *Las ciegas hormigas* is a celebration of the father. His struggle against all limits, whether they be imposed by weather or the central government, come to stand for the struggles of the Basque people.

And, most importantly, while *As I Lay Dying* could accurately be said to lack a single organizing point of view (locating that responsibility in a reader), *Las ciegas hormigas* is organized differently. The eighty-eight monologues are organized into twenty-one sections (like chapters), and the opening monologue in each comes from Ismael, the youngest son. While the monologues from the other characters are spoken (or thought) from the novel's present time, the time of the action, Ismael speaks from a point of more mature reflection somewhere in the future, thinking back to the events that define the novel. He provides, then, a single narrative thread that is lacking in Faulkner's novel. A reader is tempted to identify him with the author, whether this identification is justified or not. A reader can't get lost in *Las ciegas hormigas*.

There is a similarly fixed point of reference in the final monologue in Pinilla's novel. The Jáuregui family has struggled and, it appears, lost everything. A son, Fermín, was killed in a fall while carrying a sack of coal up the face of the cliff; the civil guards have confiscated the stolen coal. In the final scene, narrated by Ismael, the father, Sabas, who seldom speaks, speaks at length to his son. The weather has cleared and the two have walked to the cliff above the beach at Arrigunaga. The novel ends with an extended exchange, one obviously placed as a reader's guide.

Ismael has been trying to catch a giant conger eel, known locally as "El Negro." (El Negro appears again in the opening chapter of *Verdes valles, colinas rojas*.) Sabas tells Ismael that he must never catch El Negro. (Although Pinilla claimed to have come to Hemingway later in his career, there is more than a bit of *The Old Man and the Sea* in the novel at this moment.) He says to Ismael (and I will paraphrase) that he will need the memory of this example of freedom and resistance at the end of the day, when he lies in bed and thinks of the daily struggle to sustain his convictions against the press of words and ideas that will come to him from books, newspapers, radios, and other media, all delivered to destroy his dignity and individuality.

At the end, the reader is in the position of the child, passively receiving a lesson from the father. We are far from Walden and the declaration of independence. The irony here is unacknowledged. At this moment, *Las ciegas hormigas* becomes one more book with a message, more words delivered, perhaps, to deny a reader's dignity and individuality. It is as if Pinilla lost faith in (or lost track of) his narrative scheme, where it was going and what it was doing, or that he couldn't help himself and needed to intervene (compulsively) to ensure that the reader got the point.

I am inclined to argue that Pinilla was unwilling rather than unable to work within the structure of *As I Lay Dying*. While I don't have time to write at length about the three novels that were published together under the general title *Verdes valles, colinas rojas*, and that completed the project begun with *Las ciegas hormigas*, I think these novels demonstrate Pinilla's understanding that this early novel was incomplete, unfinished. This novel, too, opened a *hueco*.

In *Verdes valles, colinas rojas*, the setting remains the same, Arrigunaga, but the method is significantly revised. These later novels give even greater attention to local history, including the ways that lives are shaped or scripted by history and ideology, by governments and banks as well as local customs and local weather. And with this comes a change in the narrative style, including moments of magical realism. (If *Las ciegas hormigas* was shaped by *As I Lay Dying*, *Verdes valles, colinas rojas* was shaped by *One Hundred Years of Solitude*). Each of the three novels is, again, made up of multiple, named monologues, but in *Verdes valles, colinas rojas* the monologues shift between members of two families, Altube and Baskardo. A teacher, Don Manuel, also plays an important role in the dialogues reported by his former student, Asier Altube. The speakers in the novels represent collective identities, some shaped by the rural past and some by the industrial present. They represent collective experience and collective identities in a world shaped by forces and concerns beyond the individual and beyond the family.

And that was the point. If Pinilla began with the impulse to write an "American" novel, he ended writing Basque novels—or novels that were intended to represent the lives shaped by the forces of tradition and modernity that belonged to these people in this particular area in Europe. In this sense, the three novels are a statement on behalf of a Basque nationalism, if the Basque nation could be allowed to contain deeply divided, competing desires and objectives (which, as nationalism was represented by political parties, proved to be impossible).

As I read the clumsiness at the end of *Las ciegas hormigas* and the achievement in *Verdes valles, colinas rojas*, Pinilla did not want a reader to draw the conclusion that Brooks drew from the example of Faulkner's monologues, "the ultimate isolation of every human being from the rest of humanity." Pinilla's later novels are statements on behalf of collective experience, not individual characters or single families. Brooks said of *As I Lay Dying*, "The reader's sense of each character's isolation is strengthened by the fact that in reading the story of the Bundrens the reader is always inside some individual's mind—that person's memory of what was said or done on a particular occasion or his reflections on it or his inner meditations on his or her own plight." The writing during the twenty-year period before the publication of *Verdes valles, colinas rojas* shows Pinilla experimenting with setting, character, history, and narrative style. Pinilla began with Faulkner, ran up against what became the limits of this translation, and then he moved on.

FROM ARRIGUNAGA TO YOKNAPATAWPHA

In *What Is World Literature*, David Damrosch argued that "world literature" is not defined by a collection of great books; it is best conceived as circulation, books traveling across languages and borders, books going abroad and being read, usually in translation, in various ways and to a variety of ends. He says, "My claim is that world literature is not an infinite, ungraspable canon of works but rather a mode of circulation and of reading, a mode that is as applicable to individual works as to bodies of material, available for reading established classics and new discoveries alike." And, he says, as a novel moves into the sphere of world literature, "far from inevitably suffering a loss of authenticity or essence, a work can gain in many ways. To follow this process, it is necessary to look closely at the transformations a work undergoes in particular circumstances." I've tried to do something like that. My concern in this essay has been to consider *Las ciegas hormigas* as a critical rewriting of *As I Lay Dying*, one mediated by translation, appropriation, and local (or national or commercial) interests. And I think of this writing, the exchange that took place between Faulkner and Pinilla, as, in Damrosch's sense, an instance of world literature.

Pinilla made good use of Faulkner, but how do we name this exchange? I am hesitant to use the word *imitation*—to say that Pinilla imitated Faulkner, since I think that is simply inaccurate. There is much in his work that is both distinctively his and specific to the Basque country, including the labor. And if I were to speak of *influence*, I would be making the relationship between Pinilla and Faulkner deeper and more profound than it was, or is. The novel does not represent the kind of primal struggle with a prior text (or a master text) as charted memorably by Harold Bloom in *The Anxiety of Influence* and other, later books and essays. The roots are just not that deep.

In a compelling essay, "American Modernisms in the World," my colleague Gayle Rogers speaks of "alliances" and "routes of exchange" to describe the ways American novels, including Faulkner's novels, have traveled across the planet. I find "alliance" to be a useful term in thinking about Pinilla and Faulkner, here at the end of my essay, since it suggests a determined interaction between two parties, one that is contingent, not permanent, set in the context of multinational institutions (and "routes of exchange"), and intended to be mutually beneficial.

I chose to give Arrigunaga the initial spot in my title, "From Arrigunaga to Yoknapatawpha," to put the attention where it belongs, on a writer and his work. In the end, Pinilla wasn't receiving something; he was making something.

CHAPTER EIGHT

In Search of Yasuní

Once on the water, we could see the rain forest pushing close to the river. The town of Coca, a depot on Ecuador's Rio Napo, was already slipping away, disappearing behind a bend. It was early morning. There had been a week of heavy rain and trees had fallen into the river as the bank washed away. With the pressure of the current, branches emerged from the brown water and waved up and down, as if saying goodbye. Older branches, now blackened and leafless, broke the surface and then silently disappeared.

After an hour, we began to see wildlife: toucans and parrots, movement in the trees that suggested monkeys. On one log, I spotted four turtles sitting in a row, each with a butterfly on its head. (I took this as a sign, an offering; it turned out to be the standard postcard image from the Napo valley.) I had been on the lookout for caiman, freshwater alligators, which entertained our guides—sharp-nosed men who grew up along this river. The men were from one of the local tribes, most likely Huaorani, Kichwa, or Shuar. They wore T-shirts and baseball caps.

There were three of us on this trip: Tim, a biologist; me, an English professor; and Carly, a student from our summer program in Ecuador. We were at the far eastern edge of the settlements below the foothills of the Andes, and we were at the far western edge of the rain forests of the Amazon Basin. Between here and Manaus, the first "real" city to the east, twelve hundred miles away, far into Brazil, a brave traveler would find few roads and little else other than indigenous villages, some seldom visited by the twenty-first century.

Tim, Carly, and I were headed two hours downstream, deep into the Ecuadorean rain forest, speeding toward the headwaters of the Amazon in long, thin metal canoes, each with two 175-horsepower Yamaha outboards on the back—one to navigate downstream, two to push the boat back up. And then we would have to cross land, hop another canoe, and travel three hours down the Tiputini River to our destination, the Tiputini Biodiversity Research Station at the edge of Yasuní National Park, where we would find ourselves in one of the richest and most biologically diverse environments left on the planet. And so it was a surprise to see a column of fire reaching high into the sky as we rounded the bend and prepared to disembark.

Our motor canoe docked in a small cove tucked in beside a heliport. As we entered the area, we passed first the fiery tower and then storage tanks from a small refinery, marked *REPSOL*. We carried our packs up a long, steep flight of stairs to a covered area and what looked like passport control. There was a sign in the staging area: *It has been 96 days since the last industrial accident.* Men in uniforms checked passports, reviewed our immunization cards (yellow fever vaccinations were required), and placed our luggage on a belt to be screened.

But of course this was not an immigration desk or a customs office; we had not left Ecuador. We had entered what a couple of us began to refer to as Repsol-landia. (There is an irony here. Repsol is a Spanish oil company. While the Spanish were early to colonize what is now

Ecuador, they came late to its oil fields.) The Ecuadorean government is selling drilling rights ("concessions") to large multinationals (most of this brokered through the Chinese) with the understanding that Ecuador will get not only signing fees but royalties keyed to levels of production and a promise of future free (or low-cost) gasoline. Ecuador does not have a diverse economy. It relies primarily on tourism and the sale of oil—and the sale of oil is the larger source of income, in 2016 providing more than 40 percent of the federal budget. Foreign multinationals are given access to oil (including future reserves) with the understanding they will be responsible, by law, for maintaining appropriate safeguards for the environment. The jury is out on whether these standards can or will be enforced.

Drilling in these areas has always been controversial. There is a substantial and still-unresolved class-action suit against Chevron over the environmental damage created by Texaco (the previous owner) between the 1970s and the 1990s. The drill sites remain riddled with pockets of tar, sludge, and spooge. The groundwater is contaminated with salt and heavy metals. The 312-mile pipeline to Quito has spilled nearly seventeen million gallons of oil (six million gallons more than the Exxon Valdez left in Prince William Sound). There have been ugly confrontations with remote indigenous communities, sometimes leading to deaths on both sides. The political and legal battles are brutal, including threats of violence. Both local and world environmental action groups have this remote location on their radar screens.

After we stepped off the canoe, we were screened against a checklist of those registered to visit the Tiputini Research Station. Repsol wanted to ensure that the boat wasn't bringing yellow fever into a work area, and they wanted to ensure that we were not journalists or lawyers or activists or mercenaries or members of Greenpeace. As we left the staging area we were told: "Remember, you are not allowed to take any photographs"—no pictures until we left Repsol-landia, which meant no pictures until we reached the next river.

To get to Yasuní, then, we needed to cross from river to river (from the Napo to the Tiputini), and we had no choice but to cut across restricted land. We drove for two hours in a brightly painted, open-sided bus decorated with pictures of parrots and jaguars and toucans, a relic from an Amazon tour company, and we drove across a new gravel road, passing trucks and police cars and newly constructed villages for local indigenous workers and their families—clusters of cedar houses on stilts with corrugated tin roofs. The bus would stop now and then as a favor to pick up a mother and her children, to pick up kids coming home from school or men carrying bright bags of potatoes. The moms were very young—or so they appeared. The children would stare at us with big brown eyes. We had been given bag lunches. It was hard to decide whether we should or shouldn't offer them our Oreos.

At one point we passed a small, open evangelical church with a wooden cross over the door. These impromptu churches were a common sight in the small villages along these rivers. In the 1950s, eager young North American missionaries arrived in this area: men and women home from the war, inspired by their faith and their nation's new standing in the world, eager to spread the word of Christ and arriving with the skills necessary to fly and service small planes. The airfields along the Napo were built to support the oil companies. A town named Shell became a launching spot for missionaries intent on bringing the gospel to the natives.

In 1956, five missionaries flying out of Shell were killed by a Huaorani tribe after landing with gifts in a jungle clearing; the airplane was destroyed, the cloth-covered fuselage ripped to pieces. Their death was covered by a photo essay in *Life* magazine with the title "Martyrdom in Ecuador." Two of the wives remained in Shell with their children to continue the missionary project. The cedar-clad house of the pilot, Nate Saint, and his wife, Marjorie, has become something of a shrine.

The bus ride took two hours. We passed freshly cut timber and freshly turned soil. We drove parallel to a pipeline that ran alongside the road—one large pipe for oil, one small pipe for gas; sometimes aboveground, sometimes below, occasionally cantilevered over a stream. We passed a house with *Rap Music NY* painted on the side. We passed company signs that warned of the dangers presented by the pipeline. We passed newly cut and newly numbered roads. And we passed a hand-painted sign that said, in Spanish, *It has been 143 days since the last.* . . . Bouncing along at a fairly brisk pace, I couldn't make out the last word. It was either resurrection or insurrection.

I was in Ecuador for the month of July 2015 to teach a summer course at the Andes and Amazon Field School, a collection of thatched huts perched on the banks of the Rio Napo about seventy-five miles (by winding road) south of Coca. The Field School is run by Tod Swanson, a professor of religious studies at Arizona State University. Tod is married to Josefina, a Kichwa woman who grew up on or near the land he now owns and occupies. His mother and his father, a physician, were among the missionaries who settled in Shell in the 1950s. Tod was raised as a child in a Kichwa community; he is fluent in the language. When he went to school in Quito, the capital city, he lived with Marjorie Saint, the woman whose husband had piloted the plane destroyed in the jungle clearing.

Tod's extended family—brothers-in-law, sisters-in-law, a vast network of nieces and nephews, and those from their village—helped to build and maintain the station: a lovely, harmonious complex of wood and river stone, thatched cabanas, and open meeting areas. Tod lives there every summer with his wife and his four children. It is a beautiful place in a beautiful spot, looking out over a sharp bend in the Napo.

The advanced graduate and undergraduate students are here to learn Kichwa, most of them with the thought of future fieldwork. Many are from Brigham Young University. Tod's mission is to record and preserve Kichwa language and culture. He has a vast archive of taped songs, stories, conversations, and explanations (of, for instance, the uses of medical herbs, hunting practices, the design of ceramics, the identities of plants and animals). Kichwa people accompany us on our hikes—describing scenes, plants, or practices—while Tod (or one of the advanced students) would translate.

Tod is particularly interested in how the Kichwa people across time have defined the place and role of the human. The Kichwa exist and understand themselves not as individuals, the defining center, but as part of a network that includes not just family and neighbors but plants, trees, and animals, even rock and soil. The rain forest knows you—and you know who you are through the ways you are known by, say, the trees.

Along the Napo, there are about fourteen hundred acres of rain forest under Tod's protection. Sadly, there is little animal life left. It was hunted out years ago, once rifles took the place of bows and arrows. (The government has recently outlawed the use and sale of bushmeat.) But there is remarkable diversity in the plant life, including some huge hardwood trees that would surely have been forested had they been on unprotected land.

We hike here, as always, with Kichwa guides, like Elodia and her brother, David. Both are distinctively indigenous—short, brown-skinned, dark-eyed, and sharp-featured. Elodia had her first child at thirteen or fourteen; she is now, we figure, about forty-five. She had ten children (eight survived). While her grandson is ten years old, she also has a daughter who is nine. She is quick to laugh.

David (Da-víd) looks younger. He is friendly, fit, and engaging, not much over five feet tall. He has rock-star good looks, but he is quiet and serious—until, that is, he makes bird calls or a loud hunter's whoop at the high ground in the forest.

David was trained by his father, a great hunter who was much loved by these trees around us. David moves easily through the forest with remarkable endurance and agility. He says the trees guide him as he hunts or walks or sleeps at night on the forest floor. After his father died, for five years David was unable or unwilling to enter the forest. And then he did. And he asked for guidance. And the tall tree that most closely shared his father's spirit welcomed him and embraced him. This is what he said.

When we arrived for our hike, it was pouring rain. At the trailhead, we stumbled out of the pickup truck—ten of us. Elodia gathered palm leaves to use as umbrellas and we headed off down the trail, the mud sucking at our boots. At one point we stopped, as we often did, to talk about where we were and what we saw. Someone asked about the rain.

David said that the trees know their people, the people who belong, just as they know the plants and animals around them. For someone like David, there is, in the motion and the sound of the trees, information about who is here and who is where, and what is new and what is familiar, and this is valuable information for a hunter or for someone walking deep without direction. When there is something or someone new in the forest, the trees notice. And they are at attention. When they are unhappy or uncertain about who is entering, David said, they call for rain.

Later that night, around a fire in the thatched meeting house, I asked my students: "Well—did we learn a lesson or were we taught one?" Both, they decided.

The landing at the Tiputini Biodiversity Station was like the landing before, minus Repsol. We had had our second long boat trip of the day, and it was now late afternoon, dusk. We mounted a steep set of rickety wooden stairs to enter an open dining hall.

From the dining hall, it was a slippery, muddy hike down a hill and across a wooden bridge, with a moss-covered rope the only aid for balance, and then up a slippery, muddy path to the area where we would stay—small, cedar cabanas built on stilts, along with a larger building, "the Lab," which housed laboratories for the research scientists (all graduate students), as well as a library and a classroom or lecture hall.

The Lab was air-conditioned and included "dry boxes" we could use for our computers, cell phones, or iPads. It was hot, rainy, and humid, and the moisture, we were warned, could make a circuit board a little wonky. By ten o'clock a.m. each day, I was drenched in sweat. When it rained, and it did, I couldn't get any wetter. We were far, far from cell phone service or internet. We had no hot water and we had electricity for only three hours in the morning, three hours in the evening. Around us the forest was alive with sounds—a chorus of birds, bugs, and animals. Tim had a device that would pick up bat calls and broadcast them in a frequency we could hear, so at dusk, sitting on our porch, we had bats in the chorus as well. I could listen for hours, and I did, but I couldn't tell a monkey from a bird. Our guides were all locals, men who had grown up hunting and fishing in villages along the Tiputini. They had amazing ears and eyes and were, without exaggeration, "at home" in the rain forest. We had two days with them. I never learned to hear with anything like their precision, depth, or understanding, but I did develop new ways of seeing.

Outside the Lab was a giant ceiba tree, maybe two hundred feet tall and fifteen feet in circumference. The ceiba (or kapok) has soft wood and so, to support its height, it sends out wings or flying buttress roots, themselves more than six feet tall. There were four of them with this tree, spreading out from the base, gracefully curved like a cupped palm and shaped like large sails. They were covered in soft green moss. The area between the roots harbored a host of other plants, glossy and colorful—fern, hosta, palm, narcissus, and coleus. The ceiba is one of the few trees not covered in vines (perhaps it is too tall) or strangled by the matapalo, a vine that begins with bird droppings high in the canopy, leaving seeds in the tangle of moss and flower where they send down roots, some of which encircle the tree and choke it like a giant snake. The combination of weight at the top and pressure at the bottom brings down most of the trees we see on the forest floor.

The ceiba was a striking presence and impossible to take in at a glance. You couldn't see the top, since it was above the canopy. You couldn't quite fit the elaborate, broad lower trunk into your line of vision. It couldn't be framed by a camera—at least not if you wanted the photograph to carry any meaning. A person could fall in love with this tree. I looked for it every day.

In Kichwa, the language of the villages around our home base on the Napo, the tree is called *samona*. As the tallest tree, it is considered to be a chief, custodian of the forest. It is inhabited by two spirits, one above and one below. The spirit in the crown looks over the forest and keeps watch. If the spirit is troubled, you can hear it at night, high up in the canopy, making the crying sounds of a child. The spirit at the bottom will sometimes appear as a short man with a round head, which he uses to beat against the buttress roots. The boom resounds through the forest like thunder. The Kichwa, too, will pound on these roots if they should become lost, waiting for a sound in response.

The area at the base of the tree is a perfect place to seek shelter when it rains, but this, we were told, can be dangerous. Later, along the Napo, we asked our Kichwa guide, Pedro, about these spirits. He told the story of a young girl who had become pregnant, the daughter of his cousin's sister. When pressed, the girl confessed that she had not had sex with anyone—well, actually, only with an odd, round-faced man who kept tempting her in her dreams.

Her child was born deformed. It had a round face, small eyes, large ears, with hair on its arms and back. It looked like a bat. The parents doused the child with gasoline and burned it alive. If the mother suckled that baby, Pedro said, she would bear more and more of these spirit children.

The Tiputini Biodiversity Station was established by the Universidad de San Francisco, in Quito, in 1994, about two decades after the first major highway was built to connect the capital city with the Amazon Basin, all part of a conflicted effort by the central government to lay claim to this previously remote territory—to lay claim to its resources, primarily oil; to identify new areas for tourism; and to take steward-ship of one of the planet's last wilderness areas. Before 1975, the major highways from Quito went south to Guayaquil, a major port on the Pacific, and west to the beaches, where a traveler would also find plantations and access to Ecuador's most famous site, the Galapagos Islands. Now a major highway connects Quito to the east. For more than three hundred miles it runs up and over the Andes (highest point: the Papallacta Pass, at over fourteen thousand feet) and then drops down—the deep green hillsides cut by long, thin cascades of water—to a rich green valley that is home to several rivers feeding the Amazon. This highway was cut at great cost and great effort. It is continually plagued by landslides and washouts; it is a highway designed to support the traffic of heavy trucks.

The Yasuní National Park was created in 1979. It includes thirty-eight hundred square miles of dense rain forest and all that this forest holds. In 1989, Yasuní and the surrounding Huaorani territories were declared a UNESCO "Man and the Biosphere Preserve." Within its borders live two tribes in voluntary isolation. They have turned their backs on motorbikes and chain saws, social services and public schooling, in order to preserve control over their lives and, they hope, their lands. In the fraught language governments use to manage indigenous peoples, they are called "uncontacted," an ominous term suggesting what is true, that the next step belongs not to the hunters and gatherers but to some powerful arm of the nation.

What distinguishes the Yasuní National Park, however, is its incredible biological diversity. It is one of the two richest areas in the world for reptiles and amphibians, and it is home to the highest number of globally threatened vertebrates of any place on earth: toads, turtles, macaws, warblers, spinetails, antshrikes, Amazonian eagles, jaguars, monkeys, wild dogs, giant otters, manatees, tapirs, armadillos, and peccaries. It is the richest area in the world for trees and shrubs, and it is the richest area in the world for bats. While there is not as much global data for insects, it is safe to say that bugs belong on this list as well. According to a recent report, "a single hectare of forest in Yasuní is projected to contain at least 100,000 insect species," approximately the same number as all insect species found in all of North America.

With this concentration of life—human, animal, insect, and plant—the land within and around the Yasuní National Park stands as a last sanctuary, a kind of Noah's ark for much that has been historically concentrated in this, the Amazon Basin. And the waters are rising. The total area of rain forest in the Amazon Basin continues to shrink dramatically as timber is cut for global markets and forest is turned to grazing land to provide beef for markets in Hong Kong and Chicago. The Chinese are investing heavily in oil production and hydroelectric dams; Ecuador's government has learned to rely on Chinese investments to finance its agenda.

The money is in oil. And the area under Yasuní National Park contains the largest untapped oil field in Ecuador's piece of the Amazon Basin. There is a long and often ugly history of oil exploration on this side of the Andes. Not far from Coca, where we began our journey, is the town named Shell and another, Lago Agrio, named after Sour Lake, Texas, the original home of Texaco. The east–west highways were built to connect these oil fields with the capital, Quito. The land beyond the towns of Shell and Lago Agrio already bears the legacy of the oil boom of the 1970s: rusted pipelines; pollution above- and belowground; abandoned drilling sites and oil towns; villages and families disrupted by boom and bust, by new ways of working and living.

But the future is not all belowground. Although threatened by the world's reliance on fossil fuels, Yasuní's geography—a moist lowlands within the rain shadow of the Andes—will shelter it from the consequences of global warming, or so it is projected. While in the future much of the rain forest will have more severe cycles of wet and dry and, therefore, become something other than rain forest, the areas around the Tiputini and its tributaries are likely to remain wet year-round. They will then become a last refuge for those local species responding to climate change—a crowded, vicious, wet, and watery Noah's ark.

We spent Saturday and Sunday at the Tiputini station, and our schedule included two long hikes each day. At our first briefing, Diego Mosquero, the program director, warned us: "The trail will have steep sections. If you slip in the mud, your first instinct will be to reach out and grab something. Don't. It might be something that doesn't want to be grabbed."

I was in a group of four that included Tim and Carly along with Louisa, a biologist from UNAM (the National Autonomous University of Mexico) who was scheduled to lecture the following week at the Universidad de San Francisco in Quito but was eager to spend a few days at their research station. Our guide was Mayar Rodriguez. With twenty years' experience, he was the dean of guides at TBS; he had trained all the others.

Whatever Mayar's colonial heritage, it was worn away by time and circumstance, although along the Napo he would still most likely be called a *colono*. He was light-skinned and grey-haired but short and compact with indigenous features, including a quick smile that showed missing front teeth. He spoke Spanish and a local language; he had some English, predominately words for plants, bugs, and animals (caterpillar, swallow, kapok tree). He knew the Latin names for plants. Mayar had grown up on the Tiputini and had spent years hunting and fishing to feed his extended family. He had a hunter's eyes and ears and a local's familiarity with the voices and the spirits in the rain forest. His pack contained a high-powered telescope and a very fancy digital camera with quite amazing powers to quickly frame, focus, and capture distance shots. He was pleased to be a part of the conservation project at TBS. We joked that he had traded his gun for a camera.

The trails were deep with mud. We wore high rubber boots (also protection from snakes). My old knees struggled with the up and down of the trails, which were often quite slick; Mayar, noticing this, made me a walking stick. We walked briskly.

On the trail, Mayar would stop suddenly, walk a yard or so away to bring into view something hidden. He spotted a tiny bright red mushroom, no bigger than a plastic pinhead on a two- or three-inch white stalk. He dug it carefully from a rotting trunk and placed it in his hand. (Later, he would return it to its place in the forest.) This was a cordycep, the "zombie fungus" whose spores would spread to insects, where they would root and suck the life out of the unsuspecting bug. We saw one growing out of a now-dead ant; one growing out of a dead grasshopper; one growing out of a three-inch larva.

Mayar had the same eye for birds and monkeys. He'd stop, spot something in a tree (sometimes color, sometimes sound, sometimes movement), we'd gather as silently as we could, he'd point, and it would take the rest of us several minutes to locate the toucan, the wooly monkey, or the barbitos. While we were searching the canopy, he'd snap a photo to show us what (often) we had missed. Or, with the photo and with his help, we'd start again and end with a sighting.

What did we see? We saw seven of the eleven species of monkeys in the area: pocket monkeys (pigmy marmosets), tamarin monkeys, wooly monkeys (churungos, including one who fell about two stories from the canopy), howler monkeys, spider monkeys, an owl monkey, a dusky titi. At one point, we came upon pocket monkeys sucking sap from holes they made in an old, tall ceiba. They were driven away by larger, yellow-backed tamarin monkeys—lovely animals to see, although we were initially taken aback by their aggression. One tough-minded pocket monkey, a little guy, stayed behind to sneak back when the tamarins weren't watching. And there was a large wooly monkey above, looking down and observing the action. It was quite amazing. I had monkeys running and jumping around me the way I have squirrels on the patio of my Western Pennsylvania home.

I was the first to spot a two-toed sloth. He was slow and noisy as he made his way from branch to branch to the left of the trail. The Spanish word for sloth is *perezoso* (the lazy one); this lazy one was moving deliberately from tree to ground to have his morning dump. (Sloths only poop on the ground—and not every day.) He saw us and stopped and stared. We had clearly upset his schedule. And he started slowly, very slowly making his way back again up the tree.

We spent an afternoon at 150 feet, high up in a platform on a rise (in a ceiba tree). The platform gave us a view across the rain forest canopy. We saw birds and monkeys, but what I most remember are the branches of that tree. There at 150 feet each branch wore an elaborate, crowded garden, like a sleeve filled with ferns, ivy, coleus, creepers, and flowers, some waxy leafed, some delicate—and epiphytes, like the zebra bromeliad, which we saw in the dozens, all large, brightly colored striped urns, turned up and waiting to catch the rain.

From the ground, too, or from a slow float on the river, we saw birds: ivory-billed toucans, jacamars, cuckoos, river swallows, oropendola, parrots, barbitos (like gold finches, but larger), ani, flycatchers (yellow and black), vultures, a jay (as blue as an indigo bunting), a kingfisher, hoatzin ("stinkbirds"), hummingbirds, and curassows (turkey-like waterbirds with bright red markings). I can list them; I can number them, like acquisitions; I can check them off in my bird book. There is not much more I can do. I would often try to snap pictures of the birds and monkeys, even the sloth, but I was too slow or too unsteady; all I would get is a blur of color in a blur of green.

Sunday morning we went by boat and trail to a lake, where we used a canoe to explore (a traditional canoe, cut from a single log). I had seen some animals across the lake when we arrived and assumed they were capybara (dog-sized water rats). As Mayar paddled us out, we faced a panicky school of fish, swirling and jumping, and then we saw a giant river otter raise his head out of the water in a display of territorial defiance; he was long-necked, gorgeous, his fur spotted light brown with yellow, dripping water. He looked at first like a big snake. He showed his teeth and growled with a loud, menacing voice.

We later learned that this is a rare and endangered species. We paddled some more. The otter who had confronted us had gone to get his buddies. Strength in numbers. We had another display; this time three otters lined up in front of us, their necks raised high out of the water (these are big animals, as long as six feet), and they showed their teeth and they roared their roars. And then they were gone. It never occurred to me to grab a camera.

As we prepared to leave Yasuní, I told Mayar that I would like to buy some of the photos he had taken while we were hiking. I figured this would be simple. I'd leave some money; he could send digital images to my email address. He said it wasn't allowed. I spoke with Louisa, whose Spanish is better than mine and who might come across less like a greedy American consumer. She spoke with Diego, making a case not only on behalf of Mayar's art but on behalf of the research station. Diego said, "We just don't do that here."

"What was that all about?" Carly asked. "I don't know," I said. "Maybe they didn't want to upset the balance of things." Perhaps the reasons were local and deep—a sense that one must honor the spirit of the rain forest, not sell it. But, then again, perhaps TBS wanted control over these images. Perhaps Diego didn't want Mayar to be freelancing, to be making extra money on the side, creating competition among the guides. Who knows about balance in a place like this?

My wife and I sleep by the Rio Napo in a cabana with a thatched roof. We listen to the river at night and to the sounds of the rain forest around us. There is a small possum in the thatch by the dining hall, bats in the rafters of the hall, and a chicken who visits the classroom where I teach, all of whom I've seen. And there are two tree frogs who live in the thatch above our room. We don't see them, although we have tried. At first we thought they were *in* the room and I went hunting for them in the corners and under the bed.

They peep back and forth to each other from dusk until around ten o'clock p.m., when we fall asleep. Perhaps they go on. They are in the thatch, talking back and forth. We hear one clear peep, a single burst that says something, and it is answered by another, a peep saying something back. This goes on and on at regular intervals.

The tree frogs sound like satellites in the night sky—the ones you'd hear in 70s cartoons or space movies. Or they sound like the spring peepers around my patio in Pittsburgh. But they are not satellites, and they are not spring peepers around my Pittsburgh patio. I don't know how to see them, and I don't quite know how to name them. We sleep with them easily; it is comforting, here along the Napo, over the Andes from Quito, near the last outpost before the thick forest reaching into Peru, then Brazil.

I asked Tod about these tree frogs and what they were called. He wasn't sure. He thought maybe *piri-piri*. But then he said, "No, that's not it."

AFTERWORD

In Ecuador, with my students, I wrote every day and I would put some of my pages into the pool for class discussion. The task I set for the class was to write in the first person, to place an emphasis on description, and to write in a narrative frame. Of course they could tell their own stories. But there must be equal attention to Ecuador, to place. They were reporters. Ecuador was to be their beat, every day.

In the final week of class, they would shape their daily "fragments" into two finished essays. One could be a personal essay, their story; the other would report on what they saw, heard, and learned while living on the banks of the Rio Napo. It would be a story of Ecuador. Their job was to bring the news home to others who were not (or who would never be) there.

In writing about Yasuní National Park, I was writing about the rain forest and about conservation, conservation as a conceptual problem (or a writing problem) as well as a problem of national and global politics. It was important to me to try my hand at the genre I was teaching. For my students, I wanted to highlight moments and concerns that belonged to our written record of the trip, and I wanted my voice to be a part of what was shaping the sound and sense of our time on the river.

This was the first time, however, that my daily writing amounted to an essay I would continue to work on at home. Once I was back in Pittsburgh, I sent "In Search of Yasuní" to a number of magazines and journals that publish travel writing. I received nothing but rejection letters, although a surprising number included encouraging and detailed comments from editors. I also asked for help from colleagues in our MFA program. The most frequent comment I received was that I needed to "add more of my personal journey."

But I didn't want to write about my personal journey; I wanted to write about Ecuador. That was the writing I was teaching. I was fortunate to find a very supportive editor, Melinda Lewis, at *The Smart Set*, whose regular section, "Journeys," has included prize-winning essays by leading travel writers.

Three years later, in May and June of 2018, I again taught a summer course, this time in Cuba, a country we had always wanted to visit. We lived in the residencia of the José Martí Institute for International Journalism, located on the Avenue of the Presidents, central to a once grand, now crumbling neighborhood in Havana. The residencia was called El Costillar de Rocinante, which translates as The Ribs of Rocinante, Don Quixote's almost skeletal horse. In fact, the neighborhood includes a very large statue of Don Quixote, seated ramrod straight on his rearing horse, lance in hand, where both the man and his horse look like skeletons. It is an eerie and dramatic sight, here in the capitol city of an island nation whose people are struggling and whose interests have been thwarted at every turn by the United States and its allies.

The course was Travel Writing. I taught two, three-week intensive sections, different students in each, and I was wondering what I would find, particularly given the conditions on the ground—six hot and steamy weeks with students from all over the Arts and Sciences and the School of Engineering, all women, all writing five hundred words per day for fifteen days, writing after long hours out on the streets or after visiting some of the island's more remote towns and villages.

And I taught these courses without any of us having access to Xerox machines or printers or the internet. Everything we did was shared via a thumb drive; all the teaching was oral, even the commentary. Lots of reading out loud. Lots of conferences.

The students had chosen a short, summer semester in Cuba. A writing course was the price of admission. The students were mostly rising juniors, but the commitments to writing were as mixed and uncertain as any in a required first-year writing course. I didn't have a great experience in my last full (spring) semester writing course on campus, an advanced course on style that drew English majors. Travel Writing was my last hurrah, and, as I say, I wondered what I would find. The students had an intense engagement with Havana and the small villages we had visited by bus. But there was not much time for anything (or anyone) to settle in.

Still, the final papers were a pleasure to read—the kind of engaged, surprisingly eloquent student writing I like to share with colleagues. I was buoyed reading them. I sent a selection off to my usual audience.

I remember thinking that, for me, this moment marked the end of something, for better and for worse. I had taught intro writing courses just about every semester since 1973. I had read stacks and stacks of student papers, thousands of them. I had learned to read and to value student writing for what it is and what it does, and for what it can and can't do, particularly over time.

As I prepared this collection, *Like What We Imagine*, I was surprised to see how consistent my teaching has been from beginning to end, from Basic Writing in 1975 to Travel Writing in 2018. I was teaching writing as a way for writers to generously and productively locate themselves in worlds they don't and can't command, worlds of people and worlds of words—an appropriate lesson, I believe, for the work of academy and for life as an adult.

Although I've had invitations, I won't teach another writing course. It is too hard. And it seemed to get harder for me (rather than easier) in the final years. Why? Because I didn't want to fail, and the possibilities for failing increased as students' interests and mine grew more and more remote. But preparing students to write these essays has been the preoccupation and delight of a long career. Or so I said to myself when I got to the bottom of that last stack.

CHAPTER NINE

That Went for a Walk /
On the Camino de Santiago

"A line is a dot that went for a walk." Paul Klee, the Swiss artist, is said to have said this. I've not been able to track down where or when, but the phrase has traveled widely and is used in any number of exercise books for artists, both children and adults. It calls attention to the hand and the page, the artist and the medium, and to questions of freedom and constraint or spontaneity and inheritance. In his *Pedagogical Sketchbook* (1925), a book prepared for students at The Bauhaus, Klee wrote this version of that slogan: "An active line is a walk, moving freely, without a goal."

A pilgrimage is an active line, clearly. But the pilgrims we met on our walk were not *moving freely*. They were driven or compelled, and they were following a well-defined line marked by yellow blazes. They had a guidebook. And they had a goal.

In our case, the goal was the great Cathedral of Santiago de Compostela, said to be the burial place of Saint James (Santiago). This is the *greater* of the several Jameses in the New Testament, the first of the apostles to be martyred. In paintings or carved in retablos, he is figured as a pilgrim, walking with a staff, carrying a gourd, and

wearing a scallop shell on his wide brimmed hat as a badge. He is also figured (although, on the Camino, not nearly so prominently) as Santiago *Matamoros*—a warrior on a white horse, with a sword, slaughtering infidels or "moors" as part of the Christian reconquest of Spain.

The original pilgrimage route to Santiago stretched from Eastern Europe to the Spanish cathedral city on the Atlantic (in that spit of coastline just north of Portugal). It was one of the three great pilgrimage routes of medieval Europe. (Rome and Jerusalem marked the others.)

We were walking the Camino to fulfill a promise we had made to ourselves many years ago, after Joyce, the pilgrim in these photographs, had survived two surgeries and two long rounds of chemotherapy in treatment for two separate breast cancers. She's always there in these scenes, although she's not always easy to spot.

We began our pilgrimage in Roncesvalles, a small stone village high in the Pyrenees at the border of France and Spain. We attended the pilgrim's mass at the Iglesia de la Real Colegiata de Santa Maria (thirteenth century), and the service included readings (in many languages) by pilgrims who were staying the night in bunkbeds in the old pilgrim's hospital that was attached to the church. In his homily, the priest said that we should use our time walking the Camino to be quiet—to free ourselves from distraction and to listen for what we might hear.

After the mass, when we signed the registry, we were asked for our motive. Was ours a spiritual journey? Were we primarily interested in the history and culture of the medieval pilgrimage route to Santiago? Were we in pursuit of adventure? A physical challenge?

Actually, all of the above were true, but to the official in Roncesvalles we said, "spiritual," which would guarantee us a document at the end, the *Compostela*, prepared for us by the reception office next to the cathedral, where we would present a kind of passport full of stamps, gathered from inns and churches along the way, to prove our claim. The *Compostela* reads:

The Chapter of this Holy Apostolic and Metropolitan Cathedral of Compostela, custodian of the seal of the Altar of St. James, to all the Faithful and pilgrims who arrive from anywhere on the Orb of the Earth with an attitude of devotion or because of a vow or promise make a pilgrimage to the Tomb of the Apostle, Our Patron Saint and Protector of Spain, recognizes before all who observe this document that: _____ has devotedly visited this most sacred temple with Christian sentiment (*pietatis causa*).

We were moved by the spirit, but also by a long-standing interest in the history and culture of Spain, and the art and architecture of the medieval church.

In retrospect, though, our goal can be simply stated. The route we followed, the Camino Francés, covered 756 kilometers, or 470 miles, a little more than the distance between Pittsburgh (our home) and Chicago. It was a long walk and it traversed three mountain ranges, the highest point at about 1,500 meters. We wanted to make it all the way. We wanted to complete this long walk, step by step, hour by hour, and day by day.

Every day we would start out with *peregrinos* from all over the world— Germany, France, Korea, Japan, Sweden, Australia, the United States. But because people walk with a different pace, soon we were walking alone.

We walked usually six hours per day. We stayed in *hostals* (our own room!) and *albergues* (eight to sixteen to a room, a shower down the hall, and a chorus of snoring at night)—all in small villages, many with buildings and bridges built in the twelfth to fourteenth century to support the pilgrimage and the pilgrims. We were served the pilgrim's dinner—local wine, a salad, bread, and (usually) lentils or stew.

According to the *Codex Calixtinus* (a twelfth-century guide for pilgrims),

> the *Camino* takes us away from luscious foods, it makes gluttonous fatness vanish, it restrains voluptuousness, constrains the appetites of the flesh which attack the fortress of the soul, cleanses the spirit, leads us to contemplation, humbles the haughty, raises up the lowly, loves poverty.

We were too tired for much in the way of voluptuousness. And we learned that while the Camino may be good for the spirit, it is very hard on the feet.

"Traveler, there is no road; you make your own path as you walk." *Caminante, no hay camino; se hace camino al andar.* This is one of the slogans for the road—and it is a theme song for the Camino de Santiago. It is reproduced on postcards and T-shirts; you'll see it as graffiti; you'll find it framed, painted, or in tile on the wall in bars, inns, and *albergues.*

It comes from a poem by Antonio Machado, part of a collection of "proverbs and songs" published in *Campos de Castilla* (1912). (Castilla is one of the historic regions of north-central Spain. It is the centerpiece of the Camino Francés.) Here is the full text with a translation:

Traveler, your footprints are what make	Caminante, son tus huellas
the road you walk, nothing more;	el camino y nada más;
traveler, there is no road;	caminante, no hay camino,
you make the road as you walk it.	se hace camino al andar.
By walking you make the road,	Al andar se hace camino,
and as you look behind	y al volver la vista atrás
you see the path you	se ve la senda que nunca
will never walk again.	se ha de volver a pisar.
Traveler, there is no road,	Caminante, no hay camino,
only a wake in the sea.	sino estelas en la mar.

Robert Frost said that to be a good reader, you have to follow a metaphor to see where it leads. Then you decide if it serves. In a talk to students at Amherst College, he said:

What I am pointing out is that unless you are at home in metaphor, unless you have had your proper poetical education in the metaphor, you are not safe anywhere. Because you are not at ease with figurative values, you don't know the metaphor in its strength and its weakness. You don't know how far you may expect to ride it and when it may break down with you. You are not safe in science; you are not safe in history.

Machado's poem didn't work for me. I couldn't ride it. I had it in my head, as I had other songs and poems, to pass the time and to mark the rhythm of my steps, but I couldn't follow it on the ground. The metaphor was compelling, to be sure, *you make your own path as you walk*, but it had no descriptive truth or power, which made it ring hollow on a hard five-hundred-mile walk, a walk along a path that was well marked and that could be (and often is) walked a second time (or more). I couldn't use it to think about where I was and what I was doing.

On the Camino, there *was* a road. And it was defined by more than my footprints—by maps and signs, by daily schedules; by memories, histories, and desires; and, unless there had been a hard rain, by the dusty footprints of others. All were as present as sharp rocks, bandages, and blisters.

"Facts for the walker, fictions for the viewer." This comes from a larger display of word and image prepared by Hamish Fulton, the "walking artist" whose walks all over the world (including Spain) are represented as art in galleries and museums: collections of photos, primitive maps, names and dates, timelines and elevations, and usually a few words, words that seldom amount to sentences but offer themselves as slogans. *Eyes, Feet, Road.*

Fulton, for example, spent seven days and seven nights walking

through Myrdalssandur, an outwash plain in southern Iceland, in March 1996. The exhibit includes a poster with the details of place and time, and these words stamped in random clusters around the word "boulder" at the lower center: *stones, gravel, rock, black sand.* If you go to Hamish Fulton's website, which is certainly worth a visit, you can see photographs of his walking shoes as well as the paths they have walked. But what you can't ignore is the sound of his footsteps, loud and crisp, one after another for as long as you choose to listen.

If, in the US, we have a national road poem, a prime candidate (at least for my generation) would be Robert Frost's "The Road Not Taken." I've taught this poem often, and often used it as an opening moment in my lower division, general education course, Reading Poetry.

Frost used this poem as a test. Someone who read poems badly, who would read this poem, he said, with the eyes only (and not with the ears)—someone who read poorly would say, "Well, the poem tells us that we have to take the untrodden path." Or, "Frost says that we have to head out on our own. We can't follow the crowd." Something like that.

But if you read with your ears—listening for a sense of the character, the person speaking; listening to the situation, the dramatic moment of this utterance—then you find yourself inside the head of someone who is thinking about someday thinking back, hoping to be able to cast himself or herself in a heroic narrative. It is not a poem that offers advice. It is a poem about growing old. And it is a poem about the desire to (and the problem of) making a life (or a walk) worth something.

I shall be telling this with a sigh
Somewhere ages and ages hence:
Two roads diverged in a wood, and I—
I took the one less traveled by,
And that has made all the difference.

The poem acts out the desire to make something out of the ordinary, to give a walk a higher purpose. I would ask my students: "Who walks that way, already writing the story he or she will tell *somewhere ages and ages hence*? What are the alternatives? What else can you do with a walk in the woods?"

And I would ask them to read this stanza out loud, to find a way of inhabiting the moment that begins with a sigh. What does it sound like? Is it rehearsed? Spontaneous? Earned? Empty?

I would ask: Does it speak an eternal longing? Is this a story of artistic creation? (I would phrase those two questions in a deep, professorial voice.) Or is this person a blowhard, a show-off, a bully, a narcissist? How *does* a person become someone, become present in the world in a way that matters?

I have come to think that the speaker is like an old friend of mine who insists on telling stories of our high school football games, over and over again. My students, undergraduates usually, believe in the future, as they should. They are quicker to forgive this old man than I am.

Here is the full text of Frost's poem "The Road Not Taken." In the first two stanzas, you can see (and hear) the poet setting up not just the terms and conditions of the walk but a tone of voice to use on the road.

Two roads diverged in a yellow wood,
And sorry I could not travel both
And be one traveler, long I stood
And looked down one as far as I could
To where it bent in the undergrowth;

Then took the other, as just as fair,
And having perhaps the better claim,
Because it was grassy and wanted wear;
Though as for that the passing there
Had worn them really about the same,

Then comes the dramatic gesture, where the tone changes; the speaker waxes poetic and speaks self-consciously to an admiring audience: "Oh, I kept the first for another day!"

And both that morning equally lay
In leaves no step had trodden black.
Oh, I kept the first for another day!
Yet knowing how way leads on to way,
I doubted if I should ever come back.

And, finally, we are invited to step back to assess the moment—the speaker is rehearsing a speech he plans to deliver to a rapt audience at some point in the future. In my skeptical reading of the poem, where I think of it as a cautionary tale, the speaker is an older man speaking to the young, perhaps young women. He could be a teacher addressing his students.

I shall be telling this with a sigh
Somewhere ages and ages hence:
Two roads diverged in a wood, and I—
I took the one less traveled by,
And that has made all the difference.

Facts for the walker; fictions for the viewer.

I started to walk down a hill of purple heather. The sun was straight ahead of me. Soon it would be getting dark, the sun would sink into the Atlantic. The colours of the vast panorama before me were sumptuous. The people were still working in the fields and I asked everyone if it was far to Triacastela. Four kilometers downhill, they said. The smell of grass and clover was sweet and powerful, and it was a great happiness, for once, not to have cheated. But it was more than four kilometres and it was not all downhill. It's not far, they told me, when I asked

again. Obviously, they were used to this. They told the same story to all pilgrims. The last half an hour's walking was pure agony, but the pain was nothing to the pleasure and the expectation as the rooftops of Triacastela gradually came into view.

This is the great Irish novelist Colm Tóibín, writing about his time on the Camino de Santiago. The passage above comes from a chapter, "A Walk to the End of the Earth," in Tóibín's book of travel essays, *The Sign of the Cross: Travels in Catholic Europe* (1994). The opening to this chapter sets both context and tone: "Two months later, on a Sunday in July, I set out to walk from Leon in the north of Spain to Santiago de Compostela. I did not check the distance because I knew, from the very beginning, that I was going to cheat."

And cheat he does. It is a fallen world, right? Pilgrims know this. It is why they have to walk. With sore feet, or bad weather, or the desire for another glass of wine, Tóibín abandoned the trail to grab a cab or a train or a bus to get him to his next stop.

In Tóibín's account, stories can never be trusted; this is clear from the outset, including (I think we must believe) the stories told by writers who write such lovely sentences about grass and clover, about the vast panorama. "Soon it would be getting dark, the sun would sink into the Atlantic. The colours of the vast panorama before me were sumptuous. . . . The smell of grass and clover was sweet and powerful, and it was a great happiness, for once, not to have cheated." The writer may be a skeptic when it comes to the stories we tell, the slippage between word and deed, the temptations we face as tellers, but all the pressure here still is on a prose that can show something happening on the Camino de Santiago, something important.

Or so I was thinking. In August, I had retired from a career as a professor of English. I taught literature and composition, reading and writing. I had loved this job, all of it, pretty much nonstop, but I knew it was time to leave. For forty-five years I had measured the days, weeks, and months by stacks of student papers. They'd come in on Tuesdays. I'd return them on Thursdays. Wednesdays I would read student writing all day, often into the night. And I was pretty good about honoring this commitment. I wrote comments to direct revision, and a revised paper was due the following week. And then we'd start over again.

Revision, sending students back to work on something they (or we) had started—this was the core of my teaching, including my teaching in a class, say, on the Victorian novel. I graded on the basis of what I saw happening from draft to draft. Progress? I could point to it—or not. Revision was a next step, a going a little farther down the road. It was grace in action; it was *the heart in pilgrimage, gladness of the best, something understood*—as George Herbert once said of prayer.

And I measured my progress as a teacher by the Wednesday moments when I had to stop to say, *Wow*, or to read a sentence or two to Joyce, or to send a student paper on to friends. *You have to read this.* I came to fear that we couldn't pull it off anymore, the distance between us was too great, even though the evidence said that things were still pretty much OK.

We walked from Roncesvalles to Santiago de Compostela, passing through the great Spanish cathedral cities of Burgos and Leon. In 2016, 277,854 persons walked the Camino de Santiago. In 2017, there were 301,106. As I am writing this in early November 2018, the number has already reached 317,170. The Camino de Santiago is well known and well traveled.

And yet, for most of our time on the Camino, we walked alone. There were always other pilgrims in the towns we scheduled for the end of the day. And we would see them in the morning, drinking coffee and fresh orange juice, eating *tortilla de patatas*, although many left before we did, before the sun was up. It was common to see faces a second time during the day, but it was rare to see anyone a third time. We were in our seventies, older than most, and walked at our own determined pace.

We would start out together, of course, but Joyce walks faster than I do. This is just a matter of natural gait. I walk faster than she going uphill, but much more slowly going down. On the flat she would quickly pull ahead and sometimes disappear from view. On an average day, we'd each settle into our own stride, then after a half hour the one ahead would stop for water and to let the other, usually me, catch up. We didn't make a point of matching stride for stride six hours a day. It would have been a distraction.

There were several long climbs—one for eleven hours, two days at our pace. The downhill route was brutally steep and had long stretches of scree. This took us into the green valleys of Galicia, with stone villages that smelled of wood smoke and cow dung. We'd hear the sounds of the herds, of cows and drovers, of sheep bells and sheep dogs, tractors and Land Rovers. And, as earlier along the Camino, we would hear the distinctive call of cuckoos. They sounded just like the cuckoos in Disney movies—or in my dad's old German clock, the family heirloom that no one wanted. A surprise but no surprise. As a boy, every seven days it was my job to pull the chains and raise the metal pine cone weights to reset the clock that hung by his chair. Even then I thought the sound more than a little silly. But here, in the mountains, the sound of the cuckoos rang clear and true; it was welcoming, even reassuring.

On flatter land we walked through vineyards, wheat fields, and long tracts of sunflowers, bright yellow in the spring, but with brown, drooping faces in the fall. Because I had a winter work schedule, we divided our walk between the two seasons. Summer was too hot and too crowded.

In the spring, we saw the damage done by *jabalíes* on the banks of grass, bramble, and fern that ran along the side of the trail, but we saw no wild boar. In the vineyards, the vines had been pruned severely, right down to the old stock. Each was maybe three feet tall, stocky at the core. The remaining, trailing branches, one on each side, pointed in unison to the north and the south. Each vine looked like a tiny old man—dark, scraggly, and twisted, struggling to get up and out of the ground.

The vineyards held troops of these little old men, lined up as though for battle. I thought of my dad, ninety-eight, once a talented musician and a fine athlete, chief of staff at the city hospital, now a baby in a bed in a nursing home. When I ran out of songs or poems, and I was sick of just counting numbers, I would count his heartbeats as I walked.

In the fall, after the harvest, we could eat the sweet grapes left on the vines, now five to six feet tall and with branches trained along guide wires to support the hanging fruit. It was a dry fall, and the morning air had the spicy smell of holm oak, dry grass, and broken fern.

We walked one fall morning out of Reliegos de las Matas, a stone village (population 236) in the province of León. This was the region of sunflowers, not vineyards. Suddenly, the drove road we were walking was overtaken by a flock of sheep, at least two hundred. It was as though they came on cue. At the back of the flock were the animals with sore feet and sore joints, hobbling along—as were we by that time in our journey. And behind them was the sag wagon—a tractor with a pen that held those who could walk no further. We suspected that the sheep were marching to the *matadero*, the last stop for them on life's dusty road. This is the area famous for *lechazo*, or roast suckling lamb.

We completed our pilgrimage in October 2018. This, actually, was our second journey on the Camino. In 1973, while living in Oxford, we took our bikes via train and ferry to Santurce, north of Bilbao, to bike to Burgos and from there to Santiago. This was before the Camino was a major tourist initiative. We planned the trip by consulting history books, including Walter Starkie's *The Road to Santiago*. We took notes on the key stops in the ancient pilgrimage route, many of them distinguished by early Romanesque churches, hospitals, and monasteries, some still in ruins in the 1970s, many now well restored.

As I planned the trip in Oxford, where I was writing a dissertation, it never occurred to me to work from a topographical map. And so we were more than a little surprised to find the mountains of northern Spain. After several difficult days of biking up and down mountain roads, we abandoned our bikes to complete the journey by walking, by hitchhiking (called *auto-stop*, a safe and common practice at the time), and by bus and train. This was still Franco's Spain. He died in 1975.

While on our bikes, we would see armed members of the Guardia Civil, wearing their black patent leather, tricorn caps, guarding the passes into and out of the Basque Country.

It was on this trip that we first saw the art and architecture of the pilgrimage route, where local craftsmen had carved retablos and painted saints on canvas, all following images carried from France and beyond. San Roque, with a dog licking the wound on his leg. The young Virgin, *Purisima*, dressed in blue, standing on a cloud of angels, cradled by a quarter moon. Michael, the archangel, with a young boy's face and elaborate flowered robes, standing on the chest of the devil, a spear in his hand.

Later, we moved to Pittsburgh, got jobs, raised children, and began to collect *santos* from northern Spain, all of them carved from wood, most of them from the 1600s. For the two of us, these recalled pieces we had seen standing unguarded in the old stone churches along the way. We'd walk into town, ask at a bar, and be directed to a house

where a wounded man or a widow in black, faces marked by the struggles of the Spanish Civil War, would gather keys and open doors so that we could sit and rest.

Most of my photographs from the Camino are of a long road winding off to the horizon, with a lone figure in midrange—or in the distance. Our good friend, Mary Rawson, would say: "Received the recent installment of your flipbook. Lovely." Joyce said, "Would you please stop taking pictures of my butt." But I loved these long shots—a dot on a road that stretched far beyond what I could see. There was a hard truth in them, something about time and distance.

What I most recall of our pilgrimage is getting up every morning and putting one foot in front of the other, day after day, for seven weeks. Joyce was my guide. She is also writing about the Camino. She says, "There were days when I was tired and sore and cold, even scared, but there was never a day when I didn't want to take the next steps."

We'd both been teachers. We were now retired. For us, the long walk was a way of moving on, finding the swing and rhythm of this new thing, the pace and timing. It was like sitting down to work on

sentences—struggling at first to strike a line, then to hold the pieces together while still pushing forward, and then, finally, hearing that *click* at the end. That click is usually a pleasure, sometimes a surprise, but it is always a relief. Arriving in Santiago, we knew we had done something that mattered, at least for the moment, and we'll tell that story to anyone who will listen.

REFERENCES

Appiah, K. Anthony, and Amy Guttmann. *Color Conscious: The Political Morality of Race*. Princeton UP, 1996.

Arnold, Matthew. "The Function of Criticism at the Present Time." *Culture and Anarchy and Other Selected Prose*. Penguin Classics, 2018.

Bartholomae, David. "Back to Basics." *Journal of Basic Writing*, forthcoming.

Bartholomae, David. "Composition." In *Introduction to Scholarship in Modern Languages and Literatures* (3rd ed.), edited by David G. Nicholls, MLA, 2007, pp. 103–25.

Bartholomae, David. "Everything Was Going Quite Smoothly Until I Stumbled on a Footnote." *Writing on the Edge*, vol. 20, no. 1, Fall 2009, pp. 73–85.

Bartholomae, David. "From Arrigunaga to Yoknapatawpha: Ramiro Pinilla and William Faulkner." *Critical Quarterly*, vol. 58, no. 3, October 2016, pp. 61–85.

Bartholomae, David. "In Search of Yasuní." *The Smart Set*, November 2017, https://thesmartset.com/in-search-of-yasuni/.

Bartholomae, David. "Inventing the University." In *Writing on the Margins*, pp. 60–85.

Bartholomae, David. "Inventing the University at 25." *College English*, vol. 73, no. 3, January 2011, pp. 260–282.

Bartholomae, David. "Teacher Teacher: Poirier and Coles on Writing." *Raritan*, vol. 36, no. 3, Winter 2017, 25–53.

Bartholomae, David. "That Went for a Walk/On the Camino de Santiago." *The Smart Set*, May, 2019, https://thesmartset.com/a-long-walk/.

Bartholomae, David. *Writing on the Margins: Essays on Composition and Teaching*. Bedford/St. Martin's, 2005.

Bartholomae, David. "Writing with Teachers: A Conversation with Peter Elbow." *CCC*, vol. 46, no. 1, 1995, pp. 62–71.

Bartholomae, David, and Anthony Petrosky. *Facts, Artifacts, and Counterfacts: Theory and Method for a Reading and Writing Course*. Boynton/Cook, 1986.

Bartholomae, David, and Anthony Petrosky. *Ways of Reading: An Anthology for Writers*. 8th ed., Bedford/St. Martin's, 2008.

Bartholomae, David, with Beth Mataway. "The Pittsburgh Study of Writing." *The Best of the Independent Rhetoric and Composition Journals 2011*, edited by Steve Parks et al., Parlor Press, 2013.

Bérubé, Michael. "American Studies Without Exceptions." *PMLA*, vol. 118, no. 1, 2003.

Bishop, Elizabeth. "At the Fishhouses." *The Complete Poems: 1927–1979*. Farrar, Straus, and Giroux, 1983.

Bloom, Harold. *The Anxiety of Influence: A Theory of Poetry*. 2nd ed., Oxford UP, 1997.

Brantlinger, Patrick. *Crusoe's Footprints: Cultural Studies in Britain and America*. Routledge, 1990.

Brooks, Cleanth. *William Faulkner: First Encounters*. Yale UP, 1983.

Brooks, Cleanth. *William Faulkner: Toward Yoknapatawpha and Beyond*. Louisiana UP, 1978.

Brooks, Cleanth. *William Faulkner: The Yoknapatawpha Country*. Louisiana State UP, 1963.

Brower, Reuben. *The Fields of Light: An Experiment in Critical Reading*. Oxford UP, 1968.

Brower, Reuben, and Richard Poirier. *In Defense of Reading: A Reader's Approach to Literary Criticism*. E. P. Dutton, 1962.

Canagarajah, Suresh. "The Place of World Englishes in Composition: Pluralization Continued." CCC, vol. 57, no. 4, June 2006, pp. 586–617.

Cavell, Stanley. *Conditions Handsome and Unhandsome: The Constitution of Emersonian Perfectionism*. University of Chicago Press, 1990.

Cavell, Stanley. *Must We Mean What We Say? A Book of Essays*. Cambridge UP, 2003.

Celaya, Javier. "Interview with Ramiro Pinilla." *Dosdoce*, November 10, 2006. https://www.dosdoce.com/2006/11/09/ramiro-pinilla/.

Cobo Lozano, C. "Ramiro Pinilla, Nadal 1960." *Revista Gran Via*, n.d., p. 4.

Cohn, Deborah. "Faulkner, Latin America and the Caribbean." *A Companion to William Faulkner*, edited by Richard C. Moreland. Blackwell, 2007.

Cole, Ernest. *House of Bondage: A South African Black Man Exposes in His Own Pictures and Words the Bitter Life of His Homeland Today*. Random House, 1967.

Coles Jr., William E. *The Plural I: The Teaching of Writing*. Holt, Rinehart and Winston, 1978. Republished with two additional essays as *The Plural I and After*. Boynton/Cook (Heinemann), 1988.

Damrosch, David. *What Is World Literature?* Princeton UP, 2003.

Dennis, Carl. *Poetry as Argument*. University of Georgia Press, 2001.

Derrida, Jacques. *Of Grammatology*. Translated by Gayatri Chakravorty Spivak. Johns Hopkins UP, 1998.

Emanuel, Lynn. *Then, Suddenly—*. University of Pittsburgh Press, 1999.

Empson, William. *The Face of the Buddha*. Edited by Rupert Arrowsmith. Oxford UP, 2016.

Empson, William. *Seven Types of Ambiguity*. 1947. New Directions, 1966.

Empson, William. *Some Versions of Pastoral: A Study of the Pastoral Form in Literature*. 1935. Penguin Books, 1966.

Empson, William. *The Structure of Complex Words*. 1951. Harvard UP, 1989.

Faulkner, William. *Mientras Agonizo (As I Lay Dying)*. Translated by Augustín Caballero and Arturo del Hoyo, in *William Faulkner, obras escogidas, Vol. 1*. Aguilar, 1956.

Faulkner, William. *As I Lay Dying*. Vintage, 1991.

Foucault, Michel. *The Archaeology of Knowledge and the Discourse on Language*. Translated by A. M. Sheridan Smith. Vintage Books, 1982.

Foucault, Michel. *Discipline and Punish: The Birth of the Prison*. Translated by Alan Sheridan. Vintage Books, 1995.

Foucault, Michel. *Language, Counter-memory, Practice: Selected Essays and Interviews*. Edited by Donald F. Bouchard. Translated by Bouchard and Sherry Simon. Cornell UP, 1980.

Foucault, Michel. *The Order of Things: An Archaeology of the Human Sciences*. Vintage, 1994.

Frost, Robert. "Education by Poetry. (On Metaphor)." *Frost*. The Library of America, 1995.

Frost, Robert. "To John T. Bartlett." *Frost*. The Library of America, 1995.

Frost, Robert. "The Road Not Taken." *Frost: Collected Poems, Prose and Plays*. Selection and notes by Richard Poirier and Mark Richardson. The Library of America, 1995, p. 103.

Fulton, Hamish. *Walking: Artist.* https://hamish-fulton.com/.

Gawande, Atul. "The Learning Curve." *The New Yorker.* January 28, 2002, pp. 52–61.

Gorra, Michael. "Evasive Maneuvers." *New York Times.* July 13, 1997. https://archive. nytimes.com/www.nytimes.com/books/97/07/13/reviews/970713.13gorrat.html.

Graff, Gerald, and Cathy Birkenstein. *"They Say/I Say": The Moves That Matter in Academic Writing.* 2nd ed., Norton, 2010.

Griest, Stephanie Elizondo. "Beijing." *Around the Bloc: My Life in Moscow, Beijing, Havana.* Random House, 2007.

Haffenden, John. *William Empson among the Mandarins.* Oxford UP, 2005.

Harkin, Patricia, and John Schilb, eds. *Contending with Words: Composition and Rhetoric in a Postmodern Age.* MLA, 1991.

Heaney, Seamus. "The Government of the Tongue." *The Government of the Tongue: Selected Prose, 1978–1987,* Farrar, Straus and Giroux, 1989, p. 105.

Hearne, Vicki. *Adam's Task: Calling Animals by Name.* Knopf, 1986.

Hessler, Peter. *River Town: Two Years on the Yangtze.* Harper Collins, 2002.

Hoagland, Tony. *What Narcissism Means to Me.* Graywolf Press, 2003.

Horner, Bruce. *Rewriting Composition: Terms of Exchange.* Southern Illinois UP, 2016. See chapter 2, "Language."

Horner, Bruce. *Terms of Work for Composition: A Materialist Critique.* SUNY P, 2000.

Horner, Bruce, Min-Zhan Lu, Jacqueline Jones Royster, and John Trimbur. "Language Difference in Writing: Toward a Translingual Approach." *College English,* vol. 73, no. 3, January 2011, pp. 303–21.

Klee, Paul. *Pedagogical Sketchbook.* Faber and Faber, 1968.

Kodat, Catherine. "Unsteady State: William Faulkner and the Cold War." *William Faulkner in Context,* edited by John T. Matthews. Cambridge UP, 2015.

Koeneke, Rodney. *Empires of Mind: I. A. Richards and Basic English in China, 1929–1979.* Stanford UP, 2004.

Laskas, Jeanne Marie. "Empire of Ice." *GQ,* September 2008.

Leavis, F. R. *Education and the University: A Sketch for an "English School."* 1943. Cambridge UP, 1979.

Leavis, F. R. *The Living Principle: English as a Discipline of Thought.* 1943. Chatto and Windus, 1995.

Leavis, F. R. *New Bearings in English Poetry: A Study of the Contemporary Situation.* 1932. Faber and Faber, 2011.

Lerner, Ben. "Contest of Words." *Harper's Magazine,* October 2012. https://harpers.org/archive/2012/10/contest-of-words/.

Lerner, Ben. *Mean Free Path.* Copper Canyon Press, 2010.

Loynaz, Dulce Maria. *A Woman in Her Garden: Selected Poems of Dulce Maria Loynaz.* Edited and translated by Judith Kerman. White Pine Press, 2002.

Lu, Min-Zhan. "Conflict and Struggle: The Enemies or Preconditions of Basic Writing?" *College English,* vol. 54, no. 8, December 1992, pp. 887–913.

Lu, Min-Zhan. "From Silence to Words: Writing as Struggle." *College English,* vol. 49, no. 4, April 1987, pp. 437–448.

Lu, Min-Zhan. "Living-English Work." *College English*, vol. 68, no. 6, July 2006, pp. 605–18.

Lu, Min-Zhan. "Professing Multiculturalism: The Politics of Style in the Contact Zone." *CCC*, vol. 45, no. 4, December 1994, pp. 442–458.

Lu, Min-Zhan. "Redefining the Literate Self: The Politics of Critical Affirmation." *CCC*, vol. 51, no. 2, December 1999, pp. 172–194.

Lu, Min-Zhan. *Shanghai Quartet: The Crossings of Four Women of China*. Duquesne UP, 2001.

Lunsford, Andrea. "Rhetoric and Composition." *Introduction to Scholarship in Modern Languages and Literatures* (2nd ed.), edited by Joseph Gibaldi. MLA, 1992, pp. 77–100.

Machado, Antonio. *Campos de Castilla*. Catedra (January 1, 2006).

Machado, Antonio. *The Landscape of Castile*. Translated by Mary G. Berg and Dennis Maloney. White Pines Press, 2005.

Márquez, Gabriel García. "The Art of Fiction No. 69." Interview with Peter Stone. *Paris Review*, Issue 82, Winter 1981.

Márquez, Gabriel García. *One Hundred Years of Solitude*. Penguin, 2007.

McPhee, John. *Draft #4: On the Writing Process*. Farrar, Straus and Giroux, 2017.

Mellix, Barbara. "From Outside, In." *Georgia Review*, Summer 1987, pp. 258–267.

Meyer, Michael. *The Last Days of Old Beijing*. Bloomsbury USA, 2010.

Miles, Valerie, ed. *A Thousand Forests in One Acorn: An Anthology of Spanish-Language Fiction*. Open Letter, 2014.

Miller, Richard. *As If Learning Mattered: Reforming Higher Education*. Cornell UP, 1998.

Miller, Richard. *Writing at the End of the World*. University of Pittsburgh Press, 2005.

Moi, Toril. *Revolution of the Ordinary: Literary Studies after Wittgenstein, Austin, and Cavell*. University of Chicago Press, 2017.

Ogden, C. K., and I. A. Richards. *The Meaning of Meaning: A Study of the Influence of Language upon Thought and of the Science of Symbolism*. 1923. Harcourt Brace, 1989.

Ohmann, Richard. *English in America: A Radical View of the Profession*. Wesleyan UP, 1976.

Osnos, Evan. *Age of Ambition: Chasing Fortune, Truth, and Faith in the New China*. Farrar, Straus and Giroux, 2014.

Petrosky, Anthony. *Crazy Love*. Louisiana State UP, 2003.

Pinilla, Ramiro. *Las ciegas hormigas*. Tusquets, 2010.

Poirier, Richard. *The Performing Self: Compositions and Decompositions in the Languages of Contemporary Life*. Rutgers UP, 1992.

Poirier, Richard. *Poetry and Pragmatism*. Harvard UP, 1992.

Poirier, Richard. *Robert Frost: The Work of Knowing*. Oxford UP, 1977.

Poirier, Richard. *A World Elsewhere: The Place of Style in American Literature*. Oxford UP, 1966.

Pratt, Mary Louise. "Arts of the Contact Zone." *Profession 2006 (MLA)*, 1991, pp. 33–40.

Pratt, Mary Louise. *Imperial Eyes: Travel Writing and Transculturation*. Routledge, 1992.

Quammen, David. "Deadly Contact." *National Geographic*. October, 2007.

Raritan. "Memorial to Richard Poirier," vol. 29, no. 4, Spring 2010. For Edmundson, see the "Editor's Note."

Richards, I. A. *Basic English and Its Uses*. Norton, 1943.

Richards, I. A. *Mencius on the Mind: Experiments in Multiple Definition.* 1932. Curzon Press, 1997.

Richards, I. A. *Practical Criticism: A Study in Literary Judgment.* 1929. Transaction Publishers, 2008.

Rickert, Thomas. *Acts of Enjoyment: Rhetoric, Žižek, and the Return of the Subject.* University of Pittsburgh Press, 2007.

Rogers, Gayle. "American Modernisms in the World." *The Cambridge Companion to the American Modernist Novel.* Edited by Joshua Miller. Cambridge UP, 2015.

Rose, Mike, ed. *When a Writer Can't Write: Studies in Writer's Block and Other Composing-Process Problems.* Guilford, 1985.

Russo, John Paul. *I. A. Richards, His Life and Work.* Johns Hopkins UP, 1989.

Sale, Roger. *Modern Heroism: Essays on D. H. Lawrence, William Empson, and J. R. R. Tolkien.* University of California Press, 1973.

Sale, Roger. *On Writing.* Random House, 1970.

Said, Edward. *Beginnings: Intention and Method.* Columbia UP, 2004.

Said, Edward. "Michel Foucault, 1926–1984." *After Foucault: Humanistic Knowledge, Postmodern Challenges,* edited by Jonathan Arac, Rutgers UP, 1988, pp. 1–11.

Said, Edward. *The World, the Text, and the Critic.* Harvard UP, 1983.

Salvatori, Mariolina. "Conversations with Texts: Reading in the Teaching of Composition." *College English,* vol. 58, no. 4, April 1996, pp. 440–454.

Shaughnessy, Mina. *Errors and Expectations: A Guide for Teachers of Basic Writing.* Oxford UP, 1979.

Slevin, James F. *Introducing English: Essays in the Intellectual Work of Composition.* University of Pittsburgh Press, 2001.

Starkie, Walter. *The Road to Santiago: The Pilgrims of St. James.* 1957. University of California Press, 1965.

Steedman, Carolyn. "Culture, Cultural Studies, and the Historian." *Cultural Studies,* edited by Lawrence Grossman, Cary Nelson, and Paula Treichler, Routledge, 1991.

Steedman, Carolyn. *Landscape for a Good Woman: A Story of Two Lives.* Virago, 1986.

Steedman, Carolyn. *The Radical Soldier's Tale: John Pearman 1819–1908.* Routledge, 1988.

Steedman, Carolyn. *The Tidy House: Little Girls Writing.* Virago, 1982.

Tatlow, Didi Kirsten. "For China's Children, a Resoundingly Patriotic Return to School." *New York Times,* September 2, 2016. https://www.nytimes.com/2016/09/03/world/asia/china-school-long-march.html.

Toíbín, Colm. *On Elizabeth Bishop.* Princeton UP, 2015.

Toíbín, Colm. "A Walk to the End of the Earth." *The Sign of the Cross: Travels in Catholic Europe.* Picador, 2001.

Trilling, Lionel. *The Opposing Self.* Viking, 1955.

Walcott, Fred. *The Origins of Culture and Anarchy: Matthew Arnold and Popular Education in England.* University of Toronto Press, 1970.

Weber, Bruce. "Richard Poirier, a Scholar of Literature, Dies at 83." *New York Times,* August 18, 2009. https://www.nytimes.com/2009/08/18/books/18poirier.html.

Williams, Joseph. *Style: Toward Clarity and Grace.* University of Chicago Press, 1995.

Williams, Raymond. "Cambridge English, Past and Present." *Writing in Society,* Verso, 1983.

Williams, Raymond. "Culture is Ordinary." *Resources of Hope: Culture, Democracy, Socialism*. Verso, 1989.

Williams, Raymond. "Notes on English Prose: 1780–1950." *Writing in Society*, Verso, 1983.

Wittgenstein, Ludwig. *Philosophical Investigations*. 3rd ed. Translated by G. E. M. Anscombe. Macmillan, 1968.

INDEX

INDEX

Kichwa community, 231
King Jr., Martin Luther, 20, 114
Klee, Paul, 245
knowledge, xi, 4, 12–13, 16, 28, 77, 96
Kodat, Catherine, 210
Kolb, Peter, 198, 199

La Casa Americana in Bilbao, 209–10, 214
La Galea (magazine), 206
Lago Agrio oil field (Ecuador), 237
Landscape for a Good Woman (Steedman), 125
language, 5, 27, 47, 49, 52, 64–65, 98, 117, 119, 163, 174; attention to, 34; Basque, 205, 218; discussion of language use, 101–2, 103; diversity, 175–76; English, 101, 137, 155; exercise, 136, 137; family, 151; in history, 14, 15–16; of home, 149, 151; Kichwa, 231; learning in global context, 134; lifted, 12; of literature, 80; material attributes of, 98; as metaphor, 63; of monologues, 218; narrative, 4, 125; ordinary, 88, 96; of politics, 80; of school, 149, 151; Spanish, 6, 207; struggle with, 81; trick of, 171, 172, 173, 199; verbal or written exchanges with, 172; written, 14, 98, 131
Language, Counter-Memory, Practice: Selected Essays and Interviews (Foucault), 72
"Language Difference in Writing: Toward a Translingual Approach" (Horner, Lu, Royster and Trimbur), 174
"Las cenizas del hierro (The Ashes of Iron)" novel (Pinilla), 206
Las ciegas hormigas" novel (Pinilla), xiv, 202–3, 205, 206, 207, 214, 215, 219–21, 223–24, 225
"La tierra convulse (The Earth Trembles)" novel (Pinilla), 206
Lawrence, D. H., 80

"Leaf Storm" novel (Márquez), 215
"Learning from the Beatles" essay (by Poirier), 38–39
learning, xiv, 4, 28, 52–53, 92, 105; foreign language, 138; projects on, 69; to read along with philosopher, 110; sequenced language, 157; student, 63; student writer, 131; to walk, 181; to write, 124, 128; to writing by reading, 45
Lears, Jackson, xii, 40
Leavis, F. R., 55, 128, 136
Lerner, Ben, 75, 95–99, 103, 104, 106–8, 121, 130
Lewis, Melinda, xiv, 243
lifted language, 12
"line of force," 38
literature, 49, 63, 66, 69; American, 3, 7, 20, 68, 72; English, 46–48, 72, 81, 171; in Euskera, 205; Irish, 20; language of, 80; line of force in, 38; literature-centered pedagogy, 54; reading of, 45, 77; Spanish, 6, 207; world, 225
Llosa, Mario Vargas, 212
Lloyd, Rene, 180
"Los cuerpos desnudos" novel (Pinilla), 206
Louisa (biologist), 238, 240

MacCabe, Colin, xiv
Machado, Antonio, 250–51
Macias, Anna, 20
magical thinking, 171
Mailer, Norman, 81
Main, Fred, 85
Malvido, Gonzalo Torrente, 203
"Man and the Biosphere Preserve" by UNESCO, Yasuní as, 236
Mao Tse-tung, 140, 159
Márquez, Gabriel García, 212, 214
Marx, Karl, 91
McCarthy, Gene, 20
McPhee, John, 187
Mean Free Path (Lerner), 75

sentences, 36–37, 40; of theory in English, 85–86; of writing, ix, 8, 39, 40, 53, 77. *See also* travel writing

textbooks, 91; representations of academic genres, 129–30

"That Went for a Walk/On the Camino de Santiago" photo-essay, 245–46; arriving in Santiago, 265; completion of pilgrimage, 262; *Compostela*, 248; Frost's poem, 253–57; Fulton's poem, 252–53; green valleys of Galicia, 261; Machado's poem, 250–51; pilgrimage in Roncesvalles, 247–49, 260–61; in Pittsburgh, 263–64; San Roque, 263; Tóibín's poem, 257–59

themewriting, 55–56, 59, 73, 148

Then, Suddenly (Emanuel), 24

The Plural I (Coles), x, 51, 52, 54, 55, 58, 63, 148; assignments, 58–59; discussion of papers, 60–61

They Say/I Say: The Moves That Matter in Academic Writing (Graff and Birkenstein), 85

This is Africa (TIA), 184–85, 196, 197

Thulani (interviewee), 183, 185, 186, 192–94

Tidy House: Little Girls Writing, The (Steedman), 125

Tiputini Biodiversity Research Station, 228, 229, 233–36

"To Anthony Appiah: A Rejoinder" essay, 120–24

Tóibín, Colm, 11–12, 13–14, 258–59

transculturation, 198, 201

translingual composition, 136, 173–74

Travels into the Interior of Southern Africa (Barrow), 198

travel writing, 177–87, 191–97; beginnings and endings, 188–89; course, xiii–xiv, 243–44; editing, 189–90; fragments, 187–88; line editing, 190–91; Mary Pratt's *Imperial Eyes*, 198–200. *See also* student writing

Trilling, Lionel, 52

Trimbur, John, 174

Trimmer, Joe, 69

Tusquets (Barcelona publishing house), 206

typos in language exercise, 138

ulteriority, 35

United States Information Agency (USIA), 209

University of Cape Town, 134

University of Deusto, Bilbao, xii, 3, 7, 68

University of Pittsburgh, xiii, 20, 32, 38, 52, 68, 70, 76, 95, 135–36; composition program, 128; Min-Zhan Lu in, 153–54; PittMap program, 178; translingual composition to Chinese students at, 136; writing assignment for students in, 158

US State Department, 209–15

verb tense, errors with, 138

verb tense, shifts in, 138

Verdes valles, colinas rojas (Pinilla), 206, 223–25

"vibrant intersection," point of, 41

Victorians, xii, 18

Vitanza, Victor, 91, 92

Volverás a Región (Benet), 212

Voyage to the Cape of Good Hope (Sparrman), 198

Walcott, Fred, 31

Ways of Reading (Petrosky and Bartholomae), 86, 91

What Is World Literature (Damrosch), 225

Whitman, Bob, 6

Whitman, Marina von Neumann, 6

Whitman, Walt, 33

Wideman, John, 91

William Faulkner: First Encounters (Brooks), 216

William Faulkner: The Yoknapatawpha Country (Brooks), 215